SAHEL

MORTEN BØÅS

Sahel

The Perfect Storm

HURST & COMPANY, LONDON

First published in the United Kingdom in 2025 by
C. Hurst & Co. (Publishers) Ltd.,
New Wing, Somerset House, Strand, London, WC2R 1LA
© Morten Bøås, 2025
All rights reserved.

The right of Morten Bøås to be identified as the author of this publication is asserted by him in accordance with the Copyright, Designs and Patents Act, 1988.

A Cataloguing-in-Publication data record for this book is available from the British Library.

ISBN: 9781787385641

This book is printed using paper from registered sustainable and managed sources.

www.hurstpublishers.com

Printed and bound in Great Britain by Bell & Bain Ltd, Glasgow

CONTENTS

List of Abbreviations   vii
Maps   xi
Acknowledgements   xvii
Preface   xix

PART I
THE MAKING OF THE PERFECT STORM

1. Sahel: Actors and Ingredients   3
2. Mali: The Epicentre of the Sahel Conflict   23
3. The Neighbours: Burkina Faso and Niger   55
4. The Sahel—An Enabling Environment? Drivers of Violence and Local Resilience   111
5. Hybridity in the Sahel: Violent Entrepreneurs and Big Men   125

PART II
EVERYTHING GOES BACK TO THE BEGINNING

6. Mali: The Long Road to 2012   143
7. The Grand Empires of the Sahel: Gold, Trade, and Religion   161

PART III
THE PERFECT STORM

8. Politics in Hard Times: Religion and Protest   175
9. The New Military Regimes: Adieu France, Welcome Russia   195

10. Military Rulers and Neo-Patriotism: Branding and
    Mythmaking   209
11. The Perfect Storm?   229

Notes   241
Bibliography   245
Index   265

LIST OF ABBREVIATIONS

ADC	23 May 2006 Democratic Alliance for Change
ADEMA	Alliance for Democracy in Mali
AFISMA	African-led International Support Mission to Mali
AFRICOM	United States Africa Command
A-IBK	Alliance Ibrahim Boubacar Keita
AMUPI	Association pour l'Unité et le Progrès de l'Islam
AoSS	Alliance of Sahel States
AQIM	al-Qaeda in the Islamic Maghreb
ARLA	Revolutionary Army for the Liberation of Azawad
AU	African Union
CAFO	Coordination des Associations et ONG Féminines du Mali
CDP	Congrès pour la Démocratie et le progrès
CMAS	Coordination des Mouvements, Associations, et Sympathisants
CNRDRE	National Committee for Recovering Democracy and Restoring the State
COPAM	Co-ordination of Patriotic Organisations in Mali
CSP-DPA	Strategic Framework for the Defence of the People of Azawad
DC	Decentralisation Commission, Mali
DDR	Disarmament, demobilisation and re-integration
ECOWAS	Economic Community of West African States
ETM	Emergency Transit Mechanism
EU	European Union

LIST OF ABBREVIATIONS

EUCAP Sahel	European Union Civilian Crisis Management Mission in Sahel
EUTF for Africa	European Union Emergency Trust Fund for Africa
EUTM Mali	European Union Training Mission in Mali
FAMA	Armed Forces of Mali
FC-G5S	G5 Sahel Joint Force
FDLR	Democratic Forces for the Liberation of Rwanda
FDR	United Front to Safeguard Democracy and the Republic
FEDAP-BC	Féderation associative pour la paix avec Blaise Compaoré
FIIA	Islamic Front of Azawad
FIS	Islamic Salvation Front
FPLA	Popular Front for the Liberation of Azawad
GATIA	Groupe Autodéfense Touareg Imghad et Alliés
GIA	Armed Islamic Group
GSPC	Salafist Group for Preaching and Combat
HACP	High Authority for the Consolidation of Peace (Niger)
HCIM	Haut Conseil Islamique Malien
IBK	Ibrahim Boubacar Keitas
ICG	International Crisis Group
IMA	Islamic Movement for Azawad
IMF	International Monetary Fund
IOM	International Organisation for Migration
ISGS	Islamic State Greater Sahara
ISWAP	Islamic State West Africa Province
JNIM	Jama'at Nusrat al-Islam wal Muslimeen (Group for the Support of Islam and Muslims)
M5-RPF	5 June Movement—Rally of the Patriotic Forces
MFUA	United Movements and Fronts of Azawad
MINUSMA	Multidimensional Integrated Stabilisation Mission in Mali
MNA	National Movement of Azawad
MNJ	Niger Movement for Justice
MNLA	Movement for the National Liberation of Azawad

LIST OF ABBREVIATIONS

MOJWA	Movement for Oneness and Jihad in West Africa
MPA	Popular Movement of Azawad
MSA	Movement for the Salvation of Azawad
NATM	National Alliance of the Tuareg of Mali
NGO	Non-governmental organisation
OAU	Organisation of African Unity
PCVE	Preventing and countering violent extremism
PNDS-Tarayya	Nigerien Party for Democracy and Socialism
RAF	Red Army Faction
RPG	Rocket-propelled grenade
RSF	Rapid Support Forces (Sudan)
RSP	Régiment de sécurité Présidentielle, Burkina Faso
RUF	Revolutionary United Front
SDF	Nigerien Security and Defence Forces
TOC	Transnational organised crime
UAE	United Arab Emirates
UN	United Nations
UNDP	United Nations Development Programme
UNHCR	United Nations High Commissioner for Refugees
VDF	Volunteers for the Defence of the Homeland
WAEMU	West African Economic and Monetary Union

MAPS

1. Regional map of the Sahel and its neighbours
2. Map of Mali
3. Map of Burkina Faso
4. Map of Niger
5. Map illustration of precolonial empires and kingdoms

1. Regional map of the Sahel and its neighbours

2. Map of Mali

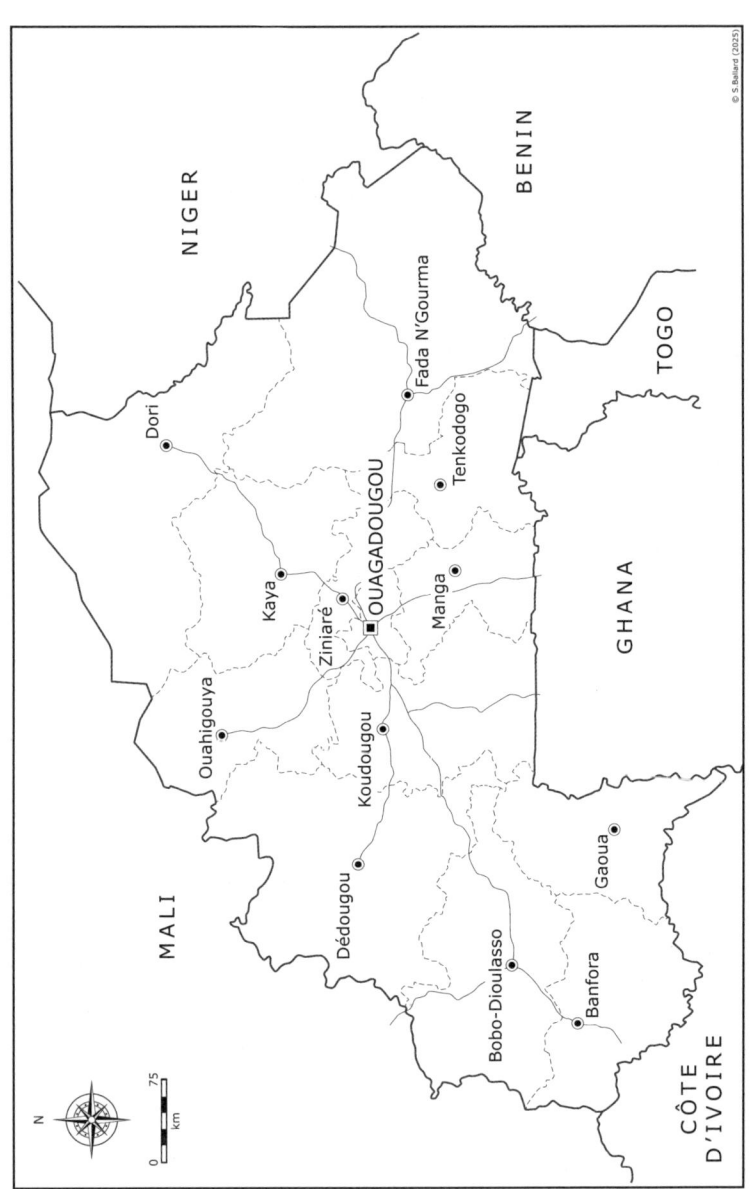

3. Map of Burkina Faso

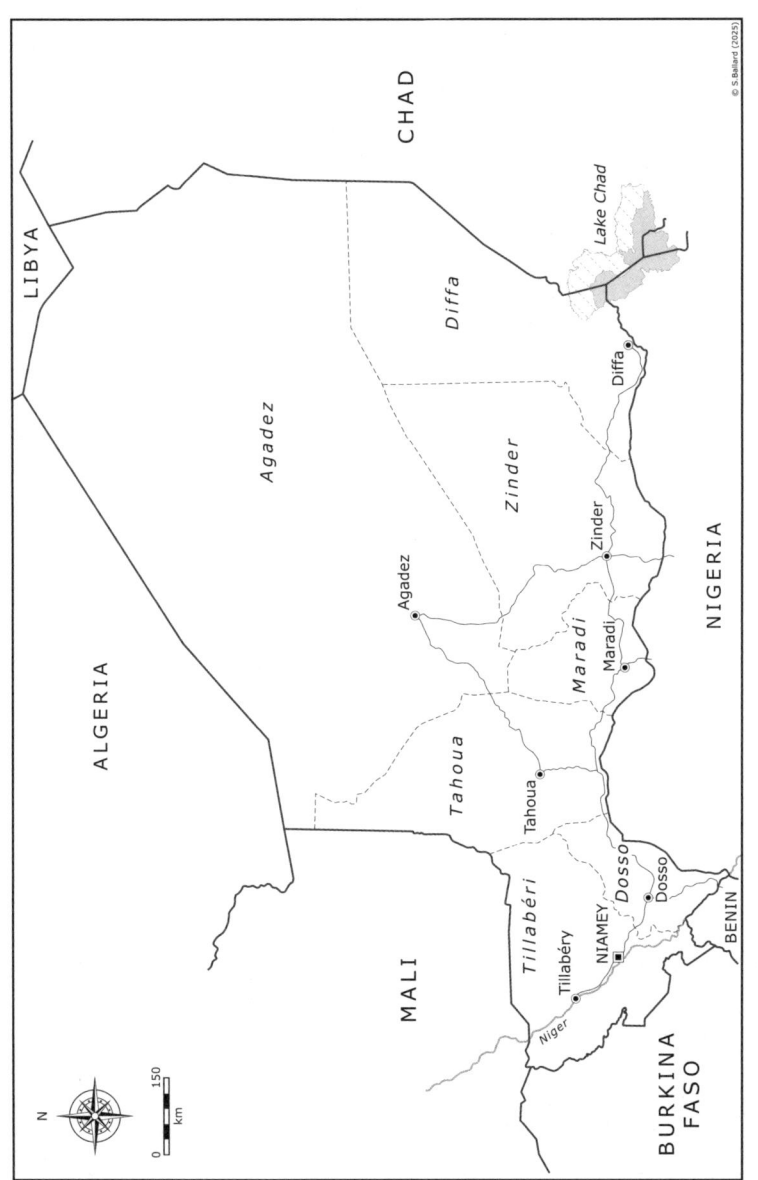

4. Map of Niger

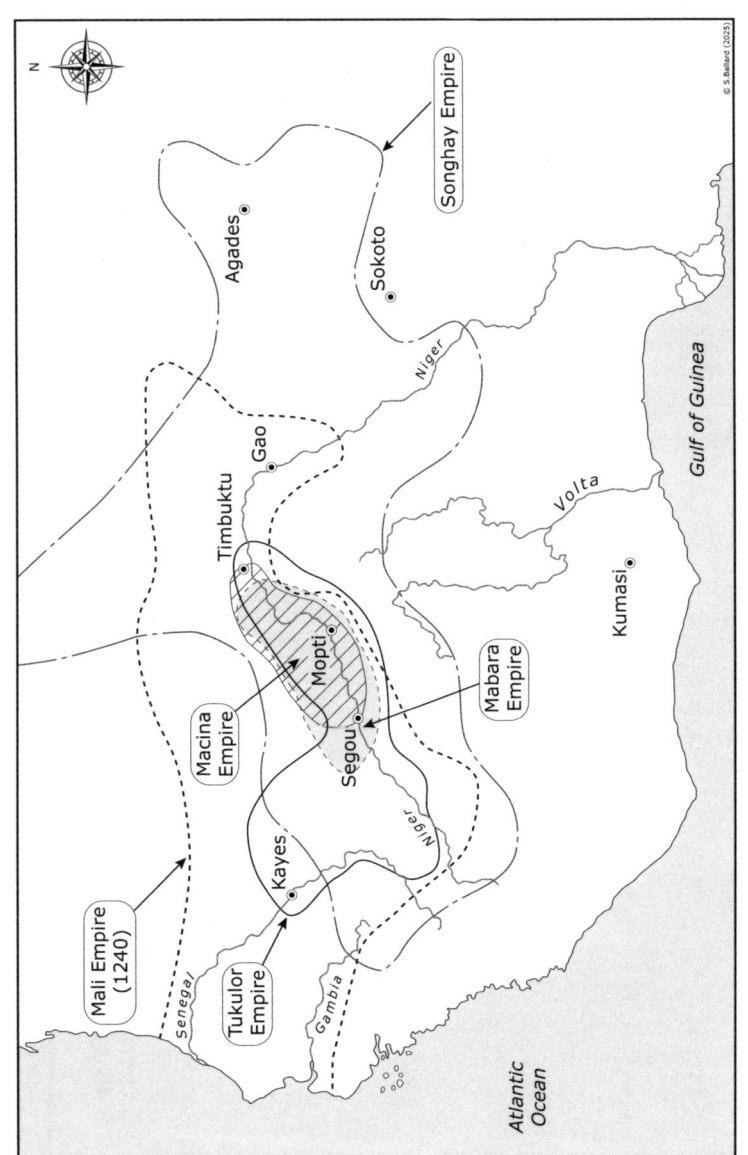

5. Map illustration of precolonial empires and kingdoms

ACKNOWLEDGEMENTS

This book has been in the making for a long time, and many people deserve a big thank you. I should start by thanking Michael Dwyer and Mei Jayne Yew at Hurst for the trust they had in this project—particularly Michael for his patience, and I know it was running thin towards the end. Writing a book while at the same time being the Principal Investigator of two successive large projects funded by the European Union's Horizon 2020 turned out to be more demanding that had I thought when signing the book contract. That said, the delays allowed me to include and discuss important events such as the coups taking place not only in Mali but also in Burkina Faso and Niger; their subsequent turn to Russia and the Wagner Group for support; and thereby the end (at least for now) of a French sphere of influence in this part of the Sahel. The European Union (EU) ponders what it should do now that its migration management deal with Niger has been trashed by the government that came into power after the July 2023 coup. Even the Economic Community of West African States (ECOWAS) is no longer what it used to be. Mali, Burkina Faso, and Niger have left the organisation to form the Alliance of Sahel States (AoSS). Volatility has become a hallmark of this part of Africa. For a researcher there is rarely a dull moment, but I am quite certain that the population of the core Sahel states would like to see less volatility in favour of being able to live more predictable lives.

Over my more than 10 years of engagement with the Sahel, I have had the privilege of working closely with some colleagues who are not just great researchers, but also very nice and warm people. A

ACKNOWLEDGEMENTS

heartfelt thank you goes out to Abdoul Wakhab Cissé, Laouali Mahamene, Issac Dakono, Yehya Maiga, Kari Osland, Adam Sandor, Francesco Strazzari, Luca Raineri, Laura Berlingozzi, Henrik Vigh, Mimmi Söderberg Kovacs, Natasja Rupesinghe, Viljar Haavik, Kristian Lefdal, Alessio Iocchi, and Andreas Lind Kroknes. Funding from the Norwegian Research Council through the JiGov Sahel project is gratefully acknowledge as it contributed to the final drafting of the manuscript.

I chose, however, to dedicate this book to my first grandchild, Iver, who was born when this book was written, in the hope that one day he may be able to travel to a more peaceful and prosperous Sahel than the one where his grandfather worked, hopefully meeting some of my friends who live there as well as their children and grandchildren.

Morten Bøås
December 2024
Oslo, Norway

PREFACE

For some time, there has been a perfect storm on the horizon in the Sahel. Several of the key ingredients have come together lately, and the consequences will be dramatic for the states in the Sahel and the people who live there, but also for Europe and the international community at large. The relationship between Mali and France, and thereby also between Mali and the EU, has become extremely tense; the situation in Burkina Faso has turned in a similar way; and during the summer of 2023 Niger followed suit. For the time being, France and Europe have lost their anchor in the three core Sahel states, and the United Nations (UN) is not doing much better, as the government in Bamako requested that the UN's Multidimensional Integrated Stabilisation Mission in Mali (MINUSMA) leave Mali by the end of 2023. The military coups in Mali, Burkina Faso, and Niger have contributed to this upheaval of previous alignments, but the problems—not only in the region, but also in its relationship to France, the EU, and thereby the Western-led international community writ large—are much deeper. It is too easy to just write off what has happened here as a case of 'democratic backsliding', where Russia acting through the Wagner Group has lured Mali away from the Western fold, and this book will explain why.

This book will thus spell out the key challenges that confront the Sahel, and it will explain why and how they constitute a perfect storm that has been in the making for more than 10 years, and how it may potentially soon be unleashed in full force. It started in Mali, and this country is still the epicentre of the crisis. Thus, the story must begin

PREFACE

with how events in Mali have unfolded since 2012. The Malian crisis that emerged in 2012 was not a shock materialising out of the blue. On the contrary, it was directly connected to events that took place in the 1990s after the signing of the National Pact, which was supposed to end the conflict between the Malian state and the country's Tuareg minority.

To present the complexity of the Sahel crisis in a concise manner to a broader readership, this book is divided into three main parts. The first part—'The making of the perfect storm'—is concerned with the period from the eruption of the Malian crisis in 2012 up until the unconstitutional regime change that removed democratically elected President Ibrahim Boubacar Keita from power in August 2020. This part covers how the Malian crisis has unfolded, the increased strength of the jihadi insurgencies, and how the conflict spread to include large parts of Burkina Faso as well as in Niger, mainly, but not exclusively, the Tillabéri region.

The second part—'Everything goes back to the beginning'—first charts the road that Mali took leading up to the events of 2012, offering answers to explain Mali's current state of affairs as a highly fragile state, where this fragility is rooted in Mali's historical context as an unsettled state, that is, a state without legitimate social contracts. It lacks a real consensus on the composition of its polity, which leads to competing identities that spill over into resource conflicts that easily are manipulated by elites for their own preservation purposes and likewise appropriated by jihadi insurgents in their bid to gain integration into local communities. This is followed by a chapter that delves deeper into the history of this part of the Sahel, discussing how some of the weakest states in the world stand on the foundations of ancient empires that were built on gold, trade, and religion before they crumbled.

In the third and final phase of this book—'The perfect storm'—we analyse the events unfolding from August 2020 and onwards, focusing not only on the advance of the jihadi insurgencies and the entry of the Wagner Group into Mali, but also how the Sahel crisis has become swept up into the geopolitical rivalry between the Western powers and Russia. The analysis of this final period of the Sahel crisis will therefore also establish an empirical foundation for a 'crystal ball' look towards the immediate future: what will happen when all ingre-

PREFACE

dients of the perfect storm come together? What might the consequences be? How will this affect the Sahel and its population? What will the ramifications be for Europe, for the African countries bordering the Sahel, and for the international community at large?

The first part of the book—'The making of the perfect storm'—will therefore begin with Mali and show how the trouble in Mali has transformed into a larger regional crisis. In Mali's case, we can identify all the key ingredients that make up the storm. Mali and the rest of the Sahel region are confronted with a whole set of serious challenges: fragile states; poverty; refugees and migrants; transnational organised crime; armed jihadist rebellions; the effects of climate change; external economic shocks, such as those resulting from Russia's invasion of Ukraine and the subsequent sanction regime enacted by Western powers; and, as events are unfolding, the broken relationship between Sahel governments and key external European stakeholders such as France—first Mali and then, like pearls falling off a string, Burkina Faso and Niger.

The increasingly hostile relationship between Mali and France after August 2020 has resulted in a complete break between the two nations. Now, Mali's transitional government, which is dominated by a group of younger army officers, has chosen to rely on Russia and the Wagner Group, a Russian private security company. This means that the conflict in Mali, and thereby also in the Sahel, has become a part of the new geopolitical conflict between the West and Russia. The icing on the cake, in early June 2023, the Malian Foreign Minister Abdoulaye Diop stunned the UN Security Council by calling the UN operation MINUSMA a failure and arguing for its immediate end. On 30 June 2023, the UN Security Council bowed to the principle that peacekeeping operations need the consent of the host government and voted unanimously to begin an immediate withdrawal of MINUSMA. Thus, while the Western members of the Security Council expressed fears that this would only lead to more insecurity, chaos, and human suffering in the Sahel, this meant the end of what has been not only the most expensive mission for the UN, billing at about 1.2 billion USD per year, but also the deadliest, as 174 peacekeepers have been killed since the start of MINUSMA in 2013. Most likely the end of MINUSMA also heralds the end of the era of large

PREFACE

UN peacekeeping missions. In fact, one could claim that Africa was the continent where UN peacekeeping as we know it went to die.

The situation in most of the other parts of the Sahel is not yet as dire as it is in Mali. However, as the conflict in Burkina Faso is quickly spinning out of control and the country has experienced two military coups in a row, there is an imminent danger of state collapse. In Niger there has also been an increase in the number of deadly jihadist attacks, and in late July 2023 President Mohamed Bazoum was removed from power by a military coup. This means that France and the EU have lost their last key ally in the region.

Even if important differences exist between the core Sahel states of Mali, Niger, and Burkina Faso, they as well as other states in the region suffer from varying degrees of fragility and weak state capacity. Individually, none of them can respond adequately to the livelihood and security challenges that currently confront their populations.

The issue of climate change underscores this point. The countries of the Sahel have contributed very little to global CO_2 emissions, yet they are in the unfortunate position of being among those that will be the most hurt by its consequences. The current projection of an increase in global temperature of 2–4 degrees Celsius will have negative consequences everywhere, but in the Sahel it will be devastating if the countries do not become more resilient to climate change. If the problem is left unaddressed, it will constitute an escalating threat to local livelihoods, with an even larger potential for increased violent conflict between farmers and herders. The explosive population growth in the region will also take its toll if systematic mitigating measures are not introduced. In Mali, the current population of approximately 20.2 million is projected to increase to over 45 million by 2050. Similar projections for Niger show an increase from the current population size of 24.2 million to about 68 million in 2050. The million-dollar question is how all these people will be able to secure a livelihood.

Addressing these development challenges is a huge task in itself, but it is even more difficult when we take into consideration that they are happening in some of the world's most fragile states, where the state's capacity to absorb external assistance and interventions is very low and large parts of the territory are currently beyond state control.

PREFACE

Despite receiving increased international attention in the form of military interventions by France (first Operation Serval and later Barkhane) and the UN's MINUSMA—supported by the deployment of a European Union Civilian Crisis Management Mission (EUCAP-Sahel) and the European Union Training Mission (EUTM) in Mali—the situation on the ground from 2013 to 2024 has gone from bad to worse. The number of jihadi-inspired insurgencies are multiplying, operating now in Mali, Niger, and Burkina Faso, and they have even begun to target the northern territories of the coastal states Benin, Côte d'Ivoire, Ghana, and Togo. The insurgents' main strength is not just in their men-at-arms, whose numbers have increased, but in their increasingly sophisticated strategies of asymmetrical warfare. They know the terrain, and most of them have also developed effective strategies towards integration in local communities. Thus, for parts of the local population, these jihadi insurgents are more relevant to their daily livelihoods and struggles than the state and its military forces. The first part of this book will therefore also offer a concise analytical description of the main insurgent groups and their strength and weaknesses.

In the second part—'Everything goes back to the beginning'—we start by locating the origins of the contemporary Malian crisis in the decisions taken to end the conflict in Northern Mali in the 1990s, showing how the making of a new conflict was built into the peace agreement. Here, we will pay particular attention to the role of the decentralisation programme (which was an integral part of the National Pact), arguing that decentralising a state as weak as Mali was at that time will not in itself lead to increased state capacity, only to a multiplicity of weaker state units. This will be followed by a concise history of the states of the Sahel, underscoring how the unsettledness of these states has deep historical roots.

History also plays a role regarding the jihadi insurgents, and to illustrate this we will delve into the Macina Empire of central Mali, illustrating how insurgencies such as Hamadoun Kouffa's Katiba Macina make good strategic use of this history, but also how such a history can be both a strength and a weakness for an insurgency that aspires to build a larger national and regional agenda. The Macina narrative gave Kouffa's men a tool for local integration, but, as this and similar narratives are very much based on the politics of place, they can form a basis for local integration but can also be a barrier to building larger alliances.

The third and final part of the book—'The perfect storm'—will spell out what the consequences could be after 10 years of the international community's inability to solve the Sahel crisis. As we move towards 2050, the Sahel will be faced with an alarming population increase, combined with increased pressure on traditional livelihoods such as farming, herding, and fishing due to the projected rise in global temperature. People will start to move in even larger numbers; some will go north to get out of the Sahel, trying to reach the Mediterranean coastline in search of a way into Europe. Others—most likely in much higher numbers—will try to get out of the Sahel the other way, moving south towards the tropical forest belt of West Africa. This is already evident in the seasonal migration of herds moving in larger numbers much further south than they used to. Herder–farmer conflicts are, for example, already on the increase in the Northern Region of Ghana, and such conflicts will only become more violent, with the Fulani and other ethnic herder groups being pitted against local farmers. Jihadi insurgents are already appropriating such conflicts, and the severity of such conflicts will inevitably enlarge the insurgents' ability to operate and recruit. The increase in violent conflict in the Sahel will even further undermine the fragile states of the Sahel. In the worst case, one or more of the core Sahel states may fall, setting in motion a larger regional breakdown of state authority.

This could happen, but it does not have to. External interventions so far have increasingly taken a narrow security approach, and there may be good reasons for providing military assistance to the states in the region, even if this looks very difficult for Europe now, with key Sahel states turning to Russia for military support and alliances. However, we should keep in mind that, when the huge international interventions started in 2013, it was French flags that were on display in Bamako, Niamey, and Ouagadougou. The French and UN interventions were very popular, but this popularity waned and was inevitably lost when the security situation on the ground turned from bad to worse. Eleven years on, in 2024, the flags on the streets are no longer French, but Russian. However, the likelihood that Russia can

PREFACE

fill the void left by the departure of France and the UN is almost nil. The security situation has not improved, and while Russia can provide some weaponry and utilise the Wagner Group, that in official Russian information is now referred to as 'Africa Corps', there is no way Russia can replace Europe as a development and trade partner. What this means is that Russia's moment in the Sahel may not last very long, and it may very well find itself in the same position as France did, with instant popularity on the dawn of intervention which quickly fades away when Russia too fails on all fronts, be it security or the economy.

What this means is that there most likely will be a way back into the region for Europe, the EU, and the UN. However, if this is to bear anything other than new disappointments, France and other key stakeholders need to seriously reconsider their previous approaches and come to terms with what went so terribly wrong. In doing so, Europe should ask itself not only what it is that these countries need, but also what balance there should be between the priorities of external stakeholders and the needs of the locals. Europe wants fewer northbound migrants and refugees, and a reduction in what it sees as a terrorist threat. But these are not necessarily the main priorities of the local inhabitants: they are more immediately concerned with their living conditions, which have come under immense pressure. What will be spelt out at the very end of the book is an agenda of how external and internal interests can be reconciled through an approach that has a security component, but one that is more focused on human protection, rebuilding legitimate state authority in close consultation with local communities, and visible local development projects than a mobile hunt for jihadi insurgents that so far has proven futile.

PART I

THE MAKING OF THE PERFECT STORM

1

SAHEL

ACTORS AND INGREDIENTS

Since 2013, the Sahel has confronted global policymakers with a whole range of serious challenges—fragile states, poverty, refugees and migrants, transnational organised crime, jihadi insurgencies. Lately, it has also served as a centre of global geopolitical conflict, as Mali, Burkina Faso, and Niger have abandoned their security and defence collaboration with France and turned instead to Russia and the Wagner Group. The question of state stability in the Sahel is therefore more prominent on the international agenda than it ever has been, and the magnitude of international assistance and international interventions in various forms has been unprecedented.

The conflict that erupted in Mali in 2012 led to military interventions by France (Operations Serval and Barkhane), the African Union (AU) (the African-led International Support Mission to Mali [AFISMA]), and the UN (MINUSMA). These various international initiatives were also supported by the deployment of an EU police and rule of law mission (EUCAP-Sahel) and an EU military training mission in Mali (EUTM).

Despite all these efforts and the signing of a Peace Agreement for Mali in Algiers in 2015, the situation on the ground has gone from bad to worse. The conflict has spilled over from the north to the central region of Mali (Sangary 2016; Ba & Bøås 2018; Sandor & Campana 2019), and Niger and Burkina Faso are also severely affected by the conflict (Thurston 2020a; Bøås et al. 2020; Haavik et al. 2022).

There were good reasons for increased military assistance to Mali, Niger, Burkina Faso, and other states in the Sahel. However, the military interventions and support programmes have not helped much. The jihadi insurgents are much closer to Bamako in 2024 than they were in 2013. Consequently, the French military intervention that was hugely popular in Mali in 2013 become increasingly controversial, and it was not an unpopular decision when the Goïta-government set in motion a series of announcements and policies that led President Macron to announce the full withdrawal of all French soldiers from Mali on 17 February 2022. This is because people simply cannot understand why the security situation continued to deteriorate as the conflict spread from one part of the country to another. In the popular imagination, other narratives emerged and gained traction, for example, the one about the conflict being a French plot to 'Balkanise' Mali in order to steal its natural resources. Not that there is that much to steal, as we will see, nor is there is any credibility to the narrative of a sinister French plot.

However, the combination of living in what must have started to seem like a permanent crisis with no improvement in sight and massive foreign interventions led by the former colonial power created an environment of suspicion that was leveraged by local political entrepreneurs. Thus, leading up to the crisis between Bamako and Paris, there were large popular protests against France in Bamako that included expressions in favour of a Russian intervention. These demonstrations coincided with and gained traction from the increasingly hostile relationship between France and the military rulers in the Malian transitional government. As events unfolded, President Macron announced a large overhaul of Operation Barkhane—what France called *Barkhane reformule*—while the rulers in Bamako let it be known that if what they defined as French withdrawal took place, they would seek support from Russia and engage the Russian private military company, the Wagner Group. President Macron and France responded that this was a red line that they would not tolerate Mali crossing. The French standpoint was supported by the EU and other European countries.

SAHEL: ACTORS AND INGREDIENTS

The complete breakdown of military assistance from France and Europe to Mali may not have seemed likely, as this would risk a full collapse in Mali. This would certainly not be in the interest of European partners, and the current government in Mali knew this. However, what seems to have been taking place was a game of poker, with several bad hands that none of the parties to the game may have sought, but still ended up playing. While we will spell out the background of the increased geopolitical tensions building up around Mali and the Sahel in the first part of the book, these questions bring yet another dimension to the perfect storm that could hit this part of the world. We will return in more detail to the timeline of mounting tensions after August 2020 in Part III of this book.

The first part will therefore explore the multidimensional crisis of the Sahel, addressing root causes and showing how the situation on the ground has evolved over time from 2012. The focus is on Mali as epicentre of the current conflict, but several severe ramifications are also felt in neighbouring countries. This is currently most acute in Burkina Faso and Niger, but the jihadi insurgencies have also started to establish themselves in the northern parts of Benin, Côte d'Ivoire, Ghana, and Togo. In exploring the security predicament that these countries are faced with, we aim to show that, as is the case in Mali, here external stakeholders struggle to find the balance between narrow security concerns and a larger developmental agenda where military security is but one part of a larger equation of political and economic issues.

The Sahel—a multidimensional crisis

Mali has been in a state of crisis since 2012, and Burkina Faso has unravelled very rapidly, while, despite the military coup in the summer of 2023, Niger still shows some resilience. However, all states in this region suffer from varying degrees of fragility and weak state capacity. Individually, none of them can respond adequately to the livelihood challenges their populations are currently faced with. This is further exacerbated by the fact that the Sahel region is in the unfortunate position of being constituted by a group of countries that have contributed very little to global CO_2 emissions but will be among those most harmed by its consequences. The current projection of an increase in global temperature of 2–4 degrees will have negative consequences everywhere, but it will be devastating to the countries of the Sahel if they do not quickly become more resilient to climate change. Thus, if left unaddressed, this constitutes an escalating threat to local livelihoods, with an increased potential for violent conflict between the two main occupational groups of rural Sahel, namely farmers and herders.

The reason for this is that these are two different types of livelihoods, but they depend on the same natural resources, namely land and water, and since ancient times herders have moved their flocks of cattle southwards during the dry season of the year towards areas where farmers dwell (Marnham 1979). However, while they depend on the same resources, they use them in different ways. Farmers need land for cultivation and water for the crops they have planted, while herders need land and water for their cattle. If resources are in abundance this is not necessarily a problem, but when resources are scarce the relationship between these two groups with different functional interests in how to utilise these basic natural resources must be regulated. The means of regulation can be traditional, or they can be managed by the modern state. The method is less important when the regulation works. The question, however, is what happens when regulatory mechanisms are weakened, become dysfunctional, or vanish entirely. The result is, as we will see, an increase in local grievances that often turn violent and can easily become deadly. In the Sahel, arguments over local access to natural resources are a primary driver of violent conflict, as is jihadi-inspired insurgencies appropriating these to gain traction over specific populations and integration into local communities.

The current situation in the Mopti region in central Mali illustrates this. Once a commercial hub in this part of the country, Mopti has undergone an economic downturn. Climatic variability impacts negatively on the productive yields of the region as irregular rainfall and the low flooding of the Niger River reduces the area of cultivable land and agricultural production, making families vulnerable to food insecurity. Pastoralists have become increasingly vulnerable after successive droughts and poor harvests of cattle fodder have led to drastic reductions in herd sizes. The livestock sector has also been hit by reduced demand and plummeting livestock prices across West African markets. Thus, compared to other south-central regions (e.g. Bamako, Koulikoro, Sikasso, Kayes, and Ségou), Mopti currently suffers from acute levels of poverty, with over 70 per cent of its population living in severe poverty and destitution.

Resource and rights-based conflicts in the inner delta along the Niger River in the Mopti region is nothing new, but conflicts over disputed access to and control over land and water resources are increasing, exacerbated by environmental and demographic pressures (Rupesinghe & Bøås 2018). With resources becoming scarcer, new as well as old cleavages over access to natural resources increasingly turn violent as people struggle to control what matters in their lives (Ba & Bøås 2018; Sandor & Campana 2019). This has opened new spaces for jihadi insurgencies. In Mopti, an administrative void has therefore emerged that neither the Malian state nor international responses have been able to adequately address. This is exacerbated by the multidimensional nature of the crisis of the Sahel: it is about conflict and chronic violence, but it is also a humanitarian crisis caused by a combination of weak statehood and stalled development, and its consequences are large-scale human displacement, with the internally displaced seeking shelter in Bamako and elsewhere in the south. This confronts the international community with huge challenges, as the very weakness of the states in the Sahel means that they lack the institutional response capacity needed to make conventional large-scale external crisis response effective (Bøås 2017).

In abstract terms, we know what is required: the states of the Sahel need stability, transparency and legitimate institutions that can extract revenues from taxes, fees, and duties to deliver economic development and services, while making their countries more resilient to climate change effects (Fjeldstad et al. 2018). The problem is how to achieve this in fragmented, conflict-prone societies where the state has eroded, if not completely vanished. The challenge that this constitutes is obvious when we consider the international community's track record in assisting state-building efforts in fragile states undergoing conflict. Most often these fall short of achieving their stated objectives, even at times making a difficult situation worse (see Tull 2019), leaving countries on an artificial international life-support system (Bøås 2019). This may prevent total state collapse if the life-support system remains in place, but it certainly does not represent a sustainable path to recovery, stability, reconciliation, and development.

For the international community to set such a process in motion in the Sahel, their assistance must be knowledge-based, and it must be based on a grounded understanding of what these states are and how they work. Unfortunately, a grounded knowledge-based approach is still at odds with the dominant perspective that views the states of the Sahel as 'lacking' what modern states are supposed to have: control of borders, monopoly on violence, procedures for taxation and dispute settlement, and a legitimate design for transfer of power from one ruler or regime to another (Eriksen 2011; Bøås 2015a).

Root causes of conflict

The peripheries of the Sahel have often been defined as an ungoverned space: a geographical area characterised by an absence of state control and state sovereignty—a lawless zone, a no-man's land—the implication being that, as state capacity has eroded and collapsed, large parts of the Sahel have turned into an 'ungoverned space', preyed upon by a plethora of forces of transnational crime and global jihad. The idea is that a narco-terrorism nexus has emerged to control these hinterlands (see, for example, Nyadera & Massaoud 2019).

As a brandable idea this may sound appealing, but it is full of flaws and misunderstandings. The point is that, while few seasoned Sahel observers would disagree with general statements such as that the Malian state is too weak, that drugs are trafficked through the Sahel, and that forces aligned to global jihad are present in this region, such pronouncements tell us very little about local conflict dynamics. These concepts are acted upon in a way that is less analytical than categorical, leading to a narrow, checklist approach to policy that may result in extremely misguided planning and interventions.

There is no doubt that crime and corruption are serious threats to state stability and human development. However, there is much more to the story of violence in contemporary Mali and the Sahel, as a wide range of different forms of political and social resistance also take place. Some of these movements are peaceful, whereas others are much more violent. Parts of this resistance (whether peaceful or violent) are secular in origin and motivation, while others are informed by religious ideas and certain specific theological points of view. At times these actors are also involved in the transportation of illicit goods and the protection of routes used to traffic them. Some of these actors are involved mainly to make a profit, while others combine self-interest with political or religious motivations. Thus, while the focus on transnational crime in the Sahel is needed and has produced some well-informed and intentioned policy analysis (see, for example, Molenaar & Van Damme 2017; Tinti & Westcott 2016), we still need more focus on the continuity between different contours of criminality, coping, and resistance, as well as the subsequent logic behind these activities. This is quite a different logic from the one towards which an 'ungoverned space' lens directs our analyses and polices (see Bøås 2015b; Raineri & Strazzari 2015; Bøås & Strazzari 2020).

The most relevant question is therefore not about the lack of authority that creates an 'ungoverned space', but rather how to understand and approach various competing forms of authority that have emerged based on different perceptions of what constitutes legitimate and effective rule. This means that the mechanisms of armed insurgencies that destabilise the existing regional order are not produced by the vacuum of power of an 'ungoverned space', but rather stem from the power structures of the state that are increasingly perceived as oppressive, dysfunctional, and corrupted. It is these power structures that are challenged by the availability of competing authorities representing different political agendas (Bøås & Strazzari 2020).

Immediately, a state like Mali may seem just like any other, just with fewer resources at its disposal. It is not up for debate that the Malian state is much weaker than most other states in the world, but the question is rather what the nature of its organisation and behavioural practices are, and what types of crime and resistance this tends to produce. Most of the recent literature on the Malian state tends to agree that in many ways it does not behave like a state in the Weberian sense of the word (Craven-Matthews & Englebert 2018). Mali is simply too lacking in terms of a monopoly of violence and control of state territory and population. Notwithstanding, the Malian state still performs certain state-like functions, along with different types of patrimonial politics in which important 'Big Men' occupy important positions (see Bøås 2012; Bøås & Cissé 2022).

The Malian state is therefore displaying a remarkable hybrid character, in that it is very present and controlling in the capital city of Bamako and surrounding areas, while in interior provinces—and particularly in the most peripheral areas—the state tends to be one among several actors competing for the role of effective and, ultimately, sovereign authority whose laws people abide by. Institutional weaknesses aside, state authorities have (and typically display) enough sovereignty to continue to interact with the international system and thereby remain the preferred recipient of donor assistance (Craven-Matthews & Englebert 2018). As we will come back to in Part III of this book, the withdrawal of French forces and MINUSMA as well as the turn to Russia have weakened the state's position as the preferred donor assistance partner, but they have not undermined it completely.

The types of state weakness present in Mali constitute fertile ground for violent insurgencies. In this case, these non-state armed groups are often and too easily described as terrorists belonging to the new African front that global groups such as al-Qaeda and the Islamic State (IS) opened after they lost territory and control in the Middle East (see, for example, The Economist 2021). This is, however, not very precise, as although the leadership of the jihadi insurgencies in the Sahel and groups with a much more global outreach such as al-Qaeda and IS share an ideological inspiration, it is far too easy to simply write off the former as African branches of 'mother' organisations. The argument advanced in this book is that the relations between the Sahel groups and al-Qaeda and IS are much closer to a branding than a branching relationship.

The question is, therefore, how we should designate these groups. Simply calling them terrorists does not offer much analytical value, and designating them insurgents does not give more mileage than describing them as non-state armed groups. That is why we will advance the term 'violent entrepreneurs' as a generic conceptual description of the non-state armed groups that operate in the Sahel (see Bøås et al. 2020). These are non-state armed groups possessing some kind of political agenda, which they implement in tandem with different types of income-generating activities. This means that at the core of their activities we find a fusion of criminality (i.e. profit-making) and some form of a larger politically motivated project. Which of these two is more important for the actors involved may change over time, but crucially neither side of this spectrum of motivation tends to become all dominant. Their political or religious projects are therefore rarely completely polluted by their self-serving income generating activities. While the nature of their activities defines them as non-state actors, this does not mean that they cannot be connected to the state or even at times occupy state positions. The example of Iyad Ag Ghaly, Ibrahim Ag Bahanga, and others of their kind, who we will return to as the book unfolds, shows that this is possible at certain times during the career of a violent entrepreneur.

Thus, while motivations may change or just coincide with each other, the ways that they seek to preserve and improve their position, both economically and politically, tend to follow similar scripts over time. They rule by force and violence, but they also distribute resources, provide or help to provide (through others) some level of order, and offer protection to (at least parts of) the population in the areas they control (or attempt to control). As these violent entrepreneurs not only operate but also have a stronger rooting in local communities in peripheral areas of the Sahel than international community actors and their national allies, understanding how local communities negotiate and navigate the new social landscape that this confronts them with is crucial (see also Bøås & Strazzari 2020; Bøås et al. 2020).

In such contexts, distinctions such as lawfulness versus unlawfulness, inclusion versus exclusion, and confrontation versus co-optation should be interpreted along the trajectory of the forces that Antonio Gramsci called 'historic blocs' (see Gramsci 2005). Crime and criminality cannot be understood if one ignores how the outlaw or insurgent is a product of social, economic, and political evolution,[1] and how the latter in the Sahelian context appears permeable to external influence. What we must consider are the hybridised strategies of government resulting from overlapping local historical paths and modern phenomena such as neoliberal transformations, democratisation, and globalisation (for example, the privatisation of public services and the increasing leverage of the illicit over the licit, see also Bayart et al. 1999), rather than to refer to more common notions such as 'failed states' that tend to measure substantive gaps vis-à-vis imported, ideal types of states (Bøås & Strazzari 2020).

Against this background, discussing today's challenges in the Sahel in terms of 'insecure spaces' (Shaw & Mahadevan 2018) infested by narco-terrorists and institutionalised state corruption that has morphed into state capture by criminal groups is simplistic and problematic, because it paves the way for apolitical analyses that overlook 'the livelihood-sustaining and security-providing aspects of alternative forms of non-state governance' (Cockayne & Lupel 2009: 10). Activities outside of the law that are carried out in such spaces can be protected and sponsored by public authorities, their proxies, other local militias, or even jihadists in a dense network where counterterror strategists too must be selective in picking their battles and their allies.

Heavily sanctioned de jure, illicit activities are often considered socially legitimate and de facto selectively allowed: the fact that they are criminalised means that they can generate large money flows. A flow of cash that lubricates the clientelist machinery in a highly segmented and economically marginal social context feeds social mobility and shapes expectations: in other words, it affects political legitimacy and builds new forms of political influence and protection (that is, stability) until a new contender appears. Inasmuch as governments have kept their distance from their impervious and inhospitable borderlands, negotiations among contenders can take place at times cordially, albeit in the shadow of arms.[2] A problem arises when a new contender, no matter whether a part of a relations system, develops and pursues an agenda that envisions a different type of political order, not only locally, but also globally.

Insurgents' order?

To come to terms with how insurgencies come about, how they seek different types of relationships with local populations, and why people choose to join them, we must acknowledge that many current insurgencies no longer fit into established analytical categories. This is certainly the case of the insurgents in the Sahel.

In his examination of the diversity of armed insurgencies in Africa at the end of the twentieth century, Christopher Clapham (1998: 6–7) distinguished between four broad groups of armed insurgencies:

1. liberation insurgencies, such as the anti-colonial nationalist movements (e.g., Mau Mau in Kenya),
2. separatist insurgencies (e.g., the Eritrean People's Liberation Front),
3. reform insurgencies (e.g., Museveni's National Resistance Army in Uganda),
4. warlord insurgencies (e.g., Charles Taylor's National Patriotic Front of Liberia and Foday Sankoh's Revolutionary United Front in Sierra Leone).

Most recent insurgencies do not fit easily into any of the categories above: the only one that is still referred to frequently is the fourth, warlord insurgencies, and even that has lost most of its acclaimed analytical value (see Bøås & Dunn 2017). Thus, while Clapham's taxonomy remains one of the best attempts to study insurgencies comparatively, the external and internal environments of contemporary insurgencies have changed significantly. It has been argued that, for insurgent groups, the objective of armed conflict is not the defeat of the enemy in battle but the continuation of fighting for profit (Keen 2006). While it is important to acknowledge the complex ways in which insurgencies have been exploiting opportunities provided to them by transformations in the global economy, explanations focusing primarily on the economic agendas of armed actors are highly problematic. Such a focus may help explain how some conflicts are sustained, but it rarely tells us much about why conflicts start in the first place. It would be a mistake, for example, to assume that the current conflict in the Sahel is only a by-product of the collusion of the forces of transnational crime with regional/international jihadists in the guise of a crime–terror nexus (see Bøås 2015b; Strazzari 2014).

To understand insurgencies and the insurgents in the Sahel—and the larger Global South, for that matter—we need a nuanced and context-specific understanding of war and violence. The conflicts are most often deeply embedded in the history of the people and place, not only in colonial history and the transformation to independent states, but dare we say in the totality of their history. Recent and distant pasts relate in direct—albeit sometimes rather unexpected—ways to ongoing processes of social change.

For example, many of the events and relationships that characterise Sahel's recent history, including politics and political violence, are intimately entangled in people's perceptions of their social and ethnic identities. These perceptions of identity are no doubt social constructs, that is representations that are constantly negotiated, changing over time, and often distorted and manipulated, particularly as a part of the discourses of domination emanating from those in power in successive colonial and postcolonial regimes (see Atkinson 1994).

Armed struggle is therefore always in a state of flux, and fighting in the desert is, from a historical point of view, quintessentially fluid and elusive, hardly centred on the notion of decisive battle (Keegan 2011). As new technologies, strategies, and pathways to resistance emerge, existing insurgencies attempt to adapt. Global and regional forces—be they political, economic, or social—impact on the context of the armed struggles in multiple, and often unpredictable, ways. In some cases, local causes of conflicts become interconnected, intertwined, and layered to produce a constantly shifting landscape. It is therefore important to acknowledge that armed insurgencies are not only forces of disorder, but equally parts of emerging systems of governance. In fact, what we see today in the cases where armed insurgencies exist over a prolonged period is that a monopolised system of governance has either broken down completely or been weakened to the extent that competing systems have emerged (Bøås & Dunn 2017).

These new systems are characterised by flexibility and adaptability, with actors competing for the role of nodal point between various networks of attempted informal governance. Such networks are characterised by a mixture of collaboration and competition. The territorial articulation of in-group identity, entitlement, and social hierarchy in the challenging ecosystem of the Sahel is historically condensed around the idea of right of way (*droit de passage*), which can be contrasted to the idea of 'paper' borders demarcating property (Strazzari 2014). At times, violent conflict flares up over who is in control of strategic territorial segments or resources. The fluidity of these networks can be reflected in the continuing existence—but changing function—of highly adaptive regional and local 'Big Men', and their shifting alliances constitute networks of governance that relate to armed insurgencies.

Regardless of the internal dynamics, new networks of power and rule are constructed that challenge—and replace—existing systems of governance. What we see are complex, often kaleidoscopic political configurations that have shifted away from any aspiration to be monopolising systems of governance and patronage and can best be understood as a multitude of shifting alliances resulting from competition among networks of patronage. Networks operate based on personal power: 'attainment of big man status is the outcome of a series of acts which elevate a person above the common herd and attract him a coterie of loyal, lesser men' (Sahlins 1963: 289). These networks vary in depth, geographical reach, and ability to penetrate the state, but all of them are unstable, changing, and constantly adaptable. While they rest on some sort of common interests, participants do not necessarily share the same goals or have similar reasons for being involved.

The elevation to Big Man status therefore does not follow one universal path. It varies in time and space and can be based on different combinations of power. However, in an area such as this where authority is always contested, it must include the ability to use force, to generate resources and, not least, to represent authority in and between the state and the informal. The historical example of the Sahel Big Man Ibrahim ag Bahanga illustrates this point. Ag Bahanga embarked on his Big Man career during the Tuareg rebellion in the 1990s as a lesser rebel leader, and after the rebellion ended he gained control of a *commune* (the lowest branch of local government) in the Kidal area of northern Mali. This did not prevent him from being involved in illicit trade and smuggling; he led other rebellions and at the same time, until his death in August 2011, maintained relationships with the neighbouring governments of Algeria and Libya, as well as certain segments of the Malian government and administration.

Thus, his status as a Big Man was not based on only one of these activities, but on the totality of them. The result was his ability to, if not control, at least influence and maintain different and partly overlapping networks that individually did not have much commonality in terms of long-term objectives and strategy (Bøås 2015a).

One can identify several Big Men along the Gao-Timbuktu axis today: Hanoune Ould Ali, Mohamed Ould Mataly, Mohamed Rouji, and Dina Ould Daya (see UN 2020). These are basically big drug traffickers (*gros traffiquants*), but they are also politically involved, as they have relations to and influence over the Malian army, different armed groups, and local official and traditional authorities.

Some of these networks and the Big Men involved in them are mainly motivated by criminality (accumulation and coping), whereas others make use of such activities to finance various projects of resistance (secular and religious). This may bring different networks and their Big Men into conflict with each other, but two conflicting networks are not necessarily prevented from collaboration and collusion at other times, suggesting that a nexus of transnational crime and global terrorism does not exist in such a way that it can be depicted as a fixed entity with permanent organisational features. Rather, the logic of these operations and networks is ambiguity and flexibility, and the actors involved are capable of adapting themselves and their resources to the ever-changing circumstances of the terrain in which they operate (see also Wedel 2009; Guichaoua 2011).

This does not mean that this plasticity knows no limits. Certain relationships and networks are not only more possible than others, but also more persistent. Ethnicity and kinship might matter, but so do the risks involved in certain relationships, no matter how profitable they may be. It is key to keep track of how the tiles of the mosaic move: relationships compose, decompose, and recompose at a level that is above the individual, where what is important are not only (or not so much) the agents of violence themselves (e.g. insurgency X or Y), but rather the nodal points in these networks of governance and violence, and their ability to keep up these networks across space and time (see also Bøås & Dunn 2017).

Thus, if we take recent conflict trends in the Sahel as an indication of the future, the field is and will continue to be characterised by

SAHEL: ACTORS AND INGREDIENTS

complicated conflicts in politically difficult terrains. These are conflicts where no clear endgames are in sight, and where UN missions or other international interventions will be left to grapple with weak states run by increasingly unpopular national leaders with dubious levels of legitimacy. Such missions and interventions could easily end up fighting or attempting to curb insurgents who are not only hard to beat militarily but whose agendas also leave little room for a negotiated settlement to the conflict. Such conflicts will also very likely take place in areas of the world where local livelihoods are under pressure from several external shocks, such as increased climatic variability, and where the states in question are rarely seen as capable of offering local populations much support. Often it will be the opposite: the state(s), and therefore those who back them, are seen locally as part of the problem and not the solution.

This 'messiness' of things to come is easily observable in several areas in which the UN and the international community at large has recently been engaged with peace operations, such as the border areas between Iraq and Syria and various parts of Africa. Here international stabilisation efforts often flounder as the international community fail to comprehend local contexts, political economies, and national sentiments. Even if there are certain commonalities that need to be thought through carefully, the conflict areas in the Sahel come with their own set of unique challenges. Thus, even if underlying cleavages and conflict lines may be relatively permanent, we are also currently faced with a new type of insurgency that does not fit within the established conceptual categories. These new insurgents we can observe are not fighting in the Sahel solely for national liberation, or separatism, or a revolution in the traditional sense, nor are they merely warlords seeking to maximise profits. However, even if their overarching objectives are none of these, they also contain traces of each of these categories of insurgencies.

What this leaves us with is a scenario where different competing Big Men vie for the role of nodal points between various extra-legal governance networks, some of which are mainly profit-driven, others combining income-generating strategies with social and political objectives (social and religious), yet others simply aiming to get by (and hopefully thrive in the future). As the constellations of these networks change, these acts and behaviours are organised, although not formally or permanently. It is possible that various strategies of criminality, coping, and resistance can be combined without necessarily losing sight of immediate and long-term objectives. The outcome is a narrative-driven space of coexistence, collusion, and conflict in which the conflation of different actors' interests, ideas, and actions will likely continue to feed analytical confusion, as well as misguided policy prescriptions (Bøås 2015a). Thus, this region becomes a social landscape in which insurgencies search for a way to insert themselves between competing systems of governance in order to install their own form of hybrid order and attempt to make it thrive.

Thus, what we are left with is a new wave of insurgencies that are both deeply local and anchored in global discourses at the same time. Branding has become an integral part of their strategy. They are religious fundamentalists, but also pragmatists, extremely capable in appropriating local grievances for their own purposes. Most of these insurgents operate in environments where local livelihoods are under immense pressure from a combination of population growth, increased climatic variability, and the inability of the state to address this adequately.

These insurgent groups are not necessarily intent on permanent territorial control, as this would entail certain costs, but rather on obtaining a social grip on targeted populations. This means that they do not fit into the dichotomy of stationary versus roaming bandits (or insurgencies) established by Mancur Olson (2000); instead, they occupy an intermediate position: these are insurgencies that operate what we call 'sporadic governance', a type of mobile governance that comes and goes, sporadically offering some governance services. As the jihadi insurgents of the Sahara-Sahel region are not seeking to capture nor break away from the state, but rather to attack the state's administrative presence (e.g. judges, police, mayors, schoolteachers) and challenge the very notion of the modern state, there is no (or only a very narrow) margin for a negotiated settlement. Negotiation, when evoked, as in the case of the Qaedist formations in Mali, is often a tactical step to consolidate positions. Finally, as most of these insurgencies are also very hard to beat militarily, the UN and the international community in general may be left to deal with conflict situations that become more and more difficult to solve.

The result is wars without frontiers or possible endgames (at least in the short to medium term). International forces and allies within the state can prevent complete state collapse and offer capital cities partial protection, but they cannot win a decisive military victory over the insurgents. Prominent jihadi leaders can be eliminated, but the trajectory of insurgencies in the Sahel shows that when one leader falls others emerge, and if one group splinters into dysfunctionality, new ones—or reorganisations of old ones—step forward.

In a scenario where no contender can impose a larger and deeper political order than its rivals, an interdependent system of various degrees of clientelism, sponsorship, and semi-autonomous Big Men emerges. It is therefore plausible that we will see more willingness on the part of international community actors, national elites, and insurgents to bargain for the 'beauty of imperfect compromises', with a growing role for politico-religious figures. Developments in Mali around the political role of important conservative imams such as Mahmoud Dicko could be a case in point.[3]

The answer to the question of how resilient constitutional democracies are in a region where an example of jihadist propaganda depicts the struggle between those who can afford air conditioning and those who cannot is ultimately dependent on how socially and politically inclusive such democracies prove to be while remaining anchored to the protection of fundamental rights. Given that the international system is increasingly characterised by competition and divergent forms of intervention, and less on rules, it is hard to envision political formulas based on national territorial homogeneity in the region. One hypothesis is that there might be a return to the ancient pragmatism of the Sahel trade, where alliances and decentralised violence are combined in a form or order that Thomas Hüsken and Georg Klute (2017) call heterarchical—a social order without state structures, but still with enough predictability for some kind of social and economic life with a long-term perspective to prevail. Another scenario is one of pervasive (para)militarisation of both 'secured' urban centres and rural peripheries. Several forms of social and territorial contracts can be combined in the hybrid order to come.

SAHEL

The challenge with predicting Sahel scenarios is that the region's future is both completely open and closed at the same time. It is open as the social landscape of the region is moving into uncharted territory, with old forms of state and non-state governance increasingly undermined by violent conflict, and immense uncertainty about hegemony and intervention characterising the current phase of the international system. However, unfortunately, it is also closed: in a region whose economy is based on circulation, the emerging security model based on enforcing demarcations and restricting mobility will increasingly be challenged by the already tangible combination of population growth and climate change effects. If anyone can acquire a more hegemonic position, this is the challenge they will be confronted with.

The Sahel—an emerging unknown social landscape

The political landscape of the Sahel has been through dramatic changes recently, and this has affected the conditions for field research, which has gone through a similar seismic shift. During my first field visit to Mali in 2008, I was astonished by our ability to gain access to high-level bureaucrats and politicians. Travelling with a friend and colleague who had worked in Mali during the 1990s, we had contacts and cell phone numbers that opened almost all doors (see Bøås 2012). People talked freely about almost anything, as long as they had an interest in telling their story or the message that they wanted to communicate.

When I returned to Mali in early 2013, I was able to use most of the same contacts, it was fairly easy to reach out to colleagues in Niger and Burkina Faso as well. Arrangements were established, and we worked together on several projects funded by the Norwegian Research Council and the EU's Horizon 2020 programme.

After 2015, the security situation in Mali deteriorated and field research became increasingly difficult. Security was a constant concern when we collected data in the Mopti region of Mali and the Tillabéri region of Niger in 2021–22 for the Horizon-funded project PREVEX.[4] However. the turning point was after the 'palace coup' in Mali in May 2021 and the subsequent coups in 2022 in Burkina Faso and in Niger in 2023. Since then, it has become extremely difficult to

SAHEL: ACTORS AND INGREDIENTS

work in these countries. Visa processes are complicated. Even if you get a visa, working on the ground with colleagues from the Sahel is difficult, and getting interviews with people in government can be almost impossible. Particularly in Mali, people are afraid to talk. Where people used to talk about everything if they thought something might be in their interest, there is now an atmosphere of fear. That's a fact for external researchers like me, but also for my friends and colleagues in these countries. Some have gone into exile; others are afraid—and for good reason—to work on anything that could be seen as political, and thereby sensitive and controversial, by the new military rulers. It has therefore become increasingly challenging to depict what is happening in the social landscapes of this part of the Sahel. Opinion polls like the Afrobarometer and Mali-Mètre show a high degree of support for the new military regimes, but to what extent they represent popular views is difficult to say (see Bøås & Haavik 2025). We may therefore be confronted with a situation where we are losing touch to some degree with the social landscape of this part of the Sahel.

This book is an attempt not only to offer a solid analysis of this part of the Sahel and what has happened here, but also to sum up over 10 years of research in this region for myself. The book is obviously based on what other people have written, my own texts, but also a multitude of fieldnotes I made during this decade. These include the references in text to the papers produced for the projects funded by Horizon 2020.

It is a story of about 10 years of misguided international interventions, failed and corrupt local governments, insurgencies that have grown stronger as the years have passed by, and consequently military coups that at least at the time of writing have popular support in the main cities. Is this book the definitive text about these 10 years of crisis? Absolutely not. It will be one of many, as more will come and some of them will undoubtedly be better. However, taking into consideration the weaknesses that will always be present when researching an ongoing conflict as multidimensional as this one, this book is hopefully accurate enough, and sufficiently sober and neutral, that it can be seriously engaged with and criticised by other researchers. That would be a debate that I would be most interested to participate in.

2

MALI

THE EPICENTRE OF THE SAHEL CONFLICT

While the key area of interest is Mali and its Sahel neighbours, some further specifications are needed, as the Sahel is enormous. The Sahel refers to the eco-climate and biogeographic zone of transition in Africa which stretches from Mauritania in the west to Ethiopia and Eritrea in the east. Here, however, the focus is almost exclusively on what historically was known as the Sudan region of the Sahel. In current parlance, this is the part of Sahel that comprises the following countries: Mauritania, Mali, Burkina Faso, Niger, and the southern parts of Algeria and Libya. The point of departure, as well as the endpoint of the book, is the turmoil in Mali, but the book will also discuss spillover effects to neighbouring countries and compare the conflict dynamics in Mali with the situation in the neighbouring countries.

Separating the Sahara to the north from the Sudanian savanna to the south, the Sahel takes its name from the Arabic word *sāhil*, which means coast or shore. This was an illustrative term in ancient times, and it is still a precise name for this part of the African continent. The reason for this is that there are two possible ways of interpreting the Sahel–Sahara: we can understand it as a great barrier, as something that separates both people and places, or conversely we can see it as a dry ocean, an area that can be navigated and travelled if you have the proper knowledge and means of transportation. The latter is a far more apt interpretation that the previous one. This is an issue we will return to when we discuss the routes of informal trade and illicit trafficking that traverse the Sahel. Thus, if we consider the Sahel not as a barrier but as an ocean of sand, cities like Agadez in northern Niger can be seen as what they really are: port cities whose bare existence depends on the availability of clients and customers, and the care and transport of goods and people.

State fragility in the Sahel

Mali, Niger, and Burkina Faso are some of the poorest and weakest countries in the world, and the fragility of these states is to varying degrees associated with instability, chronic violence, humanitarian crises, development problems, forthcoming climate change effects, and large-scale migration or displacement. This confronts the international community with grave challenges, as the lack of response capacity among the institutions of these countries has made it very difficult for international interventions to succeed. This is obvious in Mali's case and points to what we may call the 'fragility dilemma', which manifests itself in two different but related ways (see Bøås 2017).

First, these states are not only in desperate need of international assistance, but it is also very difficult to get traditional donor assistance to work effectively. The institutional and administrative response capacity is low, meaning there is only so much external aid—be it material, financial, or technical—that these countries effectively can absorb. Second, as these countries have much need of external assistance, one could easily come to think that they would be places where donors have considerable influence, but this is not necessarily the case. This is the second dimension of the fragility dilemma: for example, if we review donor engagement with Mali in the period from 2013 to August 2020, we will find that most donors became very frustrated with the democratically elected government. Government leaders, the president included, were often heavily criticised by members of the donor community for incompetence, mismanagement, and tolerance of corruption. However, this did not lead to much more than grumbling due to the fact that the donors saw no alternative to the regimes in power. What this effectively means is that being defined as a fragile state can be a bargaining asset when dealing with international donors if they do not see any clear and credible alternative to those in power (see also Bøås 2017).

As this chapter proceeds, we will first discuss the main factors in the crisis confronting Mali and neighbouring Sahel states. After this discussion, we will present the main insurgencies and explain why the idea of a Sahelian exception of collaborative cohabitation between groups leaning towards the ideologies of al-Qaeda and IS was but a moment and not one that could be sustained. Due to ideological and theological differences, but even more so because of their local alliances to different ethnic groups and different parts of ethnic groups, made this almost impossible in the long run.

We start however, with the multidimensional crisis. This is important because, while all these states may be weak and currently defined by the international community as 'fragile states', their weak statehood manifests itself very differently when faced with the current crisis. Mali may be the worst affected and will constitute a significant part of this section. Burkina Faso, which recently went through a period of turbulent political transition, is increasingly affected by insurgent groups with certain bonds to similar groups in Mali. There are reasons for this, most of which are local and national, and in this regard, we warn against viewing events in neighbouring Burkina Faso and Niger simply as spillover from Mali. It is not. The conflicts in Burkina Faso and Niger are mainly driven by local grievances, but still the larger regional conflict scenario cannot be ignored either.

Niger constitutes a different but very interesting case. In general terms, Niger shares many of the same characteristics as Mali. However, Niger has shown a much larger level of resilience to violent conflict than Mali. Niger also has a Tuareg minority, but, apart from the period 2007–9, there has not been any active violent Tuareg insurgency here. This is noteworthy, and we will return to this issue in Chapter 3, as the relative resilience that Niger continues to display despite the July 2023 military coup needs to be better understood, even if it cannot be taken for granted.

SAHEL

Mali—an introduction to the Sahel crisis

Mali is one of the world's poorest countries, ranked number 186 out of 191 countries (UNDP 2022), where most people make a living from agriculture and animal husbandry. Traditional livelihoods are threatened by violence and conflict, but also by demographic trends. Mali's current population of approximately 20.2 million is projected to increase to around 45 million by 2050. This projection is based on the current annual population growth of about 3 per cent, with each woman in Mali giving birth to an average of 5.8 children. Half of the population are below the age of fifteen, and two out of three people in Mali live on less than 2 dollars per day (World Bank 2022).

The economic outlook is equally bleak. The annual growth rate of the economy in 2020 was reported by the World Bank (2022) as having a negative growth of minus 1.2 per cent. This means that the Malian economy slipped into a recession in 2020, with real gross domestic product (GDP) estimated at minus 1.6 per cent, reflecting the adverse effects of the COVID-19 pandemic and the socio-political crisis as well as weak output from agriculture. The economy improved slightly thereafter, with an average growth in GDP per capita of about 3.5 per cent per year in the period of 2021–3. However, this is far from the growth rates of 5–7 per cent reported by the World Bank during the administration of the democratically elected Ibrahim Boubacar Keita. The message from the World Bank (2022) to the current transitional government is therefore to step up tax administration reforms in order to improve economic performance and optimise public spending. This is certainly necessary, but much easier said than done given the quagmire of conflict and political uncertainty than Mali is currently in.

The current trends that Mali is captured by—widespread poverty, population growth, violent conflict and a sluggish economy—are not sustainable in the long run, and the negative consequences they have for the population will be further exacerbated by future effects of climate change. For Mali, the combined forecasts of population growth and climate change will further decrease the amount of fertile land available for agriculture, while land is increasingly being sold off. The land being sold is most often not being used by the owner, but

MALI: THE EPICENTRE OF THE SAHEL CONFLICT

loaned or leased to someone else who now loses access to it (Bertrand 2019; Coulibaly & Li 2020). The inevitable result is greater competition for land—sometimes although not necessarily always violent, but with the clear potential for being appropriated by violent entrepreneurs in the form of jihadi-inspired insurgents. This is what has been taking place in the Inner Delta area of the Niger River in central Mali. Traditional arrangements such as customary tenure regimes have increasingly become dysfunctional or are simply unable to cope with an increasing number of conflicts, while the apparatus of modern administration (courts, etc.) is scanty, often far away, expensive to use, and often ridden by corruption and biased mismanagement (see Benjaminsen & Ba 2009).

Land rights conflicts in Mali are nothing new, but their importance as drivers of conflict is clearly increasing (Hansen 2023). The main reason for this is that land is an existential commodity in a country like Mali. It ensures survival in the present as well as being a guarantee for coping in the future. If one's access to land is threatened it must be protected, and protection must be sought where it can be found—even among jihadist insurgents if no other credible alternatives (see also Bøås & Dunn 2013). Such conflicts can emerge within communities (between different lineages) or between communities with different preferences for land use, such as between farmers and herders. Not all land rights conflicts in Mali are based on this cleavage, but as more and more land in the Inner Delta along the River Niger and its branch rivers is cultivated, there are fewer corridors available that allow access to water resources for herders and their flocks of cattle. Along the River Niger, the result is therefore a multitude of such conflicts, some of them cleverly appropriated by jihadist insurgents.

The first evidence of this occurring south of the Niger River emerged in 2013 around the town of Konna, where Fulani herders were pitted against local farmers. That same year, there were similar conflicts in the Gao area involving Fulani and Tuareg communities, where the former gained the support of the jihadi insurgency the Movement for Oneness and Jihad in West Africa (MOJWA). This trend has also spread in various parts of the Inner Delta of the Niger River, where local land rights conflicts have been appropriated by the

Katiba Macina insurgency. We will return to the situation in the Delta when we discuss the role that land rights conflicts play in the Sahel crisis; here, it is important to note that even if we see such conflicts and their appropriation by armed jihadi-inspired insurgencies as a major driver of violence, we take issue with how this is framed in the 'war on terror' interpretation of the crisis that has become the hallmark of international operations in Mali and increasingly elsewhere in the Sahel.

The Malian crisis: 2012/13—the year that refuses to end

The year 2012/13 constitutes a defining moment in the history of independent Mali as the combined forces of a military coup, the Tuareg uprising, and the advance of the jihadi insurgents exposed Mali's extreme fragility. The weakness of the state could no longer be hidden away behind images of the Flame of Peace Monument in Timbuktu, or with new promises of economic reforms, decentralisation, and peace and reconciliation efforts. However, if we are to understand what caused such dramatic events in Mali, we must not only study in detail what happened during this year, but also contextualise it. What we aim to accomplish is therefore a political analysis that not only focuses on key figures and their respective organisations, but also places them in the historical context of the trouble in Mali. This is a history of trouble that must be understood as a prolonged process of conflict, collusion, and resistance between Tuareg rebels demanding autonomy and independence for the North, jihadist insurgents, smugglers and traffickers, and state officials. These actors compete for influence and are often locked in violent conflict with each other, but also at times collaborate for economic gains or political benefit.

2012: the year of violent transformation

In early 2012, Mali was heading towards general elections. As this was taking place in a period of increased domestic uncertainty and regional instability, the Tuareg group the Movement for the National Liberation of Azawad (MNLA) and other insurgents (jihadists included) may have viewed this as the strategic moment to start a

MALI: THE EPICENTRE OF THE SAHEL CONFLICT

larger and more ambitious insurgency. It started with MNLA, but the jihadist insurgents soon managed to push the initial Tuareg rebellion into the background. This happened through a process that unfolded in four distinct but also partly overlapping phases.

The first phase was the period that spanned from the establishment of the National Movement of Azawad (MNA) in Timbuktu in November 2010 to the MNLA's first attacks in northern Mali in mid-January 2012. Key events include the return of former rebel commander Ibrahim Ag Bahanga to northern Mali in January 2011 after 2 years of exile in Libya; his death on 26 August 2011;[1] the Libyan civil war and fall of the Gaddafi regime; the subsequent return of former Tuareg rebels from Libya to Mali; and the making of the MNLA as a merger between the MNA and Ag Bahanga's group, the National Alliance of the Tuareg of Mali (NATM).

The second phase was the period between mid-January 2012 and the MNLA's declaration of independence of 'Azawad', which encompassed northern Mali, on 6 April 2012. During this period, the MNLA in collaboration with Iyad Ag Ghaly's Tuareg jihadist movement Ansar ed-Dine drove the Malian army out of the cities of the north. These military defeats led to protests in February by the families of military personnel in southern Mali. This was followed by a mutiny in the Malian army, which culminated in the coup of 21 March that removed President Touré from power and installed the National Committee for Recovering Democracy and Restoring the State (CNRDRE). The CNRDRE was chaired by Captain Amadou Haya Sanogo.

In the third phase, which lasted from 6 April 2012 to 8 January 2013, the main point to note is how the jihadi coalition in northern Mali—Ansar ed-Dine, al-Qaeda in the Islamic Maghreb (AQIM), and the MOJWA—politically and militarily outmanoeuvred the MNLA and took control of all major cities in the north. This period ended with the advance of jihadi insurgents south of the Niger River into the Mopti region and their seizure of the town of Konna, whereupon the political elite in Bamako, thinking that Bamako was next, panicked and turned to French President François Hollande for military assistance.

In the fourth phase, 8 January 2013 through 11 August 2013, the Islamist advance south of the Niger River triggered the French military intervention in Mali, Operation Serval. Together with troops from

Chad, other neighbouring countries, and some units from the Malian army, the intervention chased jihadi insurgents out of the main towns of the north. Operation Serval also attempted to gain control of the rest of the north, but with little success. In fact, it can be argued that the French troops, UN peacekeepers, and the Malian army never had more than nominal daytime control of the main towns of Gao, Kidal, and Timbuktu. The rest of the territory of the north was and remains hotly contested, something that the Wagner Group, which currently operates in Mali, has also come to experience. We will return to Bamako's new alliance with Russia and the Wagner Group in Chapters 9 and 10, but it is worth mentioning here that in late July 2024, jihadi insurgents together with other bands of Tuareg fighters may have killed as many as eighty Wagner operatives in the battle at Tinazaouaten in the north of Mali, close to the Algerian border (see Marotte 2024), and on 17 September Wagner forces in Bamako could not prevent jihadi insurgents from simultaneously attacking gendarmerie stations and the airport, where they burned the presidential airplane (see Lawal 2024). These incidents together with the fall of Assad in Syria have most certainly led to fear and confusion among regime leaders in Bamako, Ouagadougou, and Niamey.

Leaving aside the question of the durability of the Russian intervention for now, here it needs to be stated that the initial French intervention managed to create enough stability for Mali to hold democratic presidential elections. These culminated with a second round of presidential elections on 11 August 2013, won by Ibrahim Boubacar Keita with 77.6 per cent of the vote to Soumaila Cissé's 22.4 per cent. The elections returned Mali to nominal political stability, but President Keita's public approval ratings soon started to drop dramatically. The main reasons were his failure to broker a credible and sustainable peace agreement with the MNLA, defeat the jihadi insurgents, and tackle the endemic corruption that continued unabated despite his promise during the election campaign to clean up the system.

The 2018 elections

Whereas the 2013 elections took place in an upbeat and positive atmosphere, this was not the case of the summer 2018 presidential elections. Over twenty candidates participated, but there was little interest among the population. The election campaigns were not very high profile, as most candidates lacked sufficient funds to arrange a national campaign for their candidacy, and the threat of violence from jihadi insurgents was ever present in the north and central region. The fear of violence was very present, although the number of attacks and casualties were lower than expected.

In the end, a second round of voting was necessary. In the first round, on Sunday 29 July, the incumbent President Ibrahim Boubacar Keita took 41.4 per cent of the votes, but as the winning candidate needed 50 per cent + one vote, a second round on Sunday 12 August was necessary. Here President Keita faced Soumaila Cissé, who was the runner up in the first round with 17.8 per cent of the votes. Just after the results of the first round of voting were released, Cissé along with third-place Aliou Boubacar Diallo and fourth-place Cheick Modibo Diarra filed a court case. Their case was built on what they claimed were several irregularities, including that ballot boxes had been stuffed with fake votes. This case was rejected by the court, but what it shows is that the atmosphere during the 2018 elections was different from 2013, when Cissé had immediately acknowledged defeat. The voter turnout for the second round of voting in August was very low. Less than a quarter of the electorate voted, showing how little the Malian population seemed to care about this election and the outcome it would produce.

Once after the final votes had been cast, the opposition again immediately complained about irregularities, but President Keita dismissed claims that ballot boxes around the country had been stuffed with votes with his name on them. The international observers, who by and large only had been able to operate (semi-)independently in Bamako and the southern parts of the country, said that they would highlight some irregularities in their reports, but that in general they were satisfied with the process (Ba & Bøås 2018). That is to say, the international community and in particular key concerned European stakeholders were satisfied that elections were carried out and they could claim they were working with a democratically elected government against vicious jihadi insurgents and drugs and human traffickers. With the benefit of hindsight following the events of August 2020, more concern should have been given to what this would mean for the very idea of democracy in Mali, when the outcome was another Keita government that continued to fail in its fight against the jihadi insurgents while its corrupt practices became even more visible for anybody who wanted to see.

The path from Operation Serval and MINUSMA to Barkhane

In 2013, the first French military intervention in Mali (Operation Serval) in collaboration with the UN force (MINUSMA) managed to beat back the jihadi insurgents. The insurgents took some losses—including a prominent leader, the AQIM emir Abou Zeid—but nonetheless continued to prove their capacity to resist, striking within towns under the control of Operation Serval forces as well as those supposedly under MINUSMA surveillance. Thus, while entering the major towns in northern Mali may have been a swift and relatively easy military operation for the international forces, controlling this vast territory of sand proved to be much more difficult for France and MINUSMA, that would come to have a combined strength of about 15,000 troops and personnel.[2]

It is tempting to compare the situation that occurred in northern Mali in 2012/13 with the conflict that prevailed here in the 1990s. However, the crisis was no longer local; it had been internationalised via criminal networks and 'global jihad' (see Marchal 2013; Bøås 2012). Not only was the conflict in the north far more complex than it had been in the past, but the political situation also changed after the military coup of 21 March 2012 (Whitehouse 2012). This meant that it would be difficult, next to impossible, to return to the compromise of the 1990s that established the National Pact and the Governance and Decentralisation Programme (see Chapter 6). The current crisis in Mali is therefore much more severe and complex than the previous crises that Mali has experienced. Moreover, the history of previous attempts at reform also indicates that conducting combined political democratisation, economic liberalisation, and administrative decentralisation in a weak and fragile state such as Mali runs the risk of being hijacked by a combination of national elites and regional Big Men (see Bøås 2012). This is precisely what happened in the 1990s in Mali (Lecocq et al. 2013), and the events in 2012 are an unintended consequence of this. In policy circles, Mali was for a time

MALI: THE EPICENTRE OF THE SAHEL CONFLICT

in the 1990s and early 2000s heralded as a model for democratisation in Africa (Pringle 2006). However, the reality on the ground was a far cry from the idealised picture of the Flame of Peace ignited in Timbuktu on 27 March 1996 to herald Mali as model for peace, reconciliation, and democratic conflict resolution in Africa.

After the failed attempt in early January 2013 by ECOWAS and the AU to respond to the Malian crisis, France launched Operation Serval, based on a request from the transitional authorities in Bamako. This was followed by the planning of a larger AU operation. Operation Serval succeeded in pushing the jihadi insurgencies out of main northern cities like Gao, Kidal, and Timbuktu. However, reluctant to take formal ownership of the international engagement in Mali but also concerned that the planned AU operation would not be able to maintain Serval's military gains, France insisted on a stronger multilateral arrangement (see Théroux-Benoni 2014). France wanted the AU operation to be transposed into a UN force, like MINUSMA. This would also enable France to wield considerable influence over MINUSMA, where the costs and possible flaws could be more widely distributed. All this was possible because France holds a permanent seat on the UN Security Council, from which it was able to sign off on all UN resolutions on Mali (see Tardy 2016).

This did not change when Serval was replaced by Operation Barkhane in July 2014, but it expanded the scope of the French mission to include other former French colonies in the region—Burkina Faso, Chad, Mauritania, and Niger. Thus, even if Barkhane represented a wider geographical focus, it also reinforced the anti-terror approach to the Malian crisis, an approach that has been strongly promoted by French security and foreign politics (see Marchal 2013).

The argument is not that there is no need for external support for a military approach against the jihadi-inspired insurgencies but that the Malian crisis has been framed within too narrow of a hard security focus. This has come to inform how the Malian state, opposition groups, contentious political actors on the ground, and other international actors approach the crisis and the issues at stake. This is particularly pertinent in the case of successive series of governments in Bamako, as defining the crisis as one caused by foreign terrorist groups provides a convenient excuse for not dealing with the underlying internal causes of conflict and the drivers of violence. Not only has the crisis that erupted in Mali in 2012 continued unabated, but it is increasingly taking a turn for the worse. As such, there is an obvious need to re-calibrate current approaches. This should be done with an eye to the historical context, as it is impossible to make sense of the current situation without understanding the past.

What about other regional arrangements—castles in the sand?

The precarious security situation in the region is further exacerbated by the almost total absence of any functional regional arrangement. In contrast to the regional warzone that developed in the Mano River Basin in the late 1990s, the Sahel has no regional arrangement like ECOWAS, which encompassed all of its neighbouring countries, nor is there an obvious regional hegemon such as Nigeria (see Bøås 2000). ECOWAS tried to intervene at the beginning of the crisis in 2012/13 but was sidelined together with the AU by France. Since then, ECOWAS's influence has been limited to sanctioning the transitional government in Bamako after what we can refer to as the 'palace coup' of May 2021,[3] and later sanctioning the new military governments of Burkina Faso and Niger. This second round of sanctions has proven equally futile, and their only results have been these countries leaving ECOWAS and establishing a competing regional organisation (see Chapters 9 and 10).

The few other regional arrangements that exist are either dysfunctional or severely hampered in their ability to execute policy by the old rivalry between Algeria and Morocco. This is not likely to change soon, as their decaying relationship has taken a turn for the worse since August 2021. Accusing Morocco of supporting terrorism in Algeria and other subversive activities, the Algerian government cut diplomatic ties with Morocco, and in late September of that year it closed its airspace to all Moroccan planes (see Zouhir 2021).

The lack of working regional arrangements was therefore one important reason why France, Germany, and the EU placed considerable emphasis on assisting the creation of a new regional institution, the G5 Sahel. The idea was that this new regional body—created by the presidents of Mauritania, Mali, Niger, Chad, and Burkina Faso—would strengthen regional security co-operation, but also implement common projects in infrastructure, food security, agriculture, and pastoralism, all related to root causes of conflict in the region.

External stakeholders in search of a regional framework greeted the initiative with considerable interest, and perhaps it could have become a new functional framework for security and development co-operation in the Sahel. However, for this to happen external stakeholders would have needed to realise that a regional arrangement is rarely more than the sum of its member states, and the member states in question here were all fragile. This means that for the G5 Sahel to have had any chance of succeeding, external institutional support would have had to work in tandem with assistance building administrative capacity in the member countries. This was not impossible, but it would have been a slow and difficult process, with several setbacks.

What happened instead was that external stakeholders, wanting swift results on the ground, rushed the process of establishing the G5 Sahel as a regional security actor. The result was that too much emphasis was placed on hard security measures in the establishment of the G5 Sahel Joint Force (FC-G5S), and consequently far too little was placed on the development dimension of the larger G5 Sahel agenda. As the external stakeholders would have to carry most of the costs, they were mainly interested in the FC-G5S part of the G5 Sahel as an arrangement that could provide more boots on the ground. 'Boots' that could be directed towards external priorities of improved border control to reduce northbound migration flows while fighting those who the same stakeholders defined as jihadist terrorists and therefore a threat to global security.

It is in considering these external priorities that we should understand the Western donors' pledge of half a billion USD for the FC-G5S in 2018. As Carbonnel and Emmott (2018) of Reuters reported from the meeting that took place in Brussels on 23 February 2018, 'The European Union which believes training local forces will allow it to avoid risking the lives of its own combat troops, doubled its contribution to 116 million euros.' The only part of the G5 Sahel that functioned for a while was thus framed in the same narrow 'war on terror' approach as other ongoing international initiatives. This was ultimately at the expense of the development agenda of the G5 Sahel, which contained at least the potential for tackling root causes of conflict in the Sahel. European pledges of support for the Sahel by way of support to the G5 Sahel were thus in fact pledging to support European political stability, and not necessarily a sustainable investment in a peace, reconciliation, and development agenda for the Sahel.

Considerable amounts of money were invested in the G5 Sahel. However, as events have unfolded since August 2020, with a government in Bamako that is feuding not only with ECOWAS but, until the July 2023 coup, with neighbouring Niger as well, the G5 Sahel was for all practical purposes dead. In May 2022, Mali left the G5 Sahel, then Burkina Faso and Niger followed suit on 3 December 2023. Thus, although the institutional structures remained in place, what had been established to much fanfare and donor support became just another entity in a spaghetti bowl of dysfunctional regionalism in the Sahel. Consequently, on 6 December 2023, the two remaining members, Chad and Mauritania, announced the dissolution of the G5 Sahel.

The insurgents

Ever since Mali gained independence from France in 1960, the Tuareg minority of the north have been in rebellion against the state. The first rebellion took place in the early 1960s, and the second one started in 1990 (Berge 2002). As the National Pact of 1992 failed to produce tangible results on the ground, a new rebellion emerged in 2006 (Bøås 2012). This was relatively small until many Tuareg returned from post-Gaddafi Libya with masses of arms. This gave new impetus to the idea of rebellion, and a new movement was formed in 2012, namely the MNLA.[4] Whereas Tuareg independence and nationalism had been more of an alias for previous rebellions, the MNLA declared full independence of Azawad from Mali. The struggle was no longer to access the Malian state and secure positions of power and privilege for Tuareg leaders and leading lineages, but to break away from it entirely.

The little that may have existed of Tuareg unity, however, quickly disappeared. As MNLA fighters looted and plundered in the north and the Malian army ran away and engineered the 21 March 2012 coup in Bamako, the MNLA was effectively sidelined by other forces: the Tuareg Islamist organisation Ansar ed-Dine, led by Iyad Ag Ghaly, a

MALI: THE EPICENTRE OF THE SAHEL CONFLICT

veteran Tuareg fighter from the 1990s, and two other regional movements: AQIM and MOJWA. The latter two are not Tuareg movements per se but have been present in this area since around 1998, so they should not be seen solely as alien invading forces. In fact, they have achieved considerable local integration in some places and among certain communities in the north. Skilfully appropriating local grievances, AQIM and MOJWA quickly became integral parts of the conflict mosaic of northern Mali (Bøås & Torheim 2013; Bøås 2015b; Raineri & Strazzari 2015).

In the first part of the period since 2012, AQIM was at the forefront of the jihadi insurgents. This is no longer the case. Its so-called southern or Saharan unit is basically non-existent, and the relationship between the current AQIM leadership in Algeria and the jihadi insurgency in the Sahel is weak. The jihadi insurgents no longer take orders from AQIM, as they have become much more powerful than AQIM ever were. However, as AQIM was instrumental in setting the jihadi scene in the Sahel in motion, it is still important to offer a precise overview of what this group once was.

AQIM

Until the announcement of the establishment of Jama'at Nusrat al-Islam wal Muslimeen (JNIM) in 2017, AQIM was commonly viewed as the lynchpin in a crime–terror nexus that had taken advantage of the 'ungoverned space' of the Sahel. In conventional analyses, it was seen as an operational branch in a global al-Qaeda structure. However, when we look beyond the global rhetoric also employed by AQIM itself, a more nuanced picture emerges. Based on a sophisticated reading of the local context, AQIM developed advanced strategies of local integration in Mali. Its operatives knew how to combine the group's financial strength, military equipment, and religious credentials. The latter was important in an area where local administration, to the extent that it exists, is generally seen as corrupt and of little use to local people. AQIM operatives, on the other hand, presented themselves as honest and pious Muslims.

AQIM's point of origin is in the Algerian civil war, which erupted after the country's military leadership annulled the 1992 elections results. Officially, the civil war ended with an amnesty act (the Civil

Harmony Act) in 1999, but some fighters were not willing to lay down their weapons, or they were afraid that they would be accused of having committed acts of violence not covered by the amnesty. Some of them made their way across the border to Mali. It was these fighters who came to form the core of AQIM. Most of them belonged to the Salafist Group for Preaching and Combat (GSPC) that had left the Armed Islamic Group (GIA) during the latter stages of the Algerian civil war. During its first decade in Mali, the group kept its original name but changed it to AQIM in 2006 (see Lounnas 2014; Thurston 2020a).

When GSPC left GIA in 1998, the group communicated that this was its response to GIA's massacres of civilians, but it also simultaneously declared support for al-Qaeda. Three years later, GSPC withdrew its support to al-Qaeda, but then reaffirmed its loyalty and received al-Qaeda's blessing in 2003. Finally, GSPC embraced the al-Qaeda banner in 2007and changed its name to AQIM (see Thurston 2020a). It may have done this for ideological reasons, but more pragmatic concerns may also have played a role. These were men who had lost the war in Algeria and were now on the run in the sand dunes of northern Mali. Neither the Algerian government nor the international community would negotiate with them, and as such so no settlement, not even an honorary surrender, was in sight. They had little to lose and much to gain from embracing the al-Qaeda banner: it would make them look more global, and more omnipotent and powerful in the eyes of local communities (Bøås 2015a).

In 2013 and a few years thereafter, AQIM may have had as many at 1,000 men at arms and operated across the western Sahel, from Algeria and Libya in the north to Mali, Mauritania, and Niger in the south (see Laub & Masters 2015). The supreme AQIM leader Abdelmalek Droukdel was well-respected among the various units that constituted the group's southern flank, but the organisation suffered from a major deficit that soon would become apparent. Droukdel was in hiding in Algeria, while by now most of AQIM's activities were taking place in the Sahel. This meant that Droukdel's ability to influence not only day-to-day activities but also strategic planning was very limited. The leaders of the AQIM units in the south therefore became increasingly more autonomous. Droukdel rarely, if ever, met them in

MALI: THE EPICENTRE OF THE SAHEL CONFLICT

person. Electronic communication was seen as too dangerous, and consequently he relied on sending physical letters. This may have given him safety from Western intelligence services, but it is not an efficient way of supervising an insurgency taking place far away from where you are hiding. The outcome was ultimately that AQIM's position as the lead insurgency among the jihadi groups of the Sahel started to dissipate as local leaders, such as Iyad Ag Ghaly and Hamadoun Kouffa, became the face of the new front of jihad in Africa.

When Droukdel finally travelled to northern Mali in June 2020, he was killed by French forces on the 3 June. Thus one of the few remaining original jihadists in the region met his end. Even if he had remained in the shadows in Algeria, Droukdel had achieved a nearly mythical status as one of the few still alive of the generation that had started the jihadi insurgency project. Droukdel's death therefore also signalled the end of AQIM as a leading force in the Sahel, as none of the surviving AQIM leaders in Algeria held much sway over the leaders and rank-and-file of JNIM or the Katiba Macina. These latter organisations were no longer the 'little brothers' to the Algerian jihadists but had become key players in the region. Iyad Ag Ghaly and Hamadoun Kouffa were no longer just local heroes, but legends in their own right throughout the Sahel.

Ansar ed-Dine

Ansar ed-Dine translates as 'Defenders of the Faith', and the group was established in northern Mali by Iyad Ag Ghaly. Its first reported action was in March 2012. The group consists mostly of ethnic Tuaregs and is organised according to existing tribal structures. Its number of fighters is estimated at several hundreds. However, as is the case of most of the jihadi groups in the Sahel, the actual figure is not only unknown but varies with circumstances and who is considered part of it (see, for example, IISS 2017).

Its leader, Iyad Ag Ghaly, an Ifoghas Tuareg from the Irayaken clan, has been at the forefront of violent Tuareg discontent for more than four decades. Like several young Tuareg men of his generation Ag Ghaly left Mali for Libya in the early 1980s. As did many others, he left due to increased pressure on local livelihoods caused by the frequent droughts in this period. In Libya, he joined Muammar

Gaddafi's Islamic Legion and fought, among other places, in Lebanon (see Thurston 2020a). When Gaddafi closed the Islamic Legion in the late 1980s, Ag Ghaly returned to northern Mali, and in 1990 he launched his first attack against the Malian state, as head of the Popular Movement of Azawad (MPA). At that time, he was a secular rebel. However, after the National Pact of 1992 and the final peace agreement of 1996, Ag Ghaly appears to have come under the influence of the Islamic missionary movement Jama'at Al-Tabligh that had started to operate in northern Mali and gained influence among the Ifoghas of Kidal. However, this did not prevent Ag Ghaly from playing an instrumental role in negotiating the release of thirty-two German hostages who had been taken by GSPC. Ag Ghaly's involvement in in these negotiations gave clear indication of his growing importance as a regional Big Man.

In 2006, Ag Ghaly together with Ibrahim Ag Bahanga formed the May 23, 2006 Democratic Alliance for Change (ADC)—a short-lived rebellion that ended after a couple of months with a peace agreement signed in Algiers. Soon after, Ag Ghaly left Mali for Pakistan and the spiritual headquarters of Jama'at Al-Tabligh, spending some time there before the Malian government appointed him in 2007 to the position of cultural attaché at the Malian Embassy Consulate in Jeddah, Saudi Arabia. This decision was probably based on the calculation that having Ag Ghaly on a state salary somewhere else in the world would keep him from joining or organising yet another rebellion in northern Mali. With hindsight, the wisdom of this strategy is questionable, because in 2010 Ag Ghaly was expelled from Saudi Arabia for unspecified interactions with suspected extremists linked to al-Qaeda. He returned to Mali and again served as an intermediary in hostage negotiations, this time with AQIM. Later events give rise to questions as to what it was Ag Ghaly did and contributed to in these processes.

When Tuareg fighters started to return to Mali en masse after the fall of Gaddafi in Libya in 2011, Ag Ghaly was once more called upon by the Malian government—this time to act as a liaison between the government and the returning combatants. Ag Ghaly used this position to attempt to take over the leadership of the Ifoghas and the MNLA. Failing in both regards—at least partly because the leadership of the Ifoghas traditionally belongs to the noble clan and not the warrior clan to which Ag Ghaly belongs—he ended up creating Ansar ed-Dine and quickly allied his new insurgency with AQIM (Thurston 2020a).

After the French intervention (Operations Serval and Barkhane) and the establishment of MINUSMA, Ansar ed-Dine continued as a rural insurgency. It no longer has the control of cities and towns that it enjoyed in 2012, but it employs several asymmetrical warfare tactics to weaken its primary targets. Its militants employ suicide attacks, explosive-laden vehicles, and more traditional insurgency warfare carried out with rocket-propelled grenades (RPGs), mortars, grenades, and rifles. Its primary targets were the French force in Mali, MINUSMA, and of course to this day the Malian army and police force. However, it has also contributed to attacks against hotels, restaurants, and bars frequented by international personnel, thus contributing to making the international operation in Mali one of the world's most deadly. Apart from self-identifying as a Salafi-jihadist group and having declared that it aims to establish Sharia law across Mali (Sandor & Campana 2019; see also ICG 2016), Ansar ed-Dine has not really communicated a larger religious-ideological platform or agenda.

Ansar ed-Dine's partnership with AQIM, al-Mourabitoun, and the Katiba Macina led to the establishment of JNIM as an umbrella organisation in 2017. JNIM allows these groups to join forces and coordinate more closely when needed, but the member insurgencies have also continued to operate as autonomous entities. This is necessary, as they recruit from different ethnic groups and communities that often have grievances and disputes among each other. While Ag Ghaly is the leader and frontman of JNIM, his power base is still in Ansar ed-Dine and those from the Tuareg community who support this group.

The Katiba Macina

Central Mali is currently gripped by an escalating sense of insecurity, due to an increase in inter-communal conflicts, the proliferation of self-defence groups and armed non-state actors including jihadist groups and bandits. One of these radical jihadi insurgencies is the Katiba Macina, led by Hamadoun Kouffa, a well-known and respected

Islamic Fulani preacher from Niafunké in Mopti (Rupesinghe & Bøås 2018). Having been active in the region of Mopti for at least a couple of decades, Kouffa had developed a following at the Quranic schools he taught at. Later in the early 2000s, Kouffa started to cultivate a relationship with Iyad Ag Ghaly through the Tabligh organisation (also known as the 'Dawa'). When the war came to the Mopti region in 2012/13, Kouffa's following and his connection to Ag Ghaly, who by then had become the leader of Ansar ed-Dine, could be utilised to start a separate insurgency in Mopti.[5] While the Katiba Macina has a connection to JNIM (the new Sahel superstructure of Salafi-inspired insurgencies) and therefore operates under the mantle of global jihadist discourse, it ultimately thrives on appropriating local conflict, exploiting communal and inter-communal resource disputes, and igniting inter-ethnic and intra-communal tensions in order to garner support. However, while the global brand of jihad is not the major vehicle for recruitment and local affiliation, it provides the Katiba Macina with a global-religious identity and legitimacy, as well as access to resources, allies, and national and regional networks (Rupesinghe & Bøås 2018).

Mopti and the Inner Delta of the Niger River has historically been a contested space. It is rich in resources, but competing systems of governance challenge each other, and those who never see the benefits are the common people of the region. Communal conflict over access to land and water is not a new phenomenon, but it is exacerbated by population growth, climate change effects, and the presence of armed jihadi groups that have developed strategies for turning to their advantage conflicts that a vanishing and dysfunctional state is not able to deal with in a trustworthy manner. When colonial power arrived in this part of Mali after the fall of the Macina Empire in 1864 (Brown 1968), the French accepted the original management system of natural resources to an extent, but they also undermined it by establishing a parallel form of land tenure. Customary chiefs managed land under continuous cultivation, whereas the colonial administration controlled so-called 'unoccupied land' and could grant private property titles. Water and forests were placed under the control of the Water and Forest Agency—the current *Direction Nationale des Eaux et Foréts* (see Ursu 2018).

MALI: THE EPICENTRE OF THE SAHEL CONFLICT

It is the increasing corruption and dysfunctionality of these two competing systems of land governance that the Katiba Macina is currently utilising, using land conflicts that increasingly are turning violent in order to achieve local integration and, if not control of territory per se, at least a sufficient grip on the population. The Katiba Macina has, for example, achieved widespread acceptance due to its management and control of the much-prized *bourgoutiéres* (the highly nutritious dry-season pastures that pastoralists depend on for grazing their livestock) by halting access fees, claiming that the land belongs to God alone. This is in stark contrast to the rising access fees (sometimes up to 1,000 000 CFA), extracted by the Jowros, part of the noble Rimbé class who act as the gatekeepers of the pastures. These fees to access pastures have fostered much resentment among herdsmen who consider the Jowros to be corrupt, pocketing the fees for personal gain (Rupesinghe and Bøås 2018). This is but one example from this part of the Sahel that shows that, while religion is a vector in the current landscape of conflict, the underlying issues are land rights conflicts.

Thus, while its connection to JNIM suggests an ideological orientation towards al-Qaeda theology, the driving force behind the success of the Katiba Macina has been its ability to tap into local Fulani grievances in central Mali. This local agenda is bolstered by the group's ability to administer resource management systems, local mobile courts, and tariff collection systems on trade at river points.

Jama'at Nusrat al-Islam wal Muslimeen (JNIM)

JNIM was established in Mali in March 2017, as a merger between Ansar ed-Dine, AQIM, and al-Mourabitoun (Weiss 2017). The Katiba Macina was present at the inaugural meeting but was not officially mentioned at that time as a founding member of JNIM. JNIM also declared loyalty to the al-Qaeda network and to Abdelmalek Droukdel, the AQIM emir until he was killed in 2020.

Some observers have been sceptical of the groups' ability to effectively co-operate and conduct joint missions under a strategic framework (Weiss 2017). The main reason for this is the failure of previous attempts at establishing a joint command of the various Islamic insurgencies in Mali and bordering the Sahel periphery. AQIM itself at first aspired to such a role but found it difficult, almost impossible, to accommodate multiple local agendas within its organisation. This led to fragmentation, and this may be the case again, as it can be difficult to reconcile the local agendas of Tuareg and Fulani jihadists in the long term.

They may agree on some overall religious–political principles, but when it comes to the practical issues that give them the ability to integrate locally through the appropriation of local conflict, these groups tend to be at odds with each other. However, so far they have been able to keep a relatively high level of internal cohesion while simultaneously allowing local JNIM leaders flexibility and pragmatism in dealing with local populations. If JNIM succeeds in this matter in the long run, the group could grow to become a considerably higher threat to the government in Bamako than it currently is. If it successfully pools resources and acts strategically under a joint command, the group has the potential for co-ordination of larger regional operations. Much will continue to depend on the leadership qualities of Iyad Ag Ghaly. If he succeeds in this regard, it will increase the threat level in Mali, but also in neighbouring Sahel countries, as JNIM is highly influential in Burkina Faso as well as responsible for the attempt to move further south into coastal states such as Benin, Côte d'Ivoire, Ghana, and Togo.

In the video that was released from the inauguration of JNIM, Ag Ghaly did not specifically mention the Katiba Macina, but as representatives of the latter were present it is quite clear that the Katiba Macina is a member of the new superstructure of jihadism in the Sahel (see also ACLED 2023). This has given the jihadi insurgents a social platform south of the Niger River that they did not previously have. While Ag Ghaly and JNIM have not been shy about declaring a form of loyalty to al-Qaeda, it should be noted that they have made it clear that they have no interest in being involved in attacks on French or European soil. However, Ag Ghaly has also made it clear that he and his men have the right to continue attacking French and European interests in the Sahel if France and Europe continue to support what Ag Ghaly and his followers consider illegitimate governments (see also Boeke 2022). This suggests that, for Ag Ghaly and JNIM, the local agenda of Mali and the Sahel is much more important than their being a pawn in a global struggle.

MALI: THE EPICENTRE OF THE SAHEL CONFLICT

Islamic State Greater Sahara (ISGS)

When the MNLA rebellion gained ground in Mali in 2012, it armed young Tuareg and Daoussahak men and took control of large parts of the Gao and Ménaka regions. In the chaos that followed, with plunder and cattle theft directed against Fulani communities (Bøås & Torheim 2013), some young Fulani herders started to look elsewhere for allies. As the Malian state could not provide them with security, they found support in the MOJWA insurgency that operated in the same area (Benjaminsen & Ba 2020). MOJWA undoubtedly gained some local support in and around Gao, and it cunningly appropriated local grievances concerning land rights, taking the side of Fulani pastoralist groups in local land rights conflict (Bøås 2015b). In this process, MOJWA also welcomed the support of Fulani fighters from Niger in Tillabéri, across the border to the north. These served as useful recruits for MOJWA, as many of them already had experience with using force due to the years of inter-communal conflict in Tillabéri (see also Raineri 2020).

When this process started, the man who would become the first leader of Islamic State Greater Sahara (ISGS), Abu Walid al-Sahrawi, was a MOJWA commander, and when MOJWA gained control of Gao he became the governor of Gao city. Al-Sahrawi is a person of considerable interest, as he was not from this part of the Sahel at all. He was born in Laayoune, in Western Sahara, and his real name is Lehbib Ould Ali Ould Said Ould Yumani (al-Sahrawi is his nom de guerre). His family were relatively wealthy traders who fled from Western Sahara to the Sahrawi refugee camps in Tindouf, Algeria. Here al-Sahrawi joined the Polisario Front, but he left it when the UN started to plan for a referendum on the status of Western Sahara. We know that he studied social sciences at the Mentouri University of Constantine in Algeria, and he graduated in 1997. However, as the saga goes, he became depressed and disillusioned with the Polisario Front as the referendum on Western Sahara never materialised. The answer that al-Sahrawi must have found was to turn to Salafist interpretations of Islam, and around 2010 he left Tindouf for northern Mali where he joined AQIM. However, only one year later he was among the group that broke with AQIM to establish MOJWA, where he was one of the senior leaders. He served on MOJWA's Shura council, and he was the spokesperson that communicated with international media.

This would not last very long, as the French Operation Serval closed in on Gao in January 2013. Al-Sahrawi had to flee the city, and his escape was assisted by his newfound allies, Fulani fighters from the Mali–Niger border area, including some from Tillabéri (ICG 2020b). Here, in the tri-border area of Liptako-Gourma along the Malian border to Tillabéri, al-Sahrawi found an enabling environment in which he could embed himself and the fighters who had travelled with him by appropriating local grievances, which he fertilised along lines of inter-communal conflict. In August 2013, what was left of MOJWA around al-Sahrawi merged with Mokhtar Belmokhtar's al-Mulathameen group to form al-Mourabitoun, with al-Sahrawi as the operational leader.

During this period, the Malian army was not much present along the border with Niger and Operation Serval did not have the capacity to guard it, while Nigerien security forces, although present, lacked the capacity, training, and leadership to comprehend and deal with what was happening (see ICG 2020b). The result was that al-Sahrawi and the fighters who had followed him were able to regroup and start recruiting locally in Tillabéri, especially among Fulani herder communities that for a long time had felt that their land was being encroached upon by agricultural expansion in the south and increased competition from Daoussahak pastoralist communities in the north (see Bøås et al. 2020).

Thus, in a security vacuum where the Nigerien state was not completely absent but lacked control over the use of force, al-Sahrawi managed to gain not territorial control but such a tight grip on certain population groups that he was able to establish his own insurgency, namely ISGS, pledging allegiance to IS and its leader Abu Bakr al-Baghdadi in 2015.[6] This was a challenge to state security that the Nigerien government was not well prepared for, but initially this did not cause too much concern: not only did it take over a year and a half before al-Sahrawi's allegiance was formally accepted by a notification in the IS Amaq News Agency (see Joscelyn & Weiss 2016), but Belmokhtar denounced al-Mourabitoun's pledging loyalty to al-

MALI: THE EPICENTRE OF THE SAHEL CONFLICT

Baghdadi and IS. This caused a split in the group, but as we will see ISGS under al-Sahrawi was able to recruit new followers.

Utilising the strained relationship between different ethnic communities that became even more violent after the Tuareg movement Groupe Autodéfense Touareg Imghad et Alliés (GATIA), aligned with the Malian government, started to operate along the border and crossed into Niger and Tillabéri, ISGS manoeuvred to take the side of Fulani communities that were increasingly being targeted by GATIA and Daoussahak militias. Gaining access to a new pool of recruitment, ISGS was responsible for several attacks against security forces and installations in Tillabéri, but also elsewhere in western Niger, northern Burkina Faso, and north-east Mali.

In October 2017, al-Sahrawi became known internationally as his forces managed to kill four American special forces and five Nigerien soldiers in an ambush outside a town called Tonga Tonga in Tillabéri. Thereafter, al-Sahrawi was no longer the 'little brother' to the famous, almost mythical jihadi warriors of the Sahel such as Mokhtar Belmokhtar, Iyad Ag Ghaly, and Hamadoun Kouffa, but on par with them. Not only did he become bolder and more daring in his attacks, but his ambitions also increased as he began to move his forces steadily closer to the heartland of the Katiba Macina and thereby also to JNIM in central Mali.

The end of the Sahelian exception—JNIM versus ISGS

During the first years of ISGS's existence, its relationship to JNIM was mainly cordial, at times almost friendly, to the extent that the two groups even conducted some joint operations. Consequently, some observers started to write about the so-called 'Sahelian exception' or 'anomaly' (see, for example, Paquette & Warrick 2020). The Sahel was seen as the exception to the history of violent conflicts between al-Qaeda and IS, where whenever groups aligned to either al-Qaeda or IS cohabited there would be deadly conflict between them. The doctrinal differences between them were simply too huge to be reconciled in peaceful coexistence.

These doctrinal differences can be summed up in six main points (see Tønnessen 2015; Thomas 2016; Wagemakers 2016; Hafez 2017;

Bacon & Aresenaul 2019). First, the question of the establishment of the Caliphate. Is it the responsibility of the true mujahedeen to establish it immediately (as IS maintains) or can it be left as an ultimate objective of the struggle (as al-Qaeda strategies have emphasised). This may sound like a theoretical/theological debate, but it has immense consequences for other strategic decisions that these groups must make. Second, Islamic law: should Sharia be implemented at once without any compromises (IS) or should there be a gradual process that allows a certain tolerance of long-standing social and religious practices more largely to yield sustainable results in the long run (al-Qaeda)? Third, related to this is the question of alliances with other groups: are they permissible or not? The IS doctrine sees this basically as 'unbelief', while various al-Qaeda-aligned groups have a tradition of entering pragmatic alliances with others, even groups whose origin and objectives are much more secular. Fourth, sectarianism, here understood as an Islam that is Sunni and Sunni only, there is only one version of Islam and that is Sunni orthodoxy (IS), versus an interpretation that applies a slightly less strict interpretation of the *takfir* doctrine. Fifth, the *takfir* doctrine itself, which simply put is an Arab and Islamic concept of excommunication from Islam of one Muslim by another—in essence, accusing a Muslim of being apostate. While both al-Qaeda and IS are inspired by the *takfir* doctrine, in most cases IS and IS-inspired movements tend to apply it more harshly and towards much larger groups of people. A few sentences are therefore needed to describe what this concept is all about and its history.

The concept of *takfir* is not found in the Quran or in the *hadith* literature. In these holy texts, what do appear are the terms *kufr* (unbelief) and *kafir* (unbeliever), which amounts to apostasy. Since the punishment for apostasy in the traditional interpretations of Islam is the death sentence, the question of who can legitimately accuse another of unbelief has always been a source of huge debate in Islamic jurisprudence. The first historical recording of the *takfir* doctrine being put into effect dates back to the seventh century, when a sect known as the Kharijites carried out attacks against both Sunni and Shia Muslims based on accusations of apostasy. The religious reasoning was that Muslims not only have the right but also the duty to revolt against any ruler who deviates from what the Kharijites considered to be the only true and correct version of Islam. Since the Kharijites' assassination of Caliph Ali, they have been regarded as those most eager to declare others *takfir* in Islamic history.

The debate, however, continued. The *takfiri* writings of fourteenth-century Islamic scholar Ibn Taymiyyah, who directed his interpretation of *takfir* against several Muslim groups, including Shia and Sufi, has been a source of inspiration for scholars who followed him, and for IS. Ibn Taymiyyah as well as also Ibn al-Jawziyya (1292–1350) and Muhammad al-Wahhab (1703–92) have all been quoted frequently by texts produced by IS. However, what brought these ancient Islamic scholars and the *takfir* debate back to the forefront was the book *Milestones* by the Egyptian Sayyid Qutb, published in 1964. This book strongly espouses Ibn Taymiyyah's principle of *takfir*, holding that Muslims who do not follow a strict implementation of Sharia are not Muslims. While Qutb did not call for mass killings of those he considered guilty of unbelief, he argued that those who led societies that had fallen into unbelief were irredeemably corrupt and evil, and the vanguard movement of true Muslims must remove them from power through jihad (see Qutb 1964).

While al-Qaeda and those inspired by its ideology also have used ideas about unbelief and versions of the *takfir* doctrine to legitimise violence against civilian targets, it is IS that has advanced the harshest version of it, as they have targeted all Shia as apostates (see Wood 2015). While Shia Muslims are few and far between in the Sahel, how these groups understand the various interpretations of *takfir* has important consequences for how they approach local communities and their various religious practices, as well as how they go about making pragmatic alliances with groups that have a less strict interpretation of Islam. Those who lean towards the IS reading of *takfir* tend also to have a puritanical approach to the question of how the relations to local communities should be ordered (obedience to the theological scripture). These groups would consider establishing alliances with other groups that practise what they see as unbelief to be strictly forbidden, or *haram*.

The level of knowledge that the leaders of JNIM and ISGS have about the theological debates of *takfir* is relatively low, and among the rank and file it is almost non-existent. Many of the latter have probably never read the Quran, as they either cannot read at all or cannot read it in the language the Holy Book is available to them (i.e. in French or Arabic). Still doctrinal differences are debated among JNIM and ISGS, both internally and between the groups (see Cold-Ravnkilde & Ba 2022). The author has access to several recordings from sermons and attempts at dialogue meetings between JNIM and ISGS leaders. It is intriguing to note how they go to great lengths trying to mimic the global debates between al-Qaeda and IS, while when listening to these recordings it is unclear whether those speaking understand the debates they are referring to. However, it is also noteworthy that cloaking their discourse in theology also matters to them. It matters because this is their source of legitimacy, but it also matters because it is behind doctrine that an insurgency finds strategy and strategic survival choices that will enable them to stay alive and hopefully thrive in the future.

When ISGS first emerged in 2015 and a few years onwards, their relationship with the groups that would form JNIM in 2017 was cordial and included attempts at collaboration and co-ordination. One important reason for this was previous personal connections. They had a common point of origin in AQIM, and groups like Ansar ed-Dine, MOJWA, al-Mourabitoun, and the Katiba Macina all emerged from the fractures in the original Salafi insurgency in the Sahel. This means that many of those involved in ISGS and what would become JNIM already knew each other. They had fought together and shared the spoils of combat, meaning they knew how to talk to each other. Commanders spoke quite nicely about their counterparts in the other insurgency, and even more formal co-operation was discussed in Mopti between Katiba Macina and ISGS, and in Gourma between JNIM and ISGS (see Nsaibia & Weiss 2020). However, even before the war between them started in 2019, fault lines in what had initially been a cordial relationship started to emerge.

Doctrinal differences did play a role, but they were also used as a smokescreen and thereby a justification for much more worldly interests concerning local community integration. Already towards the end of 2017, JNIM started to voice concern against ISGS's targeted violence against Tuareg and Daoussakhah communities, and Iyad Ag Ghaly released a video warning against the killing of fellow Muslims

MALI: THE EPICENTRE OF THE SAHEL CONFLICT

(Nsaibia & Weiss 2020). For JNIM's leadership, all Muslims were potential allies and as such a possible pool for recruitment of new fighters, whereas for the Fulani fighters around al-Sahrawi these communities represented an enemy that had plagued their communities with cattle raids and other offences (see Bøås et al. 2020). Upholding local alliances was important for both JNIM and ISGS, but the way these alliances were structured also meant that violent conflict between them was almost inevitable.

The final straw in this regard was a decision by the Shura Council of the Katiba Macina. As Kouffa and his men advanced in the Inner Delta of Mopti, new recruits came forward from Fulani communities from elsewhere in Mopti and central Mali. As more of these emerged, it became increasingly necessary to find a solution to the question of whether these men would have similar access to the dry seasons pasture in the Inner Delta as those who originated from the Delta itself. The Katiba Macina gained acceptance and sympathy in the Inner Delta among young Fulanis when they opened access to the much-valued *bourgoutiéres*—the highly nutritious pastures that pastoralists depend upon for livestock grazing during the dry season—claiming that land belongs only to God. This free access approach stood in stark contrast to the high access fees—up to 1,000,000 CFA—that pastoralists had used to pay to the Jowros—the noble Rimbé class of the Fulani aristocracy and as such the traditional gatekeepers of the pastures (see Rupesinghe & Bøås 2018).

At first, this was a highly popular move, but it created problems with regard to the management of the commons, and the question of governance of the *bourgoutiéres* was left to the Shura Council of the Katiba Macina to figure out. The decision that they took should not have come as a surprise. The Shura Council is mainly made up by Fulani imams from the Inner Delta, and they ruled in favour of autochthony rather than the *Umma* principle of the Salafi creed. What this meant was that only those who could trace their origins back to the Inner Delta would have privileged access to the dry season pastures. As a result, several new Katiba Macina recruits started to seriously question why they should fight and likely spill their blood in a conflict that would not give them many benefits. Consequently, many of these left the Katiba Macina and thereby also JNIM, finding a new port of call with ISGS, which offered a more egalitarian approach to both this issue as well as how other spoils of war should be distributed. In JNIM, the issue of distribution tends to be more centralised than in ISGS, where fighters seem to be allowed to keep more of the bounty they gather from raids on what ISGS defines as hostile communities of unbelievers.

As hostilities increased between JNIM and ISGS, first in the Delta and in Gourma and later spilling over also to the neighbouring regions of Burkina Faso and Niger, doctrinal discourse was increasingly used to justify the violent conflict. The weekly newspaper of IS, *Al-Naba*, started to report on heavy fighting and considerable JNIM losses in battle with ISGS (see Kadivar 2020), while al-Qaeda Telegram channels reported heavy casualties on the ISGS side and explicitly stated that AQIM leader Droukdel had ordered JNIM to eradicate ISGS from the land of the true mujahedeen. JNIM issued pamphlets arguing that its slower and more calculated approach to the full introduction of Sharia was much more sustainable than the ISGS's fast and heavy-handed tactics of force and brutality, warning that the arrival of what it called the forces of the neo-Kharijites (i.e. ISGS) was a test for the true mujahedeen to separate the true believers from the false (Nsaibia & Weiss 2020: 8). ISGS retaliated through the Al-Naba newsletter, arguing that al-Qaeda never missed the chance for treachery, aiming its criticism directly at Iyad Ag Ghaly and Hamadoun Kouffa who they said were willing to negotiate with France, and calling JNIM the 'dog' of Algeria in the Sahel. Once the war had started, it became almost impossible to come to any manageable solution and as such the war has continued unabated, spreading into the Meneka province of Mali and greatly contributing to the communal violence in central Mali which has spilled over to Burkina Faso. What this means is that yet another element of the perfect storm had arrived, and the consequences would be deadly for those who lived in its midst, as they now had yet another violent conflict of mobile forces that operated without permanent boundaries between the various armed groups.

Bewildered and afraid, villagers might have JNIM in their homes one day, ISGS the day after, then the Armed Forces of Mali (FAMA) might arrive accompanied by a local militia allied to the government, and before the week was over they might also be paid a visit by a

MALI: THE EPICENTRE OF THE SAHEL CONFLICT

mobile band of either MINUSMA or French soldiers from Operation Barkhane. None of them would stay to protect, but a visit by any of them would put the local population in danger of violent scrutiny when an adversary showed up. While Mali was still the epicentre of the conflict, the violence had now increasingly come to include its neighbours Burkina Faso and Niger. The next chapter will introduce the neighbours in more detail and discuss how and why Burkina Faso up until the date of writing has been more severely affected than Niger.

3

THE NEIGHBOURS

BURKINA FASO AND NIGER

The international relations between Mali, Niger, and Burkina Faso have mainly been quite cordial. Apart from the brief border wars in 1974 and 1985 between Burkina Faso and Mali, there have not been any instances of inter-state armed conflict. However, after the military-led governments of Assimi Goïta (Mali) and Ibrahim Traoré (Burkina Faso) came to power in August 2020 and September 2022 respectively, the relationship between these two countries and Niger—which at that time was led by democratically elected President Mohamed Bazoum—became increasingly hostile, with verbal accusations flying back and forth.

This lasted until Niger too came under military rule on 26 July 2023, when the Nigerien armed forces led by Abdourahamane Tchiani assumed power and arrested Bazoum. Ever since, the trio of military regimes have knitted ever closer relations, leading to their joint establishment of the AoSS on 16 September 2023. This was followed by their joint decision on 28 January 2024 to leave ECOWAS, arguing that the regional organisation had become a threat to member states. The leaders of Mali, Niger, and Burkina Faso issued a joint statement that day saying it was their sovereign decisions to leave ECOWAS without delay (see AFP 2024a). This was a serious blow to ECOWAS as well as to the very idea of regional organisation in West Africa, as all three countries had been founding members of the block in 1975, even if they had lately been facing harsh criticism and sanctions for failing to return to civilian rule.

We will return to the question of the new military regimes and their turn to Moscow in Chapter 9, while in this chapter we will chart out the reasons why Burkina Faso so quickly fell apart when the jihadist rebellion started and why Niger, despite its poverty and weak control of its borders with Mali and Burkina Faso up until the time of writing, has managed to prevent the jihadi insurgents in its Tillabèri region from further advancing towards the capital of Niamey. Our exploration starts in Burkina Faso before moving on to Niger.

Burkina Faso

Burkina Faso is just like Mali: a poor landlocked country that exports cotton and minerals, mainly gold. Gold production has increased, and Burkina Faso is currently the fourth-largest gold producer in Africa, after South Africa, Mali, and Ghana. There is also the potential to increase the extraction of manganese, zinc, lead, copper, nickel, and limestone. However, despite this growth of the gold-mining industry and the potential to diversify its mineral production and export, Burkina Faso remains one of the poorest countries in the world, ranking 184 out of 191 countries in the 2022 Human Development Report of the United Nations Development Programme (UNDP), and the state, while never particularly strong, has been further weakened by the jihadi rebellion and military coups of 2022.

In 2022, the population of Burkina Faso was estimated to be about 22 million, with a birth rate of 4.27 children per woman, and almost 43 per cent of the population is younger than 14 years. The Mossi are its largest ethnic group (about 50 per cent), followed by the Fulani (around 9 per cent), and then several other groups. What differentiates Burkina Faso from neighbouring Mali and Niger is that, while it has a Muslim majority (mainly Sunni), a sizable part of the population practise Christianity (around 20 per cent), and as many as 9 per cent report following traditional beliefs such as the Dogon religion (INSD 2019). This apart, Burkina Faso has a weak economy and state, like

THE NEIGHBOURS: BURKINA FASO AND NIGER

neighbouring Mali and Niger, as well as—if the economy does not start to grow faster and become more inclusive and resilient to climate change—a population growth rate that is unsustainable. The challenge is that even if mineral production has increased, most economic activity among the population depends on traditional agriculture, with close to 80 per cent of the population employed in this sector. The increase in gold exports is good, but testifies to a limited diversification of the economy. Neither mining nor any other extractive industry will become the solution to the employment challenge that Burkina Faso as well as other Sahel-based countries are facing. Such sectors can help boost the economy, but the employment effect will be low.

Burkina Faso's recent political history is that of a poor country, but it used to be the story of remarkably political stability. From the coup that led to the death of Thomas Sankara in 1987 to the popular uprising that took place in 2014, Burkina Faso was under the rule of Blaise Compaoré. Compaoré's legacy will continue to be debated both internally as well as internationally, but he was a skilled regional player who managed to keep his country out of conflict. Under his administration, Burkina Faso avoided being dragged into the wars in the Mano River Basin in the 1990s through early 2000s. Compaoré also managed to keep insurgent groups away from bringing conflict into Burkina Faso, as he unofficially allowed some of them to use territory for external activities as long as they did not embark on any acts of violence within the country (Haavik et al. 2022). This is no longer the case, as Burkina Faso is facing a jihadi rebellion that, although it started in the north along the borders with Mali, has spread to large parts of the country, reaching all the way to the country's border with coastal states such as Côte d'Ivoire, Ghana, Benin, and Togo.

Weak states like Burkina Faso can be affected by the spillover of violence and conflict from neighbouring countries. Due to low infrastructural capacity and a long history of transnational circulation predating the colonial administrative architecture, some African state borders are porous and often do not do much to prevent the spread of violent conflict (Jackson 2016). For example, in the Lake Chad

Basin, the Boko Haram insurgency that originated in northern Nigeria in 2009 has spread to three neighbouring states: Cameroon, Chad, and Niger. In the Mano River Basin, Liberia imploded in 1989, and both Sierra Leone and Côte d'Ivoire subsequently had their own civil wars (Bøås 2005; Dokken 2008). However, some weak states have managed to navigate bad neighbourhoods and avoided the effects of violent spillover. Guinea, for example, remained a surprisingly stable state during the Mano River conflict (McGovern 2017).

For a long time, Burkina Faso too seemed remarkably resilient to resisting spillover effects of this kind. Based on Burkina Faso's history of religious tolerance and non-violence, several analysts and researchers considered there was very limited risk of conflict spreading from Mali to Burkina Faso in the short- and medium-term (see ICG 2013). Similarly, the UNDP programme launched in 2016 to prevent violent extremism in Africa identified Mali as an epicentre of violent extremism and Niger as the potential spillover country in this region, and did not even identify Burkina Faso as 'at risk' (see UNDP 2017). Nonetheless, the first terrorist attack struck the Burkina Faso capital of Ouagadougou in January 2016, and in November of the same year the country's first jihadist insurgency erupted. Today, Burkina Faso rivals Mali as the epicentre of the crisis in the Sahel, with jihadist insurgent groups claiming allegiance, at least rhetorically, to al-Qaeda and IS as they compete for influence and control over the territory (Penney 2019).

How can we explain this drastic transition from being considered to have relatively strong stability to suddenly slipping into devastating violent conflict? One answer lies in the complicated political transition that Burkina Faso went through when President Blaise Compaoré's 27-year reign came to an abrupt halt in 2014. When Compaoré was forced to step down, not only did he vanish from the country, but with his departure what also disappeared was a 'big man deep state', a state deeply entangled with society through its formal and informal networks of security provisions. While the many administrative flaws and human rights violations of the Compaoré administration are obvious (see Hagberg et al. 2018; Eizenga 2015), one can still argue that Burkina Faso under his rule represents an interesting case.

THE NEIGHBOURS: BURKINA FASO AND NIGER

For almost three decades, Burkina Faso showed substantial domestic stability and weathered several intrastate conflicts in its region (Haavik et al. 2022). However, soon after Compaoré's ousting in late 2014, Burkina Faso slid into violence, becoming a new battleground in the Sahel crisis that had started in Mali in 2012. The question is, therefore, was this just a case of the neighbourhood effect causing spillover from the battlegrounds in Mali (see Nsaibia & Weiss 2018), or would a more nuanced approach be better suited to explain the sudden demise of security in Burkina Faso? To suggest an answer to this question, we will draw upon Haavik, Bøås and Iocchi's (2022) conceptual framework on the inner workings of weak and resource-poor states and why they can, for a time, seem remarkably stable but sometimes also suddenly fall apart. This will illuminate how Compaoré worked to secure his rule and his country, and what happened when this state of formal and informal security networks was dismantled by the popular uprising that led to his removal. However, before we proceed, a brief section on Thomas Sankara and Blaise Compaoré is necessary.

Thomas Sankara and Blaise Compaoré

Thomas Sankara, at times referred to as the Che Guevara of Africa, was a Burkinabè solider, Marxist-inspired revolutionary, Pan-Africanist, and President of Burkina Faso following a coup in 1983. He was assassinated in 1987. Charismatic and an iconic figure, he has remained famous ever since. Currently, he is back in fashion in the Sahel and West Africa, his name arising in popular discourses about resistance against France and decolonialisation, with leaders like Goïta of Mali and Traoré in Burkina Faso wanting to be seen as his contemporary incarnation.

Sankara began his military career at an early age when the country was known as Upper Volta. After some initial military education, he was sent to Madagascar for officer training, where he both witnessed the popular uprisings of 1971–2 and was introduced to the works of Karl Marx and Vladimir Lenin. Returning to Upper Volta in 1972, he fought in the border war with Mali in 1974—a war he later would call 'useless and unjust' (Harsch 2014). A few years later, in 1976, Sankara met Blaise Compaoré on an official mission to Morocco.

Together with other young officers, they formed a secret organisation which they called the Communist Officers Group.

What followed for Sankara was involvement in politics. First a position as Minister of Information in the military government of Saye Zerbo, from which he resigned in 1982 due to what Sankara argued were the regime's anti-labour positions. After another military coup in September 1982, Sankara was briefly prime minister before he was dismissed and arrested. As the decision to arrest Sankara was very unpopular among younger officers, this gave his friend and ideological companion Blaise Compaoré the momentum he needed to organise another coup on 4 August 1983. At the age of just thirty-three, Sankara became the president of the country that the coup leaders now renamed Burkina Faso, a name which translates to 'the land of the upright people' in Mooré and Dyula (the two most spoken languages in the country). Sankara also designed a new flag for the country and wrote a new national anthem. He quickly set out to put his ideological conviction into concrete policies, aiming at a re-organisation and modernisation of both state and society.

Some of the results achieved were remarkable. Social programmes were started, including a mass vaccination campaign to eradicate polio, meningitis, and measles—over 2 million Burkinabè were vaccinated. Infant mortality fell from almost 21 per cent to 14.5 per cent, and Sankara's administration was the first in Africa to officially recognise AIDS as a major threat to the continent. Large-scale housing and infrastructure projects were started—700 kilometres of railway were built by the Burkinabè people without much external assistance, and a large-scale education and literacy programme was started. Under Sankara, the literacy rate increased from just 13 per cent in 1983 to 73 per cent in 1987 (Manning 1998). Comparing these achievements with those of the leaders that came after him in the region, it is easy to understand the current popular revival of Sankara and his legacy and ideas.

There is, however, also another side to this story. The Popular Revolutionary Tribunals that Sankara established to try former government officials for various crimes—such as corruption, tax evasion, or counter-revolutionary activities—were at first mainly showcases with light sentences which were often suspended. However, over time the courts became more corrupt and oppressive and were used to settle local conflicts. The Committees for the Defence of the Revolution, a mass movement of local armed groups, came to be used as an instrument of coercion by the state, as well as in various local conflicts between communities over land and other resources. The economy also started to experience problems. Aid and foreign investment were drastically reduced as Sankara pulled the country out of the International Monetary Fund (IMF) and the World Bank, and the nationalisation of land and mining did not increase production, but rather led to the opposite. It did not help that Sankara stripped the traditional hierarchy of the Mossi people of all powers. The Morho Naba, the traditional name of the 'chief' or 'king' of the Mossi, was not allowed to hold its traditional courts, and local Mossi chiefs were likewise stripped of power (see Englebert 1996).

It is impossible to say how this would have ended, as Sankara's rule did not last very long. On 15 October 1987, Sankara together with twelve others were killed by an armed group in a coup organised by the one who had been his closest companion, Blaise Compaoré. Justifying the coup without ever speaking openly about his own direct involvement, Compaoré accused Sankara of plotting to assassinate him and others in the regime, of jeopardising the country's foreign relations with Côte d'Ivoire and its former colonial master France, as well as neglecting the economy, which was suffering from his nationalisation policies and the lack of foreign funding and assistance. Shortly after Sankara was buried in an unmarked grave, Compaoré reversed the nationalisation policies, rejoined the IMF and the World Bank, and re-established close ties with Côte d'Ivoire and France (Harsch 2017). Effectively dismantling Sankara's legacy, Compaoré came to rule Burkina Faso for 27 years until he fell from the seat of power during massive popular protests in 2014. This leaves us with the question: what type of rule made this possible, and what happens to such a system of rule when the 'king' is gone?

Explaining the violence unleashed in Burkina Faso

While the neighbourhood effect argument—that intrastate conflicts have been shown to cluster in time and space, increasing the risk of violent conflict in proximate states—carries some empirical clout (see, for example, Buhaug & Gleditsch 2008), an important factor missing in the case of Burkina Faso is the rapid disintegration of the country's neopatrimonial security system. This system of rule tied together the political centre and the periphery, facilitating the navigation of different threats despite the obvious shortcomings of a weak and resource-poor state.

In many African states, a range of non-state actors operating beyond, in parallel, or in tandem with officially sanctioned channels have facilitated the coexistence of bureaucratic rationality and patrimonial norms as a 'neopatrimonial' form of rule, which enabled central governments to co-opt not only national elites but also regional elites and relevant actors in the peripheries (Englebert & Dunn 2019).

At the heart of this conceptualisation of neopatrimonialism lies the idea that the ruler's authority can be reproduced all the way down to the village level, with the president's clients becoming patrons for their own sets of clients by doling out resources and opportunities they have access to by virtue of their formal role in the state system. While accurate in several cases, the weakness of this argument is that, at some point in time, almost every African state has been described as neopatrimonial, lumping together a great number of very different states, which assumes that neopatrimonialism is a general phenomenon of resource-poor and thereby also relatively weak states.

Instead, it may be more apt to follow Paul Nugent's (2010) suggestion to refocus attention on networks and institutions in order to better understand how neopatrimonialism as a system of rule work in specific cases. The point is that some states, while displaying several neopatrimonial characteristics, have also developed what one may call a deep state which dominates the formal state by an organisational body with its own hierarchy and sets of norms. Weak states have to rule not only based on loose or informal personal networks and alliances but also through a more institutionalised deep state. This can be a deep state in the form of a network of individuals from the coercive state apparatus and various civilian spheres who are involved in the regular activities of the state while maintaining a shadow set of activities (Barak 2018). Such a network can be called an 'autocratic clique', which gathers political support and exerts direct influence on the regular state and society through hierarchical ties. This clique can take the form of a 'security community' composed by 'those elements of the regime most directly involved in the planning and execution of repression, intelligence gathering, interrogation, torture, and internal clandestine armed operations' (Söyler 2013). Autocratic cliques are semi-formal institutions because they lack formal recognition despite their official operation at large, and they often act with general impunity. This can be seen in the deep state's symbiotic relationship with racketeering and low-intensity warfare in territories that provide safe havens for extracting resources through trafficking and other shadowy economic activities (Gingeras 2011). This concept of the deep state can help us to refine our understanding of Burkina Faso under Compaoré's rule and how quickly the state's security unravelled thereafter. This is important for explaining what has happened in Burkina Faso, but also as there is a need to move beyond general 'neopatrimonialism' explanations and the 'fragile-states approach' that assumes fragility without explaining how such states actually work by offering an alternative conceptualisation of security governance in weak states (Bøås & Strazzari 2020).

Thus, in the case of Burkina Faso, the concept of a 'big man deep state' is used to illuminate the main characters of Compaoré's regime and the internal workings that allowed the regime to survive for decades. The embeddedness of security and military forces into economic and policy-making circles in power under Compaoré bears similarities to a deep state at the head of which sat the skilful military-turned-president ruler. Thus, a Big Man who embodies power and carries the power of the regime in himself as the embodiment of both state and regime. The words and orders of the Big Man can matter more than the country's official constitution and laws, but this does not mean that such a rule by necessity must be despotic, autocratic, and unpredictable. The kind of Big Man we have in mind is not the same phenomenon as the personal ruler described by Jackson and Rosberg (1982), whose rule is characterised by despotism and unpredictability (Haavik et al. 2022). Instead, while the Big Man described by Sahlins (1963) is powerful, his power is also based on the recognition of Big Man status by his followers, meaning that the Big Man is also indebted to them. This suggests that this concept describes a relationship based on reciprocity, and while what Driscoll (2020) calls 'Big Man Governance' has an informal character it must also have a degree of predictability and is thus rule-bound. As Utas (2012) reminds us, 'Big Men do not generally control followers. Quite the opposite: it is in the interests of followers to maintain ties with the Big Man.'

Compaoré's unquestioned personalised rule rested on his reputation as a skilled solider and army man, although he maintained a sober and discreet public persona, far from the image of the lavish Big Man present in some of the literature (see, for example, Bayart 1993). However, it is the ability to attract and maintain a following that makes the Big Man, and not his charisma per se, and the relatively unbiased nature of the redistribution of dividends with regards to kinship and ethnicity was unquestionably an important part of Compaoré's Big Man status. Most importantly, however, acting at the intersection between political negotiations and economic arrangements, Compaoré sustained—and was supported by—a small autocratic clique of key security officers, mainly belonging to the Régiment de sécurité présidentielle (RSP), of which he was the Big Man. Among this select group, strategic individuals, such as Gilbert Dienderé and Djibril Bassolé,[1] allowed the entrenchment of business, security, and politics in a network of alliances carefully built by Compaoré, who muscled his way to the top of the state and acted as the Big Man, and by doing so also became the very hub of the deep state. Through this position, he became an irreplaceable cog in the governance of Burkina. This 'big man deep state' was therefore the carefully built and apparently resilient structure that kept Compaoré's rule together, but it also rested on the rather fragile foundations of his political persona. Once Compaoré was removed by street protests in 2014, and key members of the military and the RSP were imprisoned, the 'big man deep state' started to crumble. In this very moment, the neopatrimonial arrangement working for the deep state revealed the vulnerability that had been there all along, but which only now came into visibility.

The main weakness of a neopatrimonial system, even with a more institutionalised Big Man rule at the centre of a deep state, is that it can become an engine for perpetual crisis, regardless of past stability, as the lack of more formally institutionalised structures can create fragmentation that sustains itself into even deeper levels of fragmentation (Haavik et al. 2022). As Bøås and Dunn (2017) point out, if the patronage systems fail to deliver on the promises embedded in them, neopatrimonialism becomes a source of instability. When neopatrimonial practices become unstable, as they did in Burkina Faso in the 2000s, the established modality of governance is thrown into question and begins to fray.

The Compaoré state

Emerging from the French colonial empire, Burkina Faso (then Upper Volta) was like many other African countries characterised by a combination of administrative weakness and political and economic fragility that led to the typical unsettlements characteristic to postcolonial African states. The reach of the state was limited, and authority was perpetuated through a form of indirect rule through local chieftaincies from the colonial era. The limited loyalty local rulers gave to state authorities in Ouagadougou was based on patronage networks diverting scarce resources, which created a highly personalised political leadership (Harsch 2017). The socio-political landscape during the country's first period of independence could be described as a web-like society, with fragmented and heterogeneous forms of socio-political control (see Migdal 1988). Burkina Faso's first decades were thus turbulent, characterised by a weak state dominated by a single party, which saw a series of military regimes. The most noteworthy of these was the short-lived one led by Thomas Sankara who, alongside Compaoré, attempted to strengthen state functions and public authority (Englebert 1996).

As we have already mentioned, Compaoré staged a coup against Sankara in 1987 and gradually built up a 'big man deep state' as his regime went through a controlled democratic transition in the early 1990s. Compaoré's rule saw a pyramid structure of networks of patrons and clients stretched from the topmost echelons of the government down to the village level. Compaoré's system was flexible in the sense that a local patron could himself be a client to some district patron who, in turn, could support a regional or national figure (Harsch 2017). The state did not have to provide services directly to everyone, nor did it need their direct support, since everything flowed through intermediaries. Those holding central state office could utilise the patronage system to acquire local big men as clients, which extended their influence into areas they would otherwise not be able to penetrate. In this way, the central government was indirectly but firmly connected to the peripheries. Compaoré's 'big man deep state' was thus built around a set of networks and alliances that were situated in between formal institutions and informal areas—including the military, Compaoré's political party, support groups, and clientelist structures—connecting the formal and the informal and creating a powerful, informally institutionalised structure in between these (Haavik et al. 2022).

The political–military regime

Compaoré's regime was characterised by a tight relationship between military and political elites. The army, led by Compaoré and his companions, was the main instrument of coercion and repression against real and perceived opponents, but it was also a state agency that was deliberately weakened by divisions and patronage. While this protected the ruler and his regime from possible contenders to power in the army emerging, it also resulted in grievances and riots in the armed forces (Dwyer 2017). Harsch (2017) argues that, given the regime's reliance on coercion to shore up power and Compaoré's army origins, it was not surprising that his patronage network would penetrate the security forces, blurring the lines between security personnel and those in the ruling party. Lieutenant Colonel Djibril Bassolé, the security minister (later Minister of Foreign Affairs), controlled the gendarmes while building a base of his own within the ruling party. Compaoré's most prominent client was General Gilbert Diendéré, in charge of the elite regiment drawn from the most able in the military forces, the RSP (Haavik et al. 2022).

Despite its official role as a security service for the President of Burkina Faso, the RSP was the arm of the 'big man deep state' extended into the 'security community' engaging in corrupt activities and violent extortion of resources with impunity. In other words, the RSP was involved in activities to preserve the regime but also in formal and informal networks of security provisions. While being a military branch that acted directly under the president, the RSP also operated as Burkina Faso's intelligence service. While reputed to be one of the best intelligence services in the region, it rested on the informal networks of key ally General Diendéré. It was a network cultivated over years, based on formal and informal connections with regional Big Men and clandestine operations within and outside of Burkina Faso in areas of low-intensity warfare in the neighbourhood. The RSP was both the most capable fighting force in the military as well as the state's main intelligence service. This means that the organisation was to some degree indispensable to the security of the state, while being part and parcel of a hidden and unaccountable 'big man deep state'.

The political party

The second pillar that Compaoré's regime rested upon was the political party, Congrés pour la Démocratie et le Progrés (CDP). It was an instrumental component of Compaoré's neopatrimonial state that came to represent a monopolised system of governance and patronage, though not without internal factional struggles. The CDP, with a nation-spanning clientelist system, not only created a hegemony in Burkinabè political life but also reached into the bureaucracy, armed forces, business circles, traditional chiefdoms, religious groups, and civil society (Haavik et al. 2022). Harsch (2017) describes the Compaoré state as an encompassing 'party state' that functioned on two levels: one was official, based on the rule of law and accountability through pluralist elections and constitutionalism, in essence a 'theatre play', partly to please donor agencies and Western partners. The ruling party could always subvert, manipulate, and simply ignore formal institutions when it needed to.

The second part of this state was an unofficial realm of politics in which power and at times more arbitrary forms of rule prevailed. While achieving a monopoly in the political realm, over time the power politics within the CDP resulted in internal struggles between a pro-Compaoré faction, the FEDAP-BC (Fédération associative pour la paix avec Blaise Compaoré) which centred around Compaoré's brother, François, and an oppositional faction, some of the so-called 'party-barons', among them future President Roch March Kaboré (Haavik et al. 2022).

The chiefs and business circles—the clientelist system connecting centre and periphery

The traditional chiefdoms were the third pillar of the Compaoré regime. The chiefs provided local support to the regime by making up a second, informal level of administration, thus extending the regime's reach outside the capital. Most importantly, the chiefs represented the bulk of the clientelist system. The system never existed officially, but before every important election chiefs would secretly issue voting instructions to the people. Traditional chiefs supported Compaoré not only as an expression of their gratitude for being allowed to retain power over local constituencies, but also because chiefs could claim the spoils this system of rule created (ICG 2013). However, they had to practise some restraint, as this system only functioned as a pact of stability between the centre and the periphery if these local chiefs were able to maintain respect in their local rural areas and mediate in and resolve local disputes. Thus, through local chiefs, a web of alliances could work both to neutralise threats to Compaoré's authority as well as defuse underlying community-based tensions (ICG 2020a).

Elite business circles also served as integral allies of the regime, providing it with financial resources. Oumarou Kanazaoé, who died in 2011, is an example of an important patron close to Compaoré. He allied himself with every government in Burkina Faso and made a fortune on public contracts. He played a significant role in the Compaoré regime, as he guaranteed support for the CDP in his native region of the Nord, funded the party and many of its infrastructure projects, and helped to defuse conflict as the head of the Muslim community where he united different currents (Harsch 2017). Business circles also established associations to support (or negotiate with) the regime, with the FEDAP-BC able to count on the support of rich businesspeople like Alizéta Ouédraogo and Lassine Diawara. Elected officials, the CDP, chiefs, and economic actors all had a stake in preserving the political status quo, and they made use of both repression and co-option of dissidents who were in direct contact with central authorities (ICG 2020a).

Through the 'big man deep state' lens, what this looks like is a state where the formal institutional structures, such as the military apparatus and the regime's political party, are fused with other informal structures of the state apparatus. This creates a web-like but still pyramidical social structure that enables regime stability. This points to Erdmann and Engel's (2007) argument that studies of neopatrimonial practices have placed too much emphasis on patrimonialism and neglected the state part of the puzzle that the theory neopatrimonialism initially aimed to draw attention to. However, what we aim to show as we continue our review of the Compaoré state is that if we are to understand how rulers of weak states rule, we need to give our primary attention to regime preservation strategies. Rulers of weak states do not just muddle through; they strategise, the same as everybody else. Some are just more successful than others. Compaoré certainly was one of these. For a long time he skilfully amassed his deep state resources, both domestically and in his wider regional neighbourhood.

Navigating a bad neighbourhood

As the head of a resource-poor nation, Compaoré started out as a regional troublemaker, befriending multiple rebel leaders, but he later chose to turn his country into a regional diplomatic powerhouse, making mediation Burkina Faso's trademark. The regime made itself seem indispensable by promoting its image as a poor but enterprising and well-administered country capable of resolving regional crises as well as utilising its networks to negotiate the release of international hostages taken by insurgents who were active in the regional neighbourhood (ICG 2013). The regime also maintained, for the most part, good relations with Western countries and donor agencies, on which it was heavily financially dependent. However, the role of Compaoré and his senior officials in the region was much more ambiguous than what their regular peace envoys and international summits in Ouagadougou would suggest. The regime's interests in these informal arrangements were bound up with the preservation and prosperity of the regime itself, and not the strengthening of the institutional design of the state.

Unofficial diplomacy, covert operations, and profiteering

The Compaoré regime was deeply involved in informal regional diplomacy, creating arrangements with several different non-state actors in troubled spots of West Africa: Liberia and Sierra Leone in the 1990s, and Côte d'Ivoire and Mali in the 2000s. While Compaoré engaged officially in several of these countries' various crises, he and his senior commanders and top foreign affairs personnel also engaged in unofficial activities that served several purposes, among them enriching top elites in the 'big man deep state' and feeding the patronage machine (Haavik et al. 2022).

Internally, Burkina Faso provided little opportunity for military graft and profiteering, but the political economy of war created by various conflicts in Africa provided opportunities for the regime. In the Mano River wars, while denying any involvement in the Liberian civil war, Compaoré and his trusted few supplied Charles Taylor with arms, ammunition, and troops, and opposed the military intervention by ECOWAS. In 1991, Compaoré admitted to having sent 700 troops to Liberia but claimed that Burkina Faso's involvement in the conflict was now over. However, in 1994 ECOWAS renewed allegations of the regime engaging in supply of arms and training of mercenaries (Englebert 1996).

As the Mano River wars expanded, so did Compaoré's covert operations. A UN panel found conclusive evidence of Burkinabè authorities' involvement in illegal arms dealing in Sierra Leone. The Ministry of Defence had legally purchased arms in Ukraine, with a document signed by Diendéré stating that Burkina Faso would be the sole user of the weapons. However, the arms were then smuggled through Liberia and into the hands of rebels in Sierra Leone in exchange for diamonds (UN 2000).

Burkina Faso's involvement in the Ivorian Civil War provides a good example of the deep state's duality, as it officially operated as a peace envoy securing the Ouagadougou Political Agreement in 2007 while simultaneously profiting from the conflict through providing support for the rebels, the Forces Nouvelles. Compared to Compaoré's involvement in Liberia and Sierra Leone, the engagement with Côte d'Ivoire also served significant political interests. Burkina Faso rarely exported its internal problems to the outside world, but it did export, mainly to Côte d'Ivoire, millions of migrant workers. The Ivorian Civil War and the anti-Burkinabè sentiments that fed it led the Compaoré regime to side with the Forces Nouvelles.

THE NEIGHBOURS: BURKINA FASO AND NIGER

With the southern port in Abidjan unavailable to northerners in Côte d'Ivoire, Burkina Faso became the main recipient of most of the north's exports. A UN group of experts found evidence of arms and ammunition being transported from Burkina Faso territories to rebel-held territories in Côte d'Ivoire but no evidence connecting it to the authorities (UN 2009). However, with the regime's previous engagement in arms dealing, it is hardly a stretch to assume that at least parts of the autocratic clique in the 'big man deep state' had a stake in such transactions. This is an excellent example of how good the Compaoré regime was at strategically managing various regional crises in a way that benefited the regime and its supporters. The regime succeeded in both profiteering from the conflict while avoiding a possibly destabilising refugee crisis of people of Burkinabè origin returning form Côte d'Ivoire. This is also an example of the mediation 'industry' that made Burkina Faso an unlikely diplomatic powerhouse in West Africa and, as it appeared to outside powers, an island of stability in an otherwise unstable and troubled region (Haavik et al. 2022).

The mediation industry

Compaoré and his associates built up a mediation industry that provided prestige, networks for intelligence gathering, and openings for Burkinabè businesspeople. As with the regime-controlled democratic transition, the mediation business bolstered the regime's international legitimacy, helping to secure good donor relations and preserve domestic stability by successfully handling destabilising external factors such as refugee inflows from the various conflicts erupting along the Burkina Faso's borders.

The regime hosted several international summits and conferences—the Franco–African Summit in 1996, the Organisation of African Unity (OAU) meeting in 1998, and the 2005 meeting of Francophone countries. As peace envoys, regime officials mediated political crises and violent conflicts in Togo, Niger, Côte d'Ivoire, Guinea, and Mali during the 1990s and 2000s (ICG 2013).

The mediation business rested upon the personal connections and networks of a few important elite individuals in the 'big man deep state' rather than the formal organisation of the Burkinabè Foreign Ministry. Compaoré was often present as a peace envoy—such as when he served as a representative for ECOWAS missions—and he was hailed as the craftsman of such successes as the Ouagadougou Political Agreement during the Ivorian Civil War (Niang 2016). Apart from the president, Djibril Bassolé in particular played an important role. Emerging from the security forces, Bassolé made a career as a minister serving in different posts, and he became Compaoré's most trusted diplomat, leading mediation missions in Togo, Niger, Côte d'Ivoire, and Mali. When the current civil war in Mali erupted, Bassolé travelled to northern Mali to meet with Iyad ag Ghaly (ICG 2013).

Another important figure was the Mauritanian Moustapha Ould Limam Chafi, who served as a presidential advisor to Compaoré. Chafi had intimate knowledge of the Saharan borderlands and its peoples and was one of Burkina Faso's most important unofficial diplomats. Through his connections, he helped Compaoré manage the Tuareg crisis in Niger (2007–9), and he served as a liaison between Ouagadougou and the Forces Nouvelles rebellion during the Ivorian crisis (2002–7). He was also a part of the ECOWAS negotiation team in northern Mali, and he worked to free Western hostages kidnapped by AQIM (Niang 2016). Under Compaoré, Bassolé and Chafi were two Big Men situated in between formal and informal institutions, serving the formal state of Burkina Faso but also the unaccountable 'big man deep state' that worked to their own personal benefit, but also for the survival of the regime and domestic stability of Burkina Faso.

Acquiring diplomatic prestige served as an external regime preservation strategy, allowing Compaoré to place many of his allies and clients in significant regional and international organisations. From a regime-preservation perspective, this meant that Compaoré could both reward or remove important regime allies and increase his external influence. For example, in 2000 Ablassé Ouédraogo, a former Foreign Minister, was appointed Deputy Director–General of the World Trade Organization, and former Prime Minister Kadré Désiré Ouédraogo was appointed president of ECOWAS in 2012. Second, Western donors critical of Compaoré's meddling in African conflicts during the 1990s came around due to Burkina Faso's apparent switch to more peaceful diplomacy.

THE NEIGHBOURS: BURKINA FASO AND NIGER

There are two things that stand out in Burkina Faso's unofficial and official involvement in the region under Compaoré. First, its covert involvement in Liberia, Sierra Leone, and Côte d'Ivoire shows a 'big man deep state' that is hidden and unaccountable, seizing the opportunities it finds in territories with low-intensity warfare which provide safe havens for extracting resources through smuggling and other shadowy economic activities. Such profiteering can be seen as a preservation strategy for the regime, as it lavishly rewards the top echelons of the neopatrimonial system and contributes to fulfilling the promises embedded within it by feeding the patronage machine.

Second, the formal state makes itself visible in its engagement in peace talks and international mediation. This creates prestige for the regime, while also throwing a veil over the hidden and unaccountable deep state's involvement. It was not the formal state with its formal institutions per se that was involved in these peace talks but rather the selected few from the autocratic clique in Compaoré's 'big man deep state'. The consequence was not only that these informal institutions guided Burkina Faso's diplomatic decisions but also that Compaoré and his selected few made themselves indispensable to the ability of the Burkinabè formal state to navigate its bad neighbourhood. This shows how deeply entangled the 'big man deep state' was with formal and informal networks of security provisions and how skilfully Compaoré combined his deep state resources both domestically and in his regional neighbourhood.

The 'big man deep state' falls

The managing of clients and allies of the 'big man deep state' was based on the manoeuvring of the various factions composing it. The Compaoré regime survived several army mutinies (1999, 2003, 2006, 2007, 2011), often in combination with popular protests (1999, 2011), by brokering deals between the senior military leadership close to Compaoré and the RSP and younger generations of officers. Such pacts, however, were fragile and only temporarily successful, and rifts between factions soon broke them apart. Internal struggles within the ruling circle and the need to quell street protests pushed the regime to lose oversight over peripheral rural areas where banditry ran rampant. To the banditry problem, the government responded by loosening its tight overseeing and instead promoting local security initiatives, fostering the emergence of parallel security governance systems. Meanwhile, the 2011 mutiny among junior ranks of the army overlapped with popular protests over the death of a student while in police custody. This led to the first major crack in the deep state as for the first time the RSP joined the mutiny, officially because of unpaid allowances and housing (Dwyer 2017). Compaoré rushed to give in to the demands of the RSP to regain their loyalty. This, however, provoked further protests in parts of the army that felt treated as a second-class unit, turning their anger against the RSP which was deployed to disarm the mutineers.

In October 2014, Compaoré's reign was finally coming to an end. On 28 October, protesters started to demonstrate in Ouagadougou against President Compaoré who they believed was about to amend the constitution to extend his 27 years of rule. Two days later, the regime lost control as protesters set fire to the parliament and took over the national TV headquarters. The members of parliament, sensing that the tide was against them, suspended the vote on changing the constitution (which would have allowed Compaoré to stand for re-election in 2015). Consequently, the generals of the military dissolved all government institutions and imposed a curfew. The day thereafter, Compaoré resigned and quickly fled to Côte d'Ivoire where President Ouattara gave him sanctuary.

The poor relationship between the regular army and the RSP became especially evident in the chaotic months following the ousting of Compaoré when a power struggle at the political centre eventually fragmented and dissolved the deep state with its security apparatus, regional diplomacy, and rural networks. At first, the army Chief of Staff declared himself the head of state before being sidelined by the second-in-command in the RSP, Colonel Yacouba Zida (Harsch 2017). Colonel Zida was one of the main cornerstones of the old regime, and his nomination was highly contested. After sustained pressure from civil society, trade unions, and many other societal actors, he ultimately stepped aside for a former diplomat, Michel Kafando, to be the head of a transitional government. However, in a matter of days, Zida was proclaimed prime minister, showing the continued influence of the RSP.

THE NEIGHBOURS: BURKINA FASO AND NIGER

The power struggle at the political centre reached its peak in September 2015, when the transitional government decided to dissolve the RSP, with Zida's approval, and strike a decisive blow to the RSP's ambitions to keep its grip on the state apparatus and its resources. This provoked a coup by the RSP and General Diendéré, who seized the capital and removed the transitional government. However, the regular army intervened and ended the coup in a week. Bassolé did not publicly denounce the coup, which gave it the look of being an attempt by the RSP at self-preservation and counter-revolution (Thurston 2020a). With the RSP and former regime elites out of the way, a rush to reform followed, and democratic elections were held. But, for those who had hoped for a clear break with the past, the new president, Roch March Kaboré—a former Big Man in the CDP—showed the continued influence of the old political cadres.

The political transition not only led to an internal political power struggle but also had wider consequences as the 'big man deep state' fragmented. Tensions within the army, the fall of Compaoré, the dissolution of the RSP, and the removal of former regime elites went hand in hand with a breakdown in how state security had been handled for over two decades. As much as the RSP represented a threat to the democratic transition, its dissolution also meant that the state was bereft of its most capable fighting and intelligence force. The fragmentation of the former 'big man deep state' meant that the security forces lost their key managers in Diendéré and Bassolé, greatly weakening and eventually fragmenting the security forces and the state. The transition saw the gradual promotion of officers and agents from the 'second row'—who during the Compaoré regime had never had the chance to benefit from EU- or US-led military training programmes or, more simply, to be engaged in actual security management—but they could not meet the urgent needs provoked by a decaying security situation.

Not only were 'second rows' not prepared to handle the security of the country, but they also lacked the knowledge, skills, and resources to handle the many local security initiatives established by the Compaoré deep state to deal with banditry in rural communities. Over the years, ethnic-based armed militias started to clash violently: for example, Mossi militias clashed frequently with Fulani militias, leading to increased ethnic polarisation. Following a recurring pattern, jihadi entrepreneurs stoked these tensions, hijacking local grievances and extending their grip over these communities (and their resources). The Kaboré government even accused Compaoré of having a non-aggression pact with jihadist groups—which apparently ended after his ousting. In fact, the Compaoré regime had maintained tacit agreements and dialogue with jihadist groups and smugglers. Bassolé met Iyad Ag Ghali in 2012 while Compaoré hosted meetings with Ansar Dine senior representatives in Ouagadougou. The senior advisor Chafi was central in developing these ties during the 2000s.

It is by no means certain that the security apparatus under Compaoré was significantly scaled to handle such an expansive conflict zone as the current one. However, the disintegration of the 'big man deep state' and its formal and informal networks of security provisions weakened the state's ability to prevent and handle a full-fledged jihadist insurgency.

The emergence of violent entrepreneurs

After the regime change, the state's monopoly over violence was severely undermined and even challenged by various non-state armed actors. Competing modalities of governance connected to community and ethnic militias emerged out of the fragmentation of the security realm after the regime collapse. The informal but institutionalised part of Compaoré's deep state did not completely disappear but rather was left in an economic and political vacuum. As Big Men with powerful networks and followings like Dienderé and Bassolé 'have been put in a garage' and put 'in [a] position not to harm ... at least not too much' by the Kaboré regime, new competing security governance providers over key resources (minerals, lands, waters) have emerged (Haavik et al. 2022: 331). As the state's security apparatus became ineffective, it was increasingly replaced by various local security initiatives. While the RSP and the regular army were known for their brutal security tactics, the involvement of ethnic-based and community militias was a real turning point, as these were difficult to hold accountable for their operations against 'bandits'. As a result, the aforementioned 'bandits' that these militias took arms against were soon pushed join ranks with jihadi entrepreneurs, who were now interested in posing as security providers.

Already in 2003, Compaoré's regime issued Law 32/2003, which allowed local community policing but only under the supervision of administrative agencies. Vigilante-styled self-defence groups, however, multiplied, modelling themselves after associations of traditional hunters, such as the Dozos (Hagberg 2019). Thus, even during Compaoré's rule, local security initiatives had already increased in an attempt to fill the void created by intra-army tensions. With the waning of the deep state, they have gained more autonomous power. In the western part of the country, the most prevalent of these groups were various local initiatives by the Dozos, while the central and eastern parts of Burkina Faso are mainly policed by the Koglwéogo (Compaoré & Bojsen 2020). Since 2015, the Koglwéogo have played a crucial role in many eastern territories in response to rising insecurity and banditry, often employing abusive methods. Similarly, the Rougha, the Fulani self-defence militias, also emerged as security providers in this fragmented political landscape. The Roughas' main function was to defend Fulani herders against the Koglwéogo.

Community-based security arrangements have therefore multiplied without much supervision. In 2016, the new government tried to hem them in with what is known as Decree 1052. This decree sought to establish institutional structures and legal boundaries in order to supervise local self-defence groups while delimiting their jurisdiction, circumscribing their scope, and fixing them to specific territories. Though commendable, such initiatives have come too late and are structurally inadequate to sanction potential breaches. In rural villages or semi-nomadic communities, Koglwéogos, Dozos, and Roughas are often the only armed authorities. Moreover, these groups often outnumber state police forces: in the Boulgou Province, for instance, members enlisted in the groups amount to about 12,000. In the entire centre–east region, they are estimated at about 20,000, with a presence in virtually every town and village. This shows how the waning of the deep state opened a new 'security market' that different security providers fought violently over, as in the example of the conflict between Koglwéogos and Dozos over specific territories or, more urgently, between the Koglwéogos and Fulani militias.

While the Decree 1052 should provide, on paper, a formal legitimacy—and therefore accountability—of self-defence groups, many Koglwéogo local militias refuse to abide by such rules and prefer their own internal organisation. The Koglwéogo organisational structure mirrors that of the state, with a set of officials, advisers, and spokespersons. The latter are supervised by a 'general' and his 'assistant', while officials are civilians with liaison functions between the provincial and state level. Non-abidance to state laws is not only a means of bypassing state control but is increasingly viewed by self-defence groups and local communities as necessary to ensure community protection and security.

The tensions during Compaoré's final period in power, the waning of the deep state, and the fragmentation of governance in the security realm has been fatal for Burkina. What has happened is a turn from the provision of security and stability by a deep state, where such security is orchestrated from the very top of the state, to a situation where a new government has attempted, but not succeeded, to reform the security sector and hem in local security arrangements that undoubtedly engineer an escalation of violence.

The sudden fall of Compaoré, and the progressive demise of the 'big man deep state' he dominated, strongly shook the security sector in Burkina Faso. Without Compaoré and his key allies in the RSP, the military, and the police, security on the ground was increasingly left in the hands of community-based militias, whose loyalty (and dependence) to state institutions varied in intensity and degree. This has left Burkina Faso, and its population, with a broken security sector of which jihadi insurgents have proven very adept at taking advantage. Subsequently, the military coups that followed when the new democratically elected government failed to deal with this were not surprising, as they could follow the same script as their compatriots in Mali.

Thus, while we must recognise the shortcomings of the Compaoré state, when the security system which was deeply entangled with the former regime disintegrated, it weakened the state and paved the way for Burkina Faso's remarkably swift transition into violent conflict a year later. The lack of a more formalised institutional structure ensured that the former modality of governance that had monopolised political life fragmented into competing networks, facilitating the proliferation of non-state armed actors as alternative providers of violence and security. Since the transition, the security situation has become increasingly complex and unstable, as jihadist insurgent groups have taken the fight not only to the state security forces but also increasingly to its 'proxies' and civilians perceived to support the creation of local security initiatives. The fall of the 'big man deep state' does not fully explain the current crisis, but it does offer an important nuance that complements explanations emphasising the role of grievances and conflict spillover from Mali. In this case, this helps us to understand why this led to an outcome where competing informal regimes of power, locally and nationally, set in motion a complex, competitive struggle among current and aspiring Big Men to become nodal points in emerging semi-hidden informal shadow networks of governance and control (Bøås 2015a).

Niger

Rated as one the least-developed countries in the world, Niger is situated as 189 of 191 countries on the Human Development Index of UNDP (2022). Niger has had a volatile political history, experiencing several coups and much political instability since it gained independence from France in 1960. After veteran opposition leader Mahamadou Issoufou won presidential elections in March 2011 and then another term in March 2016, some improvements on the political front seemed to make Niger more resilient to conflict than neighbouring Burkina Faso and Mali. Yes, it is correct that Niger showed a higher degree of democratic stability, but this should not have been taken for granted.

While Niger had a history of military coups, the political landscape seemed to have stabilised after Mahamadou Issoufou of the Nigerien Party for Democracy and Socialism (PNDS-Tarayya) won the presidential elections in 2011, was re-elected in 2016, and left the presidency when he reached his term limit in 2021. The subsequent presidential elections were won by what many viewed as Issoufou's handpicked successor Mohamed Bazoum, a founding member of the PNDS-Tarayya. The peaceful democratic transition of power that came about when Bazoum won the second round of the presidential elections with 55.67 per cent of the votes was seen as a sign of political and democratic maturity.

This was not to last, as on 27 July 2023 Bazoum was removed from power by a military coup led by the General Abdourahamane Tchiani who commanded Bazoum's presidential guard. While we will return to this issue in Chapter 9, here it will suffice to say that this created new problems for France and the EU who had relocated much of their military, development, and political missions from Bamako to Niamey, hoping the latter would serve as a safe harbour for their regional Sahel strategies. This proved to be impossible after the military dethroned Bazoum. Nonetheless, what remains to be explained is Niger's relative resilience, as at face value the country shares most of the traits that have contributed to the ever-deeper conflict in Mali and Burkina Faso.

Niger—a castle made of sand?

Political and social stability should never be taken for granted. Since gaining independence from France in 1960, Niger has had a volatile political history. Military regimes and different republics have come and gone, with frequent military coups and rebellions in the peripheral northern parts of the country. The Tuareg of the north have rebelled on several occasions, and the general lack of livelihood opportunities gives insurgencies leverage to recruit among youth who see little prospects for a better future. In fact, the migration industry that developed around Agadez between 2014 and 2016 was one of Niger's few growing sectors that gave people an opportunity to earn some extra money (Bøås 2020). While attempts by France and the EU to make Bazoum's Niger their donor darling in the Sahel may have contributed to the president's downfall, it is instructive to focus on two different regions of Niger to understand its relative resilience as well as potential fragility. These are the regions of Tillabéri along the border to Mali and Burkina Faso, and Agadez at the very north of the country.

Contrasting Agadez and Tillabéri

The Tillabéri region, rural and poor, but not far at all from the capital of Niamey. has become embroiled in the jihadist conflict that originated in Mali. The dominant insurgency is the ISGS. In the former rebellious and peripheral region of Agadez in northern Niger, which has quite a similar enabling environment as Tillabéri, there have hardly been any cases of people becoming radicalised and joining violent extremist insurgencies. An important question is, therefore, what explains the difference between Agadez and Tillabéri?

Tillabéri's geographical proximity to state institutions has not translated into concrete political dividends. Agadez, on the other hand, due to its remoteness and history of rebelling against state power, has increasingly been integrated into state institutions, tying centre and periphery in a codependent relation. In Tillabéri, mounting pressure on scarce resources combined with socio-economic marginalisation of youth and the encroachment of farmer–herder competition has led to the progressive hijacking of such grievances by groups like the ISGS. This is quite different from the situation in Agadez, where the attraction of violent jihadi discourses has been moderated by affirmative action by local politicians and traditional chiefs (Bøås et al. 2021).

The violence of Tillabéri

Tillabéri is the westernmost region of Niger. Bordering the capital region of Niamey, it is relatively new as an administrative unit, created in its most recent form by Nigerien Law No. 58–31 of 14 September 2002. Tillabéri is, like many of the other conflict-affected parts of the Sahel, a border region. Benin lies to its immediate south, Burkina Faso to the west, and Mali to the north and west. However, contrary to the other conflict-affected regions in the tri-border zone of Liptako-Gourma that Tillabéri belongs to, it is not a peripheral zone in geographic terms. While its sister regions in Burkina Faso and Mali are located far away from their respective capitals, the city of Tillabéri, the administrative centre of the region, is no more than 130 kilometres from Niamey. Nonetheless, this region has been the most violent and conflict-prone part of Niger.

This begs the question why Tillabéri? What is it about Tillabéri that made the region slide into a state of violence and displacement so quickly? There is little statistical evidence that suggest that this region has suffered more economic or political neglect than other regions in

Niger (see Nigerien National Institute of Statistics 2012; Tillabéri Regional Development Plan 2016). What is happening in Tillabéri is thus not only an unprecedented turn in the conflict in the Sahel, as up until late 2019 Niger had been spared from the violence sweeping through large parts of Burkina Faso and Mali, but it also implies that yet another string of local communities—now in a region close to its nation's capital—has come under the influence of violent entrepreneurs. We therefore need to understand why large-scale violence has suddenly become such a defining characteristic of Tillabéri. Is it just a consequence of the geographical proximity to the border to Mali in combination with the fact that Niger is a weak state that cannot properly control all its borders (Nsaibia & Weiss 2018), that is, a result of the neighbourhood effect that increases the risk of violent conflict in nearby states (Buhaug & Gleditsch 2008; Dixon 2009). If this is the case, then Mali is the proverbial black hole of the region, causing weak neighbouring countries to implode. The idea of regional implosion (Bøås 2003; Dokken 2008) is worth examining, but this hypothesis does not account to much more than a description of what has happened. Insurgents spill over borders because they can, and neighbouring countries are too weak to resist.

Herder–farmer conflicts have a long history in many parts of the Sahel (Benjaminsen & Ba 2009), Tillabéri included, and claims have been made that the specific political economy of Tillabéri as a centre of cattle-breeding and transhumance, and the conflicts this has caused historically, may offer some insight into how a region that, while never entirely peaceful, has unravelled so rapidly into violence (Assanvo et al. 2019; ICG 2020b). This is a hypothesis that cannot easily be disregarded, as herder–farmer disputes constitute a source of local grievances as well as violent conflict in several places in the Sahel, Tillabéri included. However, we also need to investigate how the weakness and dysfunctionality of the state implies that the sovereign power that was supposed to regulate such conflicts has if not disappeared became one among many actors who seek to govern in return for local support and profit (Bøås et al. 2020). To understand what has happened and continues to happen in Tillabéri, we need to analyse how insurgents seek local integration through the appropriation of local conflict.

THE NEIGHBOURS: BURKINA FASO AND NIGER

Insurgencies tend to emerge in a context where alternative modalities of governance are in competition, leading to a shifting and often unstable landscape of authority and rule. Earlier (see Chapter 2), we analysed how AQIM's rise to prominence in parts of northern Mali was directly related to its ability to capitalise on the fragmenting systems of governance typified in the warlord system that preceded its ascendancy. The question is therefore whether the same goes for the ISGS, the main insurgency in Tillabéri. If this is the case, then treating it as a warlord movement or as a mere by-product of global jihad could be highly erroneous. In general, to focus exclusively on the military–strategic or religious dimensions of Sahel insurgencies would fail to capture the multiverse of functions that such violence is performing in this part of the world.

For various reasons, the capacity of ruling elites to maintain the systems of reciprocity that the patron–client relationship relies upon has been undermined. This has resulted in both a crisis of legitimacy for many ruling elites and the perceived bankruptcy of the established state system. As neopatrimonial practices become unstable, the established modality of governance is thrown into question and begins to fray. While the logic of neopatrimonialism remains vital, we now see multiple conflicting networks emerge, often with each of them constructing a competing system of governance (Bøås & Dunn 2017). One can argue that the postcolonial systems reflected a degree of stability because they were tied by their parasitical relationship to formal state institutions. Today's networks, however, are characterised by their flexibility and adaptability, where actors compete for the role of nodal point between various networks of attempted informal governance that collaborate, but also compete, and are at times in violent conflict with each other over the issue of control (Bøås 2015a). Thus, we argue that a grounded understanding of the Tillabéri predicament requires both an awareness of the ongoing crises of established systems of governance and the realisation that these insurgencies reflect not the absence of authority but the emergence of alternative and competing modalities of rule and governance (Bøås et al. 2020).

The insurgencies of the Sahel have different capacities for governing and governance. Some clearly have some capacity to provide a certain degree of order, whereas others are basically roaming movements without much stationary territorial control (see Olsen 2000). However, between these opposite poles we also find many insurgencies that operate what we call 'sporadic governance'. This is a type of mobile governance that comes and goes. Such insurgencies do not attempt to gain more permanent territorial control, but rather aim for social control of a targeted population by combining unpredictable coercive activities with sporadically offering some governance services. If the sovereign power in question is not able to prevent the coercive activities of an insurgency, nor offer governance services of a higher quality, this may give the insurgents a considerable social grip over local populations. The question to explore is how and to what degree do ISGS and other insurgents operating in Tillabéri fit into this framework?

Tillabéri—the livelihood of people and place

Tillabéri is ethnically diverse, with a presence of most of the important ethnic groups in Niger, including Fulani, Songhay, Gourma, Hausa, Tuareg, and Zarma. The main economic activities are agriculture, raising livestock, and fishing, with some mining activities also taking place (Tillabéri Regional Development Plan 2016). However, for the Fulani and Tuareg groups of Tillabéri, pastoralism is the main economic activity. The type of pastoralism that has been practised here for centuries is transhumance, which is the seasonal migration of livestock and people between fixed seasonal pastures. This can take place across both internal and international borders. This is an activity of such economic and social magnitude that it is officially regulated in the ECOWAS Protocol on Transhumance from 1998. Such an international regulation is necessary in a system of various sovereign states, but it will only work if both the international organisation, in this case ECOWAS, and the member states have sufficient power and economic resources to support the Protocol and its regulatory mechanisms. This is not the case anymore in many places in the Sahel, as is evident in Tillabéri, where informants claim that transhumance is not within the state's capacity to organise and regulate (see Bøås et al. 2020).

Most pastoralists in Tillabéri depend on some form of transhumance during the long dry season, and for those with large herds this is particularly important. However, pastoralists claim that pasture is becoming increasingly insufficient, especially during the dry season, due to a combination of an expansion of agriculture supported by government policies, overgrazing, and less rainfall during the rainy season. The consequence is that many pastoralists have smaller herds. Pastoral marginalisation due to state-led agricultural policies and new land legislation is a common reoccurring theme in African studies (see Benjaminsen & Ba 2009) and is increasingly recognised by international organisations as a key driver of local conflict (see UNECA 2017). Local herder informants in Tillabéri claim that local state officials tend to privilege agricultural expansion over pastoralists' needs for sufficient pasture (Bøås et al. 2020).

The expansion of agriculture into traditional pastureland is not a new phenomenon in Tillabéri. Here, as elsewhere in the Sahel, this is a process that started during colonial times and increased as the newly independent state sought to both modernise agricultural production as well as clamp down on the nomadic lifestyle of pastoralists in order to achieve increased control over this population (see, for example, Bonfiglioli & Watson 1992). The pastoralist answer to these challenges has been to continue to practise transhumance, but travelling even longer distances, but for most pastoralists this answer to the livelihood challenges of living in such a precarious environment as Tillabéri is no longer an option, or it is an option that includes several difficult and dangerous choices. As a herder explained in a town close to the Malian border:

> Currently we can no longer go to areas where we used to pasture our animals—the conflict situation makes transhumance very difficult. We are facing two problems. On the one hand the existence of bandits or jihadists—I do not know what to call them—who take *zakat* samples from our animals;[2] on the other hand, there are the SDF [Nigerien Security and Defence Forces] operations which persecutes us. These SDFs confuse any Fulani or Bella with a jihadist, they commit atrocities in our area.[3] (Bøås et al. 2020: 122)

The livelihood challenges of insecurity preventing transhumance and what this leads to—namely that pastoralists are forced to buy much more animal feed than they used to at a much higher price (due to increased demand)—was a grievance that came up frequently during interviews and focus group sessions with Tillabéri herders in 2020. The consequence for the herders is that, somehow, they must raise money to buy animal feed, whether by selling cattle or engaging in other types of activities. The only alternative is to continue to practise transhumance, which means they must navigate an increasingly violent landscape of jihadi-insurgents, bandits, and SDF battalions. This is not only costly, as herders are likely to have to barter away some cattle in return for safe passage, but also dangerous, as armed robberies are frequent and sometimes lethal.

Choosing between these options is not an easy decision, but for most Fulani or Tuareg herders giving up this way of life is not an option either. This therefore tends to leave the people who live in this region between a rock and a hard place, as their choices will have consequences not only for the herders themselves, but also for the farmers and others who dwell here.

Tillabéri: between a rock and a hard place

The living conditions in Tillabéri have dramatically worsened as insecurity has soared since 2018, affecting both farmers and herders (see FAO 2020; WFP 2020; OCHA 2019), but this has happened before in this region. Waves of inter-communal violence over land disputes between farmers and herders due to droughts had already started in 2008 (ICRC 2011; Assanvo et al. 2019), and these were exacerbated by the proliferation of light weapons in the region after the fall of Gaddafi in Libya and the trouble in Mali that came to the fore in 2012 (Bøås & Torheim 2013).

The farmer–herder conflicts that erupted in 2008 created a climate of fear that hindered both farming and herding. This resulted in a loss of livestock as well as insufficient produce from farming to ensure food security. Consequently, already by 2011, ICRC had provided over 27,000 farmers and herders with 3-month food rations and special seeds to generate rapid harvests (ICRC 2011). While the waves of inter-communal violence that started in 2008 eventually died down, new clashes were brought about by the trouble that started in Mali, and both Fulani and Tuareg pastoralist communities on each side of the Mali–Niger border were affected by the jihadist insurgencies that gained ground on the Malian side.

THE NEIGHBOURS: BURKINA FASO AND NIGER

Clearly, the spillover from the war in Mali and farmer–herder conflicts in the context of a state that lacks both the institutional strength as well as the sovereign power to effectively regulate farmer–herder relations is an important factor. However, farmer–herder conflicts do not simply emerge out of nowhere. They are caused by something, in this case by droughts that reduced the area of land available for both farming and grazing cattle (see ICRC 2011; FAO 2020; WFP 2020). Similarly, there is also no doubt that Tillabéri is the victim of violent spillover from the conflict that erupted in Mali in 2012, and the Nigerien state is not strong enough, and command and control mechanisms over troops in the field are too weak, to handle it.

However, this explanation does not tell us much more than that this has happened. It does not help us understand why what was initially a small and weak band of insurgents has so quickly managed to wield such influence over a population that lives merely 130 kilometres from the strategic centre of the capital area. Did the government in Niamey fail to apprehend the threat that these insurgents represented or is the answer better identified in the strategies utilised by the insurgents regarding the local population and the state's failure to resist this? The argument here is that the conditions present in Tillabéri when the current wave of violence started are best characterised as an 'enabling environment'—ripe for a violent entrepreneur such as the ISGS emir, Adnan Abou Walid al-Sahraoui.

Tillabéri—an enabling environment?

An 'enabling environment' is an area where the combination of economic recession, rising unemployment, and low and declining levels of education makes it likely that some disadvantaged communities or individuals will have become so alienated from the state and local society that they could be persuaded to support, join, or implement organised violence inspired by political or religious extremist ideology. If and when this happens, these structural factors that constitute the 'enabling environment' will have translated into an array of deep-seated grievances that serve as emotional entry points for heralds of such ideologies to garner support (see Rupesinghe & Bøås 2018). This can, for example, happen if an armed group tries to target those who are most vulnerable or who feel most vulnerable in a society, offering them a means of escaping despair and aimlessness in favour of the dead certainty of violent resistance (see Bøås & Dunn 2013). Thus, armed groups tend to recruit among the poorest and least-educated areas, targeting destitute young men who may perceive that they have little, if anything, to lose by joining and may therefore be more malleable to indoctrination by the group targeting them.

The living conditions in Tillabéri have always been precarious, but since 2008 life has been particularly hard. Herd sizes are diminishing while at the same time the area is experiencing rapid population growth: the fertility rate is 7.6 children per woman, and the average household size is 8 persons (Tillabéri Regional Development Plan 2016). The Tillabéri region has significant natural resource potential for development. It is still Niger's main centre for cattle-breeding, and it contains the country's most important water resources. The Niger River (450 kilometres of which flow through the region) and the seven smaller connected rivers (Gorouol, Dargol, Sirba, Gouroubi, Diamongou, Tapoa, and Mékrou) are important reservoirs for irrigation and water for cattle (Tillabéri Regional Development Plan 2016). However, the region's full potential is far from realised, and repeated droughts and the failure to invest in drought and climate change resilience means that local communities suffer dramatic decreases in food security due to to smaller herd sizes and a fall in agricultural production (FAO 2020; WFP 2020; OCHA 2019).

The government response to this negative development could have been more effective, but it should also be underscored that it is almost impossible to initiate large-scale projects to increase climate-change resilience for famers and herders in an environment of unpredictable violence. The sad fact is that this becomes a vicious cycle not easily broken, as increased food insecurity leads to more violence which again makes it even more difficult to implementing countermeasures to food insecurity.

Tillabéri also has mining potential, as possible deposits of minable gold, coal, iron, and phosphate have been discovered, but this have not been realised, and the current security situation does not allow for anything beyond scattered alluvial mining.

Our point is that Tillabéri has development potential based on centuries-old traditions of cattle-breeding that, with more efficient water and irrigation systems, could bring about more resilient food and income security. However, the development of the rural sector is confronted with a range of barriers, including climatic variability, animal diseases, the predominance of traditional systems of food production, market supply circuits that are disorganised and difficult to access due to an insufficient and degraded road network, and insufficient investment in farming and pastoralism (see Tillabéri Regional Development Plan 2016; OCHA 2019; WFP 2020). The result is that food and animal feed deficits have become chronic and even structural in parts of Tillabéri (particularly the north). Likewise, if the security situation had allowed it to be systematically organised, the mining industry could have given the region much-needed employment opportunities and on top of that an economic boom. The challenge is that if the existing but untapped economic potential is not utilised in an efficient, transparent, and legitimate manner, Tillabéri will continue to be marked by a continuous deterioration of the productive base, high population growth, and spiraling insecurity that will constitute an even greater threat to its economic and social foundation.[4]

What has been described above is certainly a serious development challenge, but the same description could also be given to other regions of Niger. This suggests that, while these factors contribute to Tillabéri's status as an enabling environment, what sets this in motion are the following factors. First, as we have shown, there is a history of farmer–herder conflicts in this region, and the fact that this is the main cattle-breeding area of Niger suggests a high probability of herder–farmer conflicts. Why? The answer is because herd sizes are larger than elsewhere in the country, and agriculture has increased due to population pressure combined with access to water (e.g. the Niger River and its connected tributary rivers). This has created a history of inter-communal violence in the region. Second, while historically these conflicts have waxed and waned, spillover from the conflict in Mali has increased their intensity. Third, what has really ignited the fire of violence that has swept through Tillabéri since 2018 is the increased ability of the ISGS insurgents to integrate into local communities by appropriating local grievances and inter-communal conflict through a combination of coercive activities, offering some basic services as protection, and the establishment of some mobile courts. This process did not emerge suddenly out of the blue in 2018 but has been in the making since January 2013, when the French military operation Operation Serval started to expel jihadist insurgents from towns in northern Mali like Gao. One of those who fled Gao was the current ISGS emir al-Sahraoui (ICG 2020b).

ISGS: neither stationary nor roaming

In Chapter 2, we saw how al-Sahrawi first rose to prominence as a MOJWA commander and governor of Gao city, and then had to flee when Operation Serval closed in on the city in 2013. He was assisted in his escape by newfound allies among Fulani fighters from the Mali–Niger border area, including some from Tillabéri. Here, al-Sahrawi found a new enabling environment into which he could embed himself and his fighters by appropriating local grievances and lines of inter-communal conflict.

In this period, the Malian army was not present in the border area, Operation Serval did not have the capacity to guard this area, and Nigerien security forces, although present, lacked both the capacity, training, and leadership to comprehend and deal with what was happening. The result was that al-Sahrawi and the fighters who had escaped with him from Gao could regroup and start recruiting locally, taking advantage of Fulani herder communities in Tillabéri that for a long time had felt that their land was being encroached upon by a combination of agricultural expansion and increased competition with Daoussahak pastoralist communities. Thus, in a political vacuum where the state was not completely absent but lacked complete control over the use of force, al-Sahrawi managed to gain not territorial control but such a firm social grip on certain population groups that he could establish his own insurgency, namely the ISGS, which pledged allegiance to IS and al-Baghdadi in 2015.

When the Nigerien state finally realised what was happening, it attempted a military operation to uproot the jihadi insurgents. This campaign started in early 2017 and lasted until around June 2018 (see ICG 2020b). In this campaign, the Nigerien military forces were supported by Malian militias allied with the Malian state and the French Operation Barkhane. The Malian militias were the Movement for the Salvation of Azawad (MSA), which consisted mainly of young

THE NEIGHBOURS: BURKINA FASO AND NIGER

Daoussahak fighters, and GATIA (see Chapter 2). These groups are the remnants of the 2012 Tuareg rebellion of MNLA that in 2015 during the Algiers peace process signed a deal with the government in Bamako.

However, while the Algiers peace process for all practical purposes is almost completely dead as regards bringing peace to Mali, groups like GATIA and MSA stuck to the agreement for a long time, becoming not only the hired hands of the successive government in Bamako but also useful allies on the ground for Operation Barkhane. In return, these groups received money and weapons, but also the possibility to involve themselves in several income-generating activities such as cattle theft and smuggling. In Mali, if a group could prove itself a useful auxiliary for a government mainly concerned with regime security (Bamako) and a French intervention force that needed tactical allies on the ground, it could act with a high level of impunity. In this case, GATIA and MSA mainly operated in Mali's Meneka region, but they also were allowed by the Nigerien army to cross the border into northern Tillabéri. As a Fulani activist explained in an interview on 3 November 2019 in Niamey:

> Jihadists are not based in villages or among the communities. They have their own small bases in the bush, where food and weapons are stored. They are extremely mobile, and hundreds of fighters can gather in a couple of hours: they communicate skilfully, like in Vietnam, they are everywhere and nowhere. Local people often protect them, because jihadists are seen as having contributed to the stability of the community against the Tuareg raids: we fight for our right to stay; if MNLA had won, we would all have abandoned our places. (Bøås et al. 2020: 127)

Thus, not only did al-Sahrawi find sanctuary after he had to flee from Gao, but he and his fighters also quickly managed to achieve a certain level of local integration. This was not in the form of complete territorial control, but was enough to get a better social grip on the local Fulani population than Nigerien state security forces.

What al-Sahrawi and ISGS therefore had to offer is a very rudimentary form of governance: a mobile governance that comes and goes, but one that is seen as more reliable and enforceable than the one that the Nigerien state has to offer these communities. What this suggests is therefore not only that an insurgency like ISGS is neither stationary nor completely roaming, as the dichotomy of Olsen (2000) suggested, but also that ISGS is quite deliberately utilising a hybrid strategy that combines the two more fixed positions that a non-state armed movement can take. The semi-permanent presence it has in the local population offers ISGS some respect and support as well as fear, while at the same time it avoids the costly affair of controlling and attempting to hold territory. This way of doing things is much cheaper, and the violent approach of the SDF has pushed several young herders (not only Fulani) to support and even join ISGS.

It is therefore hardly a surprise that the Niger state's military campaign achieved little against the insurgents. However, the violence that the Nigerien army unleashed further alienated the local population from the state. As a herder in the Tillabéri municipality of Banibangou complained:

> [The army] do not play their role of protecting populations, we are sometimes more afraid of the SDF than of bandits or Jihadists. The SDF can on a false testimony or unverified information kill us or kill our children or send them to high security prisons in Quallam or Niamey. The SDF whose mission in principle is to protect the population, but it is the opposite: on February 5th, 2020, an SDF mission went to my camp and killed two of my children, I was forced to flee. (Bøås et al. 2020: 128)

Thus, there is little doubt that the failure of the Nigerien counter-insurgency strategy has helped al-Sahrawi and his men gain some legitimacy, support structures, and new recruits locally. Even some circles among the political elite in Niamey realised this, and for a while the Nigerien government had second thoughts about its counter-insurgency strategy and a process of dialogue was started.

For a while ISGS was pushed back, the dialogue process that the government started came to nothing. There are several reasons for this. While local Fulani communities' trust in the government and willingness to enter the process was questionable, the main problem was the lack of state capacity to see the process through. The dialogue process was led by the High Authority for the Consolidation of Peace

THE NEIGHBOURS: BURKINA FASO AND NIGER

(HACP).[5] The HACP was first initiated in 1995 as the Office of the High Commissioner for the Restoration of Peace in order to monitor the implementation of the Peace Accords with the former Tuareg rebellion in northern Niger, and it transformed into the HACP in 2011. The HACP is attached to the Presidency of the Republic, who is in charge of prospective analysis, prevention, and management of crises and conflicts in all regions of Niger.

In the case of Tillabéri, the HACP approach was to initiate a disarmament, demobilisation, and re-integration (DDR) programme by working through local community leaders. These were supposed to convince local rank-and-file jihadi insurgents to surrender in exchange for immunity and possibly new jobs in the security and defence forces. These positions were supposed to be available to young men from local communities along the border, particularly from Fulani villages. It was a good idea, but the HACP was not able to see it through. Few joined, and even fewer young Fulani men. Some did surrender, but the overall figure was low. People simply did not trust that the army would defend them against the jihadists, who would clearly see this as treason and inflict punishment not only on those who joined but also on their communities. The recruitment process to the security and defence forces was seen as opaque, and local people complained that even young Fulani men who wanted to join were discarded by the army. This added to the lack of trust of the HACP that already existed, as this organisation was led by a Tuareg general close to President Issoufou. Consequently, local Fulani communities tended to see him as a possible ally or friend of the Tuareg and Daoussahak militias that had attacked their communities along the border.

Thus, as the dialogue ran on empty in the dry soil of Tillabéri, new waves of violence came to the fore with local communities caught between a rock and a hard place. However, al-Sahrawi and ISGS also managed to show local communities that they had more than violence to offer. The insurgents killed people they saw as collaborating with the government, but by and large avoided killing civilians more broadly. And, more importantly, they started to offer some rudimentary basic services. They have at times helped retrieve stolen cattle as well as established some local courts to rule over land disputes and other issues that matters to local communities (Bøås et al. 2020).

Just as we have learnt from studies of similar processes in central Mali (see Rupesinghe & Bøås 2018), these courts quickly gained a reputation for honesty and competency. This does not suggest that they are that great, just that they are considered to be more efficient and less corrupt than official state courts which also at times rule in such matters. ISGS is therefore more than just another user of force; it has an agenda of governance and ordering, albeit a weak one, with the governance on offer sporadic and haphazard. It comes and goes with an armed movement that is hyper-mobile but has enough local presence to gain a considerable social grip on certain local populations.

Negotiating livelihoods during a war without frontiers

The violence in Tillabéri is far from the way violence is used in a conventional war. What is taking place here is a war without frontiers, in which all antagonists are highly mobile, moving in and out of local communities. ISGS, bandits, Malian government-allied militias, the SDF, G5-Sahel forces, Operation Barkhane, everybody is on the move, trying to get a grip on local populations with the means that they have at hand. Amid all this movement are local populations, left to negotiate their livelihoods, for which they too depend on mobility. This is how a herder in Bankilaré, Tillabéri explained it:

> These are young people riding motorcycles in the area, it's not been long before the G5 Sahel came to our village, they took more than 20 motorcycles and burned these motorcycles, and a few days later bandits came to threaten the people. The bandits are young people from all ethnicities (Fulani, Tuareg, Mossi, Songhay). They spent three days in our village. We do not sleep because they track us, and the authorities and the SDF think that we are colluding with them; we are caught between two fires. (Bøås et al. 2020: 129)

The question for local populations is who you can trust in exchange for what—who is most likely to produce something necessary for survival given the state of precarity that people live in? The answer for some, but clearly not for all, is the ISGS. Local people do complain about the strict religious practices the jihadi insurgents attempt to enforce. Marriages are not the celebrations they used to be, music is forbidden, and women have much less freedom than they used to have. However, for some this is just another price that must be paid to whoever can guarantee some level of protection for their pastoral livelihood.

Thus, if this situation continues, the social fabric of these societies will continue to evaporate and even more young people will search for the authority of the gun, which is becoming one of the most reliable ways of negotiating a livelihood. Those who cannot or will not do so must continue to endure life in an enabling environment of violent extremism, where the best bet for survival is pragmatic silence and the willingness to accept the order (or unorder) of whichever wielder of force has the most predictable presence in your daily life.

This suggests that the rise of support for jihadism in Tillabéri among some Fulani communities is conditional. The armed challenge to the Nigerien state does not originate from an 'ungoverned space' of disorder, but rather from the violent rejection of dysfunctional modes of governance by a state that is remote, weak, and often coercive. On the other side of this coin is the governance of the ISGS, which may be sporadic but at least provides an alternative form of order which some local Fulani see as more legitimate, less costly, more efficient, and not corrupt (take, for example, the Sharia courts that rule on local land disputes and other matters of importance in daily rural life).

What all of this adds up to is a landscape of violence where the spillover effects from the conflicts in Mali have clearly played a role. The history of farmer–herder and likewise herder–herder conflicts, such as those between Tuareg and Fulani communities, also matters, but what has really set Tillabéri on fire is the combination of the failure of the Nigerien state, the indiscriminate violence of the SDF and their allies (the Malian militias), and the jihadi insurgents' ability to use this to achieve a level of local integration through their ability to appropriate local conflict lines and grievances. This is not the first time that heavy-handed state response strategies have been the primary cause of recruitment to violent extremism, and it will unfortunately most likely not be the last. Until a more permanent order comes into being, the inhabitants of Tillabéri will just have to continue to adjust to negotiating their livelihood in a war without frontiers.

The relative peace and resilience of Agadez

Situated at the intersection of both intra-continental and trans-continental migration paths, Agadez is a crucial hub on the trans-Saharan route connecting West Africa to the shores of the Mediterranean since ancient times. As such, Agadez has been a melting pot of people and goods crossing the region, both northbound and southbound (Austen 2010). In more recent times, external interventions from Western powers have made Agadez a crucial point in local and international mobility and, in turn, a target of the processes of the externalisation of Europe's border management.

Agadez and northern Niger have seen times of rebellion and warfare. The last major episode was in 2007–9, when the Niger Movement for Justice (MNJ), an organisation of Tuareg rebels, started to target camps belonging to the Nigerien army and attacked some foreign commercial interests connected to the uranium mining around the town of Arli—a mining town and headquarters of the French company Areva NC (see Emerson 2011). While causing some casualties and a few disruptions in the production and transport of uranium (Keenan 2008), the conflict never reached large proportions. It ended in 2009 with first a ceasefire agreement, followed by an amnesty for the rebels, some of whom were also integrated into the military forces of Niger. Ever since, the Agadez region has been relatively peaceful, and what remained of the MNJ showed no interest in restarting their rebellion when MNLA started their war in Mali in 2012. What factors can help us understand Agadez's relative peace and resilience to the effects of violent entrepreneurs?

The region of Agadez shares many similarities with surrounding regions that have been significantly affected by violent dynamics. Structural characteristics such as socio-political isolation, environmental degradation and climate change, lack of employment, trafficking flows, and general insecurity are also present in Agadez. Surprisingly, though, in the case of Agadez such factors have not led to the outcome that we find in Tillabéri (or elsewhere in Mali and Burkina Faso). The last major attack was in 2013 and was performed by an al-Qaeda commando who came from abroad. Kidnappings, once rampant, have declined. Thus, apart from some minor inter-ethnic clashes which have not escalated or had any connection to jihadi insurgents, the region has remained peaceful to the extent that local and international preventing and countering violent extremism (PCVE) programmes have been relocated to other regions in Niger.

Prominent explanations tend to focus on the approach taken by the Nigerien state after the end of the Tuareg rebellion in 2009 to the powerbrokers of Agadez (Guichaoua & Pellerin 2017). This approach differs substantially from what one observed in the case of Mali (Raineri & Strazzari 2021). Local peacebuilding institutions like the HACP and the Comité de Paix d'Agadez have managed to obtain national and international support, including from the EU, to foster prevention policies in which the co-optation of local leaders strengthens state capacities of oversight and reduces the physical and social space that jihadi insurgents might exploit.

Traditional authorities—the imams and the Sultanate—also tend to dismiss the idea that radical religious views can take root in Agadez. This is reportedly because traditional social and religious norms retain widespread legitimacy, binding people to local Sufi brotherhoods, such as the Qadiryya. The locally based Observatoire des Réligions also represents a bridgehead between religious associations and the Ministry of the Interior, helping the latter to supervise religious discourses (sermons, radio communications, etc.) while removing 'inflammatory content' from public spaces, such as mosques and the media (Bøås et al. 2021).

Ethnographic research tempers some of these claims. Like elsewhere in the Sahel (see Ibrahim 2017), radical religious views such as Salafism and Wahabism have gained traction in Agadez. Salafist mosques are mushrooming in the town and its hinterland, and a few thousand students are reportedly enrolled in Salafist-leaning Quranic schools. If accurate, this would represent 10–25 per cent of the number of pupils enrolled in Sufi-leaning Quranic schools. Salafism appears to be more attractive to disenfranchised social groups who are poorly socially integrated into Agadez' customary religious norms—this is particularly the case for non-Tuareg Nigeriens who have settled in Agadez after migrating from the south of the country, including Hausa and Kanouri communities living in the sprawling outskirts of the town. Most of the Salafi imams and preachers in

Agadez also tend to be Hausa from the south of Niger or from northern Nigeria. Some are members of the Izala, the radical group from which Mohamed Yusuf, the founder of Boko Haram, originated. Nonetheless, while Salafi imams have described how they often meet frustrated youth who ask for moral and practical guidance as to how to act and fight the evil of disbelievers, these same religious leaders have a proven track record of dissuading these youths from violence (see Bøås et al. 2021).

This suggests that even 'radical' religious leaders can provide a valuable contribution to prevent and counter violent extremism, the same as any other religious leader, and possibly even more so because of their perceived legitimacy, moral probity, and political independence vis-á-vis the state. However, while it is important that the state of Niger has taken a different approach to its peripheral northern region than the one taken in Mali, combined with the solidity of local norms and institutions, there is also a political economy explanation that marks Agadez as something significantly different than the theatres of conflict elsewhere in the Sahel neighbourhood. This is Agadez's economic function as a port city in an ocean of sand and the transmigration boom of 2014–16, and how this contributed to the transformation of the city.

Agadez—port town, boom town, closed town

In 2015, it became evident that Agadez had become the key migration hub of the southern leg of the Central Mediterranean Route: approximately 180,000 of the migrants and refugees who landed in Italy had passed through this town (Bøås 2020). The reason for this is that the functional logic of Agadez is that of a port town in an enormous sea of sand. It is a place where everybody who travels through the northern regions of Niger must stop. It is the last port of call to rest, to acquire new supplies such as food and water, and not least to organise the next leg of the journey through the desert to Libya. There are few if any alternatives in this regard.

Placed at the centre of the region of Agadez in northern Niger in the midst of a desert landscape, the city of Agadez is the departure point for two routes connecting Niger to Libya and Algeria. As a port town, Agadez needs customers, and the migration flows have there-

THE NEIGHBOURS: BURKINA FASO AND NIGER

fore provided a most welcome financial injection. Interviews with members of the local population have shown that during the large migration flows of 2015–16 almost everybody in the city of Agadez benefited: those involved directly in the transportation of refugees and migrants, but also those who could offer housing, catering, and money transfers, as well as shopkeepers, their staff, and all the informal brokers who helped migrants orient themselves during their stay in the city (Bøås 2020). Even local authorities did not perceive transmigration as a security threat. Instead, migrants moving through the city were regularly taxed. Migrants paid an informal tax to the police when they entered the city, and on departure the Agadez municipality collected another tax of 1,100 CFA. It is estimated that during the busiest periods this may have given the municipality an additional income between 3–7 million CFA per week (see Carayol 2019).

As the number of migrants was fairly consistent, local transporters used to depart from the *gare routiér* in large convoys, often made up of more than 100 trucks, each carrying about 50 migrants who each had paid approximately 150,000 CFA for the journey from Agadez to the Libyan border. Due to the risk of being attacked by bandits in the desert, the convoys were escorted by local security forces from Agadez up to the city of Dirkou before entering Libyan soil. There is thus good reason to believe that many—maybe even the majority—of the inhabitants of Agadez share the opinion that the town not only benefited from transmigration, but also managed it quite well. The following quote from an interview conducted in November 2019 with a man in his mid-thirties who had previously worked as a driver transporting migrants to the Libyan border is an opinion shared by many:

> Before in almost all the neighbourhoods where migrants were staying, the population of these neighbourhoods benefitted. Traders, motel owners and the people who privately housed them benefitted. Now all of this has changed, it is not like before ... It was the international community that prevented migrants from coming. In the past migration management was done as follows: once the migrants arrived in Agadez at the bus station, they were greeted by someone who would take care of them during their stay in Agadez, hosting them at home and finding them a vehicle to continue.[6]

This was not going to last, as a new law was introduced that would change this completely. With the increasingly high number of migrants and refugees arriving in Europe through the Central Mediterranean Route and reporting that they had travelled through Agadez, Niger became a target of the EU's attempt to externalise its border controls in North Africa and the Sahel. The most striking example of this was what is known in Niger as Loi 2015–036. The EU was a strong advocate of this law, and without the massive amounts of aid it provided, it is highly unlike that this law would have come into being. While receiving such aid may have been convenient for the administration of President Mohamed Bazoum, Loi 2015–036 and the procedures and state interference that followed was highly unpopular locally. The reason for this is that the law criminalised providing assistance to migrants and refugees who would potentially cross the Nigerien border north of Agadez. In essence, this made a local livelihood based on offering a wide range of services to migrants and refugees a crime punishable by Nigerien law.

The implementation of Loi 2015–036 in Agadez

What would come about was a significant transformation of the economic and security landscape of the city. Police started to seize the cars that were used to transport migrants, and several drivers of the seized vehicles were given up to 5 years in prison. Most of the activities connected to migrants' presence in the city were also shot down, as feeding and accommodating migrants had suddenly become a criminal act punishable by the law.

As transit migration had come to represent an important economic resource for Agadez, it should not have been a surprise to anybody that the new law was not met with much enthusiasm by the local population. Both ordinary people and powerbrokers in Agadez argued that the government in Niamey was sacrificing the local economy to satisfy the EU's demand that Niger should do more to reduce transit migration. However, while local discontent was high, the swift implementation of Loi 2015–036 significantly reduced the number of northbound migrants in Agadez. The EU agency FRONTEX (2017) stated that in the immediate aftermath of the implementation of the law, the number of migrants heading towards Libya and Algeria

THE NEIGHBOURS: BURKINA FASO AND NIGER

decreased by almost 95 per cent. However, a range of issues emerged after the implementation of the law that questioned the sustainability of this attempt by the EU to externalise its border management, and in the end it contributed to the fall of the leader who willingly or unwillingly came to be the face of Niger's status as a client of Europe, namely Mohamed Bazoum (we will return to the issue of the fall of Bazoum in Chapter 9).

While numbers were drastically reduced, the transport of migrants did not stop completely but reconfigured in smaller numbers and along alternative paths and routes. What this means is that the transit migration business morphed from an open activity that took place in the middle of the city to a clandestine activity. For those who continued their involvement in the transit migration business, this meant that they had now really become smugglers who operated through dangerous and sometimes criminal methods.

As the new border control operations that Loi 2015–36 brought about were concentrated on the traditional routes connecting Agadez to Dirkou (the Libyan route) and Agadez to Arlit (the Algerian route), those who conducted the business of transporting migrants started to circumvent these routes. The region of Zinder emerged as a new hub for migrants transiting through Niger. New routes blossomed from the city of Tanout in Zinder, where the transporters who had now become smugglers could more easily gather migrants due to lack of control posts. From Tanout transporters headed north, transiting through Chad or the region of Kawar in northern Niger to avoid border control patrols. After crossing the Well of Hope in the north of the region of Agadez, they eventually reached Libya.[7] While less patrolled and controlled by border guards, police, and the Nigerien army, these new routes were not only much longer but also more dangerous. Migrants were exposed to isolated desert regions for longer amounts of time, and the risk of being attacked by bandits was much higher. This meant that, while fewer migrants reached the shores of the Mediterranean and thereby had a chance to cross the ocean, they were also exposed to much higher risks if they attempted this journey.

As the risks have increased, so have the costs for the migrants. Migrants who want to make the journey through these longer routes will have to pay about 350,000 CFA to reach Gatrone (the first Libyan city on the border with Niger), compared to the 150,000 CFA that transporters used to charge from the city of Agadez. Moreover, since these new routes are almost inaccessible, in case of vehicle breakdown there is the high risk of getting stuck in the desert and dying if help does not come (Border Forensics 2023). Second, while in the past migrant convoys moved with security forces, this is obviously not the case anymore, meaning that the risk of being attacked by bandits is significantly higher. While migrant death tolls in the Sahara Desert are unknown, and the few estimates that exist are very rough—an estimate from the International Organization for Migration (IOM) is that 520 migrants died along the route from Niger to Libya in 2022.[8] There is every reason to believe that more migrants die along the new routes than what was the case prior to the implementation of Loi 2015–36.

Because of the increased exposure to banditry, the transporters have also started arming themselves. This has spilled over to a general increase in the level of violence in the region. Some of the former transporters have also moved to other illicit businesses, since the risk of getting imprisoned made the transit-migration industry less attractive. Some turned to smuggling drugs such as tramadol, cannabis, and cocaine, while others pursued new careers as armed bandits.

More worrying is the observation that these new smuggling operations have become the domain of tightly organised and highly armed trafficking networks. As already mentioned, after Loi 2015–36 took effect, a large portion of the drivers of the migration convoys left the business, some of them arrested while others decided to leave for fear of prison or heavy fines. The vacuum that this created left the field open for organised traffickers already operating in the region to enlarge their operative spectrum. In this sense, smuggling has transformed from a free market activity with low entry costs (just access to a vehicle and knowledge of the routes), to a cartel form of market controlled by a few networks, and therefore a market with high entry costs (see Raineri 2018). Indeed, the criminalisation of smuggling made this activity riskier but also more lucrative for those who decide to engage in it. In other words, we may say that the criminalisation of smuggling coincided with a rise of value of migrants, who have become a considerably more attractive illegal resource than they used to be. Today, involvement in the transit-migration business requires a high level of capital, both material and non-material. Vehicles and desert knowledge are still essential assets, but recourse to violence has also become an indispensable skill. Beyond that, being part of a network represents by far the most important commodity. Moreover, as migrants have increasingly become an illegal source of wealth, it means that migrants who go into debt—that is, who cannot pay the full amount demanded by the smugglers—run a huge risk of being sold to Libyan militias and held for ransom in the infamous 'prisons' scattered all over the Libyan soil.

International migration management

As Loi 2015–36 took effect, the result was a re-configuration of the intertwined space/market nexus of the city of Agadez. However, while the implementation of Loi 2015–36 represented an undoing of the city as a key pillar of West Africa northbound mobility, Agadez's very nature as a transit city remains a defining characteristic. The only difference is that this no longer benefited the local population. As the joint intervention of both national and international institutions has deterred migrants moving through Niger towards Libya and Algeria, the transit of southbound migrants coming from the north has assumed higher relevance. The establishment of institutions such as the IOM and the United Nations High Commissioner for Refugees (UNHCR) in Agadez has profoundly contributed to this transformation.

Both organisations received entitlements to establish refugee/migrant camps on the outskirts of the city of Agadez, as well as operational transit centres scattered along strategic nodes connecting the migration routes towards both Libya and Algeria. Although the IOM's presence in Niger dates back to 2006 (Boyer & Mounkaila 2018), it is over recent years that the IOM has raised its profile. Since 2012, when the IOM's intervention was crucial for evacuating 114,500 West African migrants stranded in Libya to Niger, the operative landscape of the organisation in the country has expanded a lot.

Under the banner of promoting 'safe, orderly and dignified migration', the IOM's contribution to migration management in Niger is devoted to a number of tasks that can be summed up as three policy areas: border management, capacity building for local institutions dealing with migration,; and promoting assisted voluntary return for migrants.[9] All these activities are financed by the EU Emergency Trust Fund for Africa (EUTF for Africa) and respond to a number of issues, especially providing assistance to local security forces, training in capacity building to improve border controls; participation in desert patrolling operations; and providing software and instruments for data collection on migrants.

UNHCR, on the other hand, supports national authorities in improving the identification and protection of potential asylum seekers. To this end, the Niger government has established a National Eligibility Commission for the status of refugee, in order to process potential cases among migrants transiting through Niger, co-operating with the EU's aim of moving asylum procedures to third countries (Van Dessel 2019: 451). Moreover, UNHCR has implemented the Emergency Transit Mechanism (ETM) that is a system of evacuation for potential refugees held by Libyan authorities in the infamous migrants' prisons in Libya. UNHCR officials in Libya select people to relocate them to Niger and then eventually to Western countries. People benefiting from the ETM are those nationals to whom refugee status is assured on a regular base (i.e. Eritreans, Sudanese, and Somalis).

As northbound migration has been undermined, southbound migration proceeding from the north has gained momentum. In this respect, the aforementioned institutions have proved essential. In 2014, the Niger government signed a bilateral agreement with Algeria on repatriating Nigerien nationals from Algeria to Niger. However, informally the agreement has been extended to all foreign nationals residing in Algerian territory. In 2020, around 16,000 people were deported from Algeria to Niger. Migrants can be swept up by police raids in Algerian cities and then detained for several days before they are expelled from the country. Migrants who have been taken by the Algerian police and deported to Niger complain of being beaten and having their properties and passports confiscated. The migrants marked for deportation are taken to the Algerian city of Tamanrasset, close to the border to Niger.

In Tamanrasset, the migrants are placed on convoys that leaves them at the so-called 'Point Zero', 15 kilometres from the city of

THE NEIGHBOURS: BURKINA FASO AND NIGER

Assamakka in Niger. Some spend almost two days in the desert before they make it to Assamakka. Here, they will be handled by the Direction de la Surveillance du Territoire—the division of the Nigerien police responsible for border control—and IOM staff. Many arrive traumatised due to deprivation and distress. After receiving emergency care, migrants are carried to the IOM transit centre in the city of Arlit where they spend one night, before eventually being taken to the main IOM centre in the city of Agadez. The centre has a normal capacity of 400 hundred individuals, but if needed this can be increased to up to 1,000 people. Migrants are allowed to stay with the IOM on the condition that they accept to be repatriated through a voluntary return programme to their country of origin. If they refuse, they are excluded from any form of assistance provided by the IOM (accommodation, food, and medical and psychological care). Eventually, these returning migrants will be taken to the IOM transit centres in Niamey before being repatriated to their countries of origin.[10]

In addition to the flows of migrants deported from Algeria, there are the refugees and asylum seekers arriving from Libya via the UNHCR's ETM. In addition to them, several individuals, mostly Sudanese nationals, are reaching Agadez autonomously, knowing they can get access to the refugee status and from there possibly be relocated to a Western country. Most of them have escaped from detention in Libya's prisons or come directly from UNHCR camps at the Chadian–Sudanese border.

Consequences for the city of Agadez

Over the last few years, Niger's role as a transit country has been deeply transformed, as has the role and functionality of Agadez. The effort of both national and international organisations to transform local practices and behaviour towards migrations is evident. The town of Agadez in particular bears the marks of the events, whereby migration has shifted from being a factor of popular prosperity to an asset of dispossession controlled by exterior players. Against this background, several features concerning the international, national, and local spheres are at stake, resulting in a complex web of changing power relations and socio-economic balances, privileging some actors at the detriment of others.

The trajectories of the migrants have changed tremendously. Today, most migrants transiting through Agadez are those deported by Algerian authorities at the border with the Nigerien city of Assamakka and transferred to Agadez in the framework of the IOM's voluntary return programme. Since migrants are accommodated at the IOM centre in the city's outskirts, they have little or no contact with local communities. All the services once provided by Agadez inhabitants are now furnished at the IOM facility. The same goes for the refugees and asylum seekers at the UNHCR centre located 15 kilometres outside Agadez. It is therefore not unheard of for Agadez citizens when interviewed to claim that the benefits of transit migration have been captured by international organisations to the detriment of the livelihood of local inhabitants.

They consider it discriminatory that, while northbound migration has been declared illegal, southbound migration has been encouraged. The criminalisation of the transmigration economy by the EU and the Niamey government in tandem has deliberately dispossessed local communities from an economic activity that up until the establishment of Loi 2016–036 had improved their lives. In other words, one may say that in Agadez the disappearance of the informal free market has coincided with the emergence of a formal monopolistic market managed by a combination of organised criminal networks for northbound migration and a southbound migration network controlled by IOM and UNHCR. Beyond that, the migration management issue exacerbates even more tensions considering its implementation has not been followed by any effective compensation measures for the local economy. In an environment characterised by lack of resources, the Agadez population consider both IOM and UNHCR migrants/asylum seekers privileged recipients of care and goods (food, accommodation, healthcare). In the past, migrants used to stay for a period of time, living among the local population and buying goods and services from them. Today, on the other hand, local population feels migration is generating socio-economic pressure, as the economic benefits associated with migrants end up either with organised criminal networks or with IOM and similar external organisations.

THE NEIGHBOURS: BURKINA FASO AND NIGER

Has migration control undermined local legitimacy?

While it would be wrong to assume that it was President Bazoum's support for the EU's attempt to curb migration routes through Niger that led to the coup (see Salih 2023), Bazoum's close association with the law certainly did nothing to increase his popularity. But the downfall of Bazoum and thereby also of democracy in Niger is due to much more than misplaced policies from the EU. Nonetheless, as it had done in the case of Sudan, where EU gave support to the infamous Rapid Support Forces (RSF) of strongman Mohamed Hamdan Dagalo (a.k.a. Hemetti), the EU failed to listen to the warnings that its external migration policies could have destabilising effects. With Bazoum gone, replaced by a military junta that has revoked Loi 2015–036, the EU has lost not only its investments but also any control of this part of the Central Mediterranean Corridor.

In the EU's and various European countries' Sahel strategies, stability in the region of Agadez was considered a pillar for international security. Over the years, local institutions—which are an amalgamation of traditional authorities with local Tuareg elites and former rebel leaders—have proved crucial in preventing the spread of conflicts. For example, the mediation of local authorities (especially those who were part of the 1991 rebellion) was essential to avoid the outbreak of a new rebellion in Agadez after the fall of Gaddafi in 2011. The local leaders have walked the tightrope of delicate mediation between both local and national/Niamey interests. The EU-initiated regime of migration control has upset this equilibrium, undermining the relations between local constituencies and regional institutions. As emerged during an interview with a former driver in Agadez, 'The whites impose things on us, which are not in our interest but in their interest, I wonder why our authorities accept certain things like preventing migration.'[11]

As a country with a precarious 'centre/periphery' dimension, what is occurring in Agadez has important effects on Niger's power relations. Dominated by the overlapping of both synchronic (urbanism/ruralism; sedentary/nomadism; agriculturalism/pastoralism) and diachronic (pre-colonial; colonial; and postcolonial orders) cleavages, Niger's political sphere appears as a space undergoing an almost permanent process of disputation over established authority and public legitimacy. The hybridisation that started with democratisation in 1993 merged the ashes of an authoritarian past with a traditional/neoliberal contemporaneity.

Niger has thus, at least up until the July 2023 coup, existed in a centrifugal and centripetal political dynamic that encapsulates both local and national politics. As argued by Benjaminsen and Lund (2001) as well as Scheele (2009), local legitimacy in the Sahara and the Sahel rests on actors' capacity to forge external connectivity with other authorities. This notion sheds lights on two issues: on the one hand, it stresses the horizontal distribution and lack of hierarchy of regional power, on the other it draws attention to the *enjeu permanent* of legitimacy (Sikor & Lund 2009). Niger's vast territory and its ethno-cultural wealth have forced colonial and postcolonial rulers to rely on local authorities to varying degrees. Based on an interdependent constraint, the dialogue between local rulers and the state has developed ties binding Niamey to its various regions, departments, and communes. Far from being a one-way relationship, this entanglement is key to regulating the political balance in the country. Local Big Men's decision to enter a national party and attend local elections often proves to be a strategy for exploiting Niamey's connection and extending their authority in peripheral regions. At the same time, relying on a local Big Man is itself a salient tool for national parties aiming to find local legitimacy and, in the case of the ruling party, to find appeasement in case of turmoil.

It is therefore not a coincidence that the role of the former government party, the PNDS-Tarrayya, over time aimed to increase its influence in the Agadez region through a process of co-opting local elites. This began during the first election of former President Mahamadou Issoufou in 2011. To protect local peace, the Issoufou government established close ties with Tuareg elites through the appointment of local Big Men to high-ranking government positions in Niamey, as well as at the local level. This foreshadowed the Issoufou government's laissez-faire approach to the transport of migrants and refugees, in return for social peace (Guichaoua & Pellerin 2017).

The social peace—not only within Agadez, but also between Agadez and Niamey, and between various local and national power brokers—was therefore built on a neatly formulated compromise of informal migration management as a 'free' market with relatively low entry costs, but from which both local people and those in power as Big Men in the national police and army could benefit from. The law that the EU pushed through, and that Bazoum as president in waiting and Minister of the Interior accepted in 2015 on the condition of increased aid to Niger, cracked the social and economic compromise on migration management and left the door open for something else.

First and foremost, this saw the rise of the professionalisation of criminal networks, transforming what used to be a free market to one that was clandestine and cartel-like. However, in such an unsettled and administratively weak state as Niger, this may also have been a contributing element to the discontent that leading military officers started to express towards Bazoum after he was elected as Issoufou's successor in 2021. While the July 2023 coup also dealt a blow to the EU's attempt at external border control once the new regime revoked Loi 2015–036, it is interesting to note that, contrary to Burkina Faso where the military rulers are losing control of the country's peripheries, this has not been the case (yet) in Niger. The Nigerien resilience still holds.

And while one can argue about how resilient Niger is based on the ongoing violence in Tillabéri, an argument of geographical scale can also be made. Agadez's advantage is that it is far away. It is far away from Niamey, but it is also far away from the main fields of violence of the Sahel. Tillabéri, on the other hand, is much closer to the capital, but it is also so much closer to the main theatre of operation for the insurgents of JNIM and ISGS, as well as FAMA and its militia allies. It is therefore easier for Niamey to keep a relative peace in Agadez than it is to subdue the insurgents of Tillabéri. This may sound like a paradox, but so much of the Sahel is a paradox.

It will, however, be of interest to see how the decision taken by Niger's military rulers on 16 March 2024—the government's spokesman, Colonel Major Amadou Abdramane, announced that the government had ended the agreement from 2012 that allowed military personnel and civilian staff from the US Department of Defense to operate in Niger—will affect the stability of Agadez and Niger. Abdramane said that the accord with the United States had been imposed on Niger in violation of the 'constitutional and democratic rules' of Niger's national sovereignty (CNN 2024; Al Jazeera 2024).

This is clearly a loss for the United States, as on the south-easternmost part of Agadez lies what is officially called Nigerien Air Base 201, but is, as most locals would say, 'the American' base. Officially, it is owned by the Nigerien military, but for all practical purposes it paid for, built, and operated by the US military (see Penney 2018). This airstrip is large enough to operate C-17 transport planes as well as MQ-9 Reaper drones, and it has been used to survey and conduct strikes against Salafi militant groups, including JNIM and ISGS. When viewed from afar, Agadez may seem like a peripheral hinterland, lost in time and space, but for this purpose (just as it is for irregular migration) the town in perfect. Its location in the wider Sahel region is central. Medium- to long-range drones operated from a base in Agadez could reach all over the Sahel and large parts of territory bordering sub-Saharan Africa. From a military point of view, this gave the US Africa Command (AFRICOM) a significant strategic advantage. Plus, it was expensive, supposedly costing $110 million to construct. Now, all of this may be lost to the United States, but there remains the question of what this means for the relative resilience of Niger. This is one of the key questions that we return to in Chapter 9, but first we need to look deeper into what type of enabling environment this part of the Sahel is, and what constitutes the relationship between drivers of violence and local resilience.

4

THE SAHEL—AN ENABLING ENVIRONMENT?
DRIVERS OF VIOLENCE AND LOCAL RESILIENCE

We define an enabling environment as a geographical area where the socio-economic conditions caused by a combination of specific factors create a situation where violent extremism in various forms and manifestations is likely to occur. These factors range from economic recession and rising poverty to high levels of unemployment, low and declining levels of education, social and violent insecurity, and a sense of alienation and marginalisation from the state people are supposed to belong to, often in combination with heavy-handed counterterrorism measures from state security forces (Bøås & Osland 2025; see also UNDP 2016).

While acts of violence in the Sahel, including what must be defined as violent extremism, tend to be justified on religious or political grounds, the path to participation often starts with much more material grievances. Concerns over insecurity, unemployment, lack of economic opportunities, and not least various conflicts over local access rights to resources such as land, water, grazing land, or trade routes are frequent causes of conflict and may initiate an individual's journey into violent extremism. The state may be seen as having played a role in creating these grievances, and in some cases it has been too weak to subdue local conflicts, leaving a space that jihadi insurgents could exploit. This creates a conducive local environment that insurgents can utilise to appropriate local conflict in order to achieve a level of local integration, for example, by offering to protect a local community or support it in struggles over land rights or access to water. This has happened frequently in the Sahel, as its states are relatively weak and insurgent groups exert a high degree of social, if not necessarily territorial, control. This allows them to present alternative ideas about how life should be based on their interpretation of religious texts and practices.

Nonetheless, even in an environment conducive to violent extremism in the form of jihadi insurgents, most people are not radicalised (see Bøås & Osland 2025). An important question that this chapter will try to clarify is, therefore, what turns an enabling environment into one where violent extremist ideas and groups that espouse these ideas gain traction to the extent that they come to dominate the social sphere and their violent actions are accepted? This is obviously a pertinent issue in the Sahel, but the inverse of this question is equally important, as we must also ask why some communities remain resilient to these forces of violence even when all the factors supposed to facilitate the manifestation of radicalisation and violent extremism are present. In this chapter we will utilise field data collected by the author from the Mopti and Segou regions of central Mali to illustrate both how an enabling environment can turn violent, but also the local community resilience that does exist even in such an enabling environment. While the situation in Mopti and Segou depends on several unique contextual factors, other factors such as the poverty people are faced with, the livelihood crisis, and the complex relationship between farmers and herders can be found all across the parts of the Sahel that this book is concerned with.

The occurrence of violence

In several parts of Mali, Niger, and Burkina Faso, disadvantaged individuals or even entire local communities have become so disenfranchised from the state and society at large that they could be susceptible to supporting, joining, or implementing organised violence inspired by religious extremist ideology. If and when this occurs, the

THE SAHEL—AN ENABLING ENVIRONMENT?

enabling environment can provide agents of violent extremist with entry points for their ideas. Non-state armed groups can promise a way out of destitution and despair. Recruiting among the poorest and least educated is a tactic of violent extremist groups with proven success, particularly when targeting young men, who are considered easier prey for indoctrination and socialisation into the worldviews of non-state armed groups. Those targeted in this way may be in a situation where they feel that they have little, if anything at all, to lose by joining or supporting an armed jihadi insurgency. This can happen, and it happens in the enabling environments of the Sahel, but we also need to stress that there is no evidence of a path dependency between living in an enabling environment and becoming a violent extremist. An enabling environment simply means that most of the factors that, according to key texts on violent extremism (see UNDP 2016), are present in the area in question.

Violent extremism does not occur in a social vacuum, and in the Sahel most of the usual factors attributed to the manifestations of violent extremism is present. Poverty is widespread, and many communities experience economic and political marginalisation. This may lead people to feel a sense of alienation from a state that they feel has never cared much for their well-being, safety, or security. Young people are particularly prone to perceived and real marginalisation placing them on a path to alienation, which could then make them more inclined to fall prey to extremist religious–ideological manipulation and indoctrination (see UNDP 2016). We also know from our own studies that the chances that this will happen increase with the presence of two other factors: rights-based grievances that, if expressed, can be met with very heavy-handed state responses (see Bøås 2015b; Bøås et al. 2020).

What this means is that while rising poverty and increased inequality, dysfunctional and deteriorating educational systems, and a sense of living in an unsecure environment all matter as potential drivers of violent extremism, we cannot ignore the role and responsibility of the state. Thus, the real driver of violent extremism is often the state, either indirectly—through its inability to give its inhabitants a sense of meaning, belonging, and economic safety—but also directly, when the state responds in a heavy-handed manner to radical expressions of resistance against a life that for many does not give them even the faintest promise of upward social mobility. Both of these expressions of state complicity in the spread of violent extremism are clearly visible in the case of the Sahel.

Under such circumstances, what often emerges is a scenario of competing authorities. This happens most frequently when state authority is weak and lacking in legitimacy. When a state lacks the capacity or willingness to care for and protect its citizens, the latter will start viewing the state as dysfunctional and corrupted. This leads to grievances against the state that can be leveraged by violent entrepreneurs who utilise extremist ideologies and discourses. The competing authorities that we describe as violent entrepreneurs (see also Chapter 2) are non-state actors who use violence. They have some form of political agenda, but it works alongside different types of income-generating activities. They rule by force and violence, but they also distribute (some) resources, provide some level of order, and offer protection to (parts of) the population in the areas they control, or attempt to control. Their presence among rural communities is often stronger than that of international community actors and their national allies (Bøås 2015b).

Most of the violent entrepreneurs we are concerned about are local in origin, but some may have some local–global connections. By this, we mean that the form of violent extremism that we mostly are confronted with here is local, but with global connections. We therefore need to distinguish between local–global connections where groups deliberately, purposefully, and strategically navigate their way to becoming active operational entities in larger global networks of extremist ideology, and those that mainly employ such strategies as a branding exercise, in order to look more powerful and global than they are (Bøås & Dunn 2017).

The Sahel is increasingly presented as the new global frontier of jihadi-inspired violent extremism (Council on Foreign Relations 2023; Demuynck & Böhm 2023). However, while the most important non-state armed groups are inspired by the religious doctrines of either al-Qaeda or IS, this does not mean that they have become operational branches of global jihadi networks. Their struggle is almost exclusively local and regional. While the leadership of these groups tends to be ideologically motivated, the majority of those who join these groups are recruited less on religious grounds than on grievances over lack of employment, education, and social mobility, as well as the prevalence of violent conflict and the subsequent lack of security in the area where they live.

When all these factors are present, this can lead to what we call decisive moments, when extremist ideas catalyse violence and violent acts. Typically, this may be a situation where chaos erupts due to unforeseen incidents, creating a cloud of uncertainty about the events that have transpired. Central to this chaos is often the belief that an act of injustice, violence, or another bad act has been committed against 'us', for example, a local community—this is a perception which may or may not be accurate. The critical aspect, however, is that these people feel an existential threat, a profound sense of injustice, or deep insecurity.

While it is crucial to understand these moments in which an idea is transformed into violence, it is equally, if not even more, pertinent to understand why a situation does not reach its decisive moment, even in an enabling environment where all the factors discussed above are present. We thus must also give due attention to the cases where this does not happen, as these may very well tell us much more about how to prevent violent extremism than focusing only on why it occurs after the event.

Drivers of violent extremism

State fragility, corruption and bad governance, an education system that does not work, heavy-handed state security approaches, and misplaced international interventions are present almost everywhere in the Sahel, and the situation in central Mali offers a vivid illustration. Here, the region of Mopti is situated at the crossroads between the north and south of Mali. While most of the population are Muslims, the region is also a melting pot of all of Mali's major ethnic groups. The region is densely populated, and the region is not only ethnically diverse but it also consists of different socio-economic groups: pastoralists (Fulani and Tuareg), sedentary farmers (Bambara, Dogon, Malinke, and Songhay) and fishermen (Bozo).

Thus, what the Inner Delta brings together are three different types of livelihoods—herders, farmers, and fishers—each with an interest in using the scarce resources of water and land, but for fundamentally different purposes. In the Inner Delta, these issues have never been easily reconciled. As population pressure increases, traditional authority wanes and state authority becomes increasingly dysfunctional and corrupted. As these resources are essential for survival, the right to access them must be defended by all means necessary. As the French intervention of 2013 (first Operation Serval and later Operation Barkhane) failed to defeat the jihadi rebellion (see Bøås 2015b), one jihadi faction—the Katiba Macina—started to operate in the Mopti region. When the state issued a heavy-handed response from its security forces that profiled young Fulani herdsmen as 'jihadis' and 'terrorists', the situation in Mopti reached a decisive moment. Not only did support and acceptance of the Katiba Macina start to grow among parts of the Fulani population in the region, but other ethnic groups also started to organise and arm their militias for the sake of the security of their local communities.

What emerged was a cocktail of different armed non-state groups of jihadi insurgents and ethnic self-defence groups. Consequently, the relations between various local communities that had traditionally been cordial, if not exactly friendly, have fragmented and polarised. The Fulani widely understand the self-defence groups of the Songhay and the Dogon—the Donzos and the Dana Amassagou respectively—as being driven by the aim of expelling and killing every Fulani in the region in order to claim their land and cattle. As one local Fulani leader expressed it, 'Their goal is to create disorder to seize and steal our properties. Once we have left the area and abandoned our hamlets, they will take our properties. Their goal is to exterminate every Fulani and take our land' (Bøås et al. 2021: 13).

However, the Dogon and Songhay communities in Mopti see the Donzo and the Dana Amassagou as defenders who define their cultures and aim to 'make their land secure', while they claim that the Katiba Macina are violently forcing them to submit to an extreme version of Sharia theology. To the Songhay and Dogon communities, the Katiba Macina represent not only a new and unknown danger that hides in forest bases and roams the region on motorbikes, but even more crucially an attempt to establish Fulani hegemony in Mopti.

Most of the Donzo and Dana Amassagou militias have been provided with some weapons and ammunition by the Malian army and intelligence by a network of informants and collaborators. There is some level of collaboration between these proclaimed self-defence militias, but there is no higher line of authority of command and control between them and the Malian army that has provided them with weapons. Each of these groups tends to be organised in accordance with its own local hierarchy. Their sources of income are usually derived through 'taxation' of the communities from which they originate, meaning local villagers either voluntarily or out of fear contribute to the militias' upkeep and supplies. However, while receiving some material support from their home villages, these militias also fund themselves through raids against other local communities that they see as their enemies—mostly, but not exclusively, Fulani communities (Bøås et al. 2021).

As Fulani and Dogon communities seem to increasingly stand on opposite sides in violent conflicts, it is easy to conclude that an ethnic element has been added to an already complex conflict. However, interestingly, both Fulani and Dogon respondents expressed the view that this is 'neither a religious conflict nor an ethnic one, but an economic conflict caused by bad governance' (Bøås et al. 2021: 18). This suggests that the root cause is not necessarily extremist ideology, religious views, or ethnic tensions, but a conflict over scarce resources that has exploded into violence due to desperation and fear of losing access to the land and water resources that are essential for local communities' survival. Unmanaged inter- and intra-community conflicts have therefore obliterated what little trust in the state may have existed, and parts of the population of Mopti have instead sought the justice, security, and consideration that either jihadi insurgents like the Katiba Macina or self-defence militias such as the Donzo and Dana Amassagou can offer them. The current relative strength of these non-state armed movements therefore correlates with the weakness of local government and the inability of state security forces to deal with conflicts constructively. Instead, FAMA's practice of arming of proxies has only led to more violence and insecurity, and an arms race throughout the region.

Going more deeply into ethnographic detail, this underlines the complex micropolitics that can create a decisive moment that enables insurgents to gain social traction and local community integration.

This snapshot from fieldwork data from the commune of Bandiagara in Mopti reveals how inter-communal conflicts over access rights (to farmland, pastures, water, and trading routes) can drive a community to collaborate with jihadi insurgents. After the 2016 municipal elections in Bandiagara, the losing candidates from the ADEMA-PASJ party were worried about being excluded from local decision-making processes. They feared losing their representation in the municipality assembly and thereby their ability to voice concerns on land rights and other essential issues. Consequently, two prominent local party leaders brokered a deal with the Katiba Macina in the hope of gaining by force what they had lost in the elections. Using Bandiagara as a base, the Katiba Macina started attacking neighbouring villages and taking control of fertile land that their new allies in Bandiagara could utilise (Bøås et al. 2021).

These findings dovetail with other studies. For example, Bøås, Cissé and Mahamane (2020) argue that a key strategy of jihadi-inspired Sahel insurgencies is to appropriate local conflicts, usually related to land usage, in order to integrate locally. In the case outlined above, we also see that the opposite can be the case: local opportunists can exploit the presence of armed groups in the vicinity to reverse local power configurations. Poorly managed conflicts cultivate a spirit of revenge, and in the region of Mopti (but also elsewhere in the Sahel) communities have turned to extremist groups to both take revenge and protect themselves and their property. This is not unique to Fulani communities; it also happens in the Dogon, Bambara, and Songhay communities in Mopti.

Following these lines of argument, we can see that in areas where states are lacking in capacity and legitimacy, and where international responses are haphazard, ad hoc, and severely underfunded, local rights-based conflicts turn violent. This opens social spaces and physical landscapes onto which violent insurgencies inspired by radical ideology can manoeuvre and appropriate local conflict (Bøås 2015b).

The jihadi insurgents of the Sahel have become increasingly adept in utilising existing local conflicts—active as well as dormant—to gain traction locally. However, it is also important to note that key factors that drive violence and jihadi recruitment are the poverty, marginalisation, and lack of economic opportunities that exist here at the margins of the Malian state. This suggests that, at least initially, those who join such armed movements are more concerned with material factors and less with religious beliefs. This is most likely also why existing survey data shows huge support for a negotiated solution to the conflict (Bøås et al. 2021). This is an issue that we return to in Chapter 11, as this points to possible ways out of the quagmire that the Sahel currently finds itself in if the storm starts to abate. We will devote the next part of this chapter to discussing the fact that most people are not radicalised and that there are also cases of resilience at play.

Cases of non-occurrence in enabling environments

Although it might seem naive to discuss cases of non-occurrence of radicalisation in environments as enabling as those in Mali, Niger, and Burkina Faso, this perspective gains depth when we explore local understanding as to why people join groups like the Katiba Macina or JNIM. In surveys conducted by Bøås et al. (2021), in Mali only 10–15 per cent of the respondents believed that acquaintances who joined violent extremist groups did so due to religious conviction. Instead, a majority indicated issues such as state repression, poverty, unemployment, and lack of education as the primary drivers. Some of the respondents in Mali who closely knew someone who had joined the Katiba Macina mentioned that their feeling abandoned by the state was the decisive reason for doing so (Bøås et al. 2021). This is noteworthy, as it suggests that when extremist ideas become widespread in local communities in Mopti, this should not be seen as a sign of an anti-state rebellion but rather as a craving for a state that works for its people.

This insight is important, as it challenges the prevailing notion in mainstream scholarship about the primary motivations for joining violent extremist insurgencies. If extremist beliefs are not the main driver, it would imply that these conflicts are more rooted in material conditions than previously thought. This revelation also highlights the likelihood of more moderate religious views being prevalent in these societies than is commonly assumed. What this indicates is that, despite a minority of young folks joining insurgencies with extremist ideologies, there may still be significant resilience within local communities against extremist ideas.

The region of Segou has shown much more resilience towards the forces of violent extremism than its neighbour Mopti. While Segou is slightly closer to Bamako, there are also clear indications that the jihadi insurgents have met more discursive resistance in Segou than what has been the case in Mopti. The question is, why? Research indicates that the relative lack of violent extremism in Segou can be explained by stronger social cohesion (see Bøås et al. 2021). The region has experienced fewer access-based conflicts between farmers and herders than Mopti has. This suggests that traditional authority is less under the threat of being eroded by this kind of potentially violent competition and has therefore been able to maintain traditional values that reduce causes of conflict both within and between local communities. One important reason for this is that Segou has been exposed to different land dynamics than Mopti. Ever since the 1930s, agricultural production in Segou has been oriented around exports. Under the Office du Niger, a wide development plan was implemented to transform farming in Segou to the export-oriented production of millet, niébé, sorghum, peanut, maize, and cotton. The area of Southern Segou in particular has been an area of agricultural expansion through irrigation systems and mechanisation efforts (see Croix et al. 2011). This has created an environment prone to investment and encouraged an entrepreneurial mindset to which the 'liberation' semantics used by violent extremist groups under the guise of Islam and 'jihad' seem to have less appeal.

Land dynamics in Segou have been less affected by the crisis of pastoralism, as the higher concentration of land used for intensive agriculture and urban expansion means that the there is limited land available for herding. In neighbouring Mopti, however, the competition between state agents and traditional authority over land management, combined with increased pressure for grazing land from pastoralists, has created a vicious brew of local discontent that has spilled over into violence. Thus, as Segou has experienced less competition over access to land between farmers and herders, traditional authority has also been less compromised by such conflicts and has been able to continue to uphold social values that reduce conflict both within and

THE SAHEL—AN ENABLING ENVIRONMENT?

between local communities. This is important, as we have established that the appropriation of local conflict in and among local communities is one of the key strategies of the jihadi insurgents, and decreasing local conflict is therefore key in keeping them out.

This is supported by in the fact that Segou is historically an important centre of Sufism and Islamic teaching. Contrary to other places in Mali and the Sahel, Sufism has here seen a revitalisation of traditional praxis due to the development of new Sufi figures who stand at the crossroads between charismatic leadership and the newly emerging stylistic trends of youth movements (Soares 2010). The most important of these figures are Cheick Soufi Bilal and Soufi Lassana, two religious entrepreneurs who have attracted large audiences and groups of followers, particularly among urban youth, following the example set by Cherif Ousmane Maidani Haidara, a prominent Sufi preacher who through his association, Ansar Dine (no connection to Iyad Ag Ghaly's Ansar ed-Dine), has renovated the public narrative of Islamic practice in Mali and argued strongly against the project of 'Sunni reform' forwarded by Wahhabi leaders (see Holder 2012). The followings gathered by Haidara, Bilal, and Lassana have been galvanised by a renewal of Sufi discourses and practices, and have formed a bulwark in Segou against Salafi-leaning forms of religious extremism.

The continued strength of Sufi-inspired religious practices in Segou is also closely tied to the relationship in this area between religion and traditional authority (the so-called *Islam confreique*). The Tall family, for example, still has considerable influence in the political and economic affairs of Segou. This family are the descendants of al-Haji Umar Tall, leader of the Tijaniyya Brotherhood and of the short-lived Toucouleur Empire (1848–93), which had its capital in Segou (Robinson 1988). While the empire is history, the patriarch of the Tall family is still a much sought-after advisor in political, economic, and religious affairs who uses his influence to spread a Tijani-aligned vision of jihad that is fundamentally peaceful and stresses the avoidance of violence (al-Karjousli 2016).

What we can draw from this is that, first, when there is a relative absence of local conflict that violent extremists can appropriate, it is easier for local traditional authorities to maintain their position as institutions of arbitration that earn local respect and legitimacy as they continue to provide public good. Second, if this also contributes to an economy that has a certain level of inclusivity, as seems to be the case in Segou, that fosters an environment of economic entrepreneurship of peaceful activities, which can be an important source of local resilience against violent extremism.

Concluding comments

The Sahel constitutes an enabling environment of high unemployment, lack of resources, weak governments, and few possibilities for social mobility, especially among the youth. However, while most people living here have many good reasons for being angry, few become radicalised to the extent of taking up weapons. In fact, one can argue that most people are not radicalised and that many of these communities still have a high level of resilience.

What can external stakeholders learn about societal resilience from such cases? While the importance of contextual understanding cannot be over emphasised, on a generic level, what these cases where there is a lack of violent extremism seem to have in common is, first, a long history of moderate religion and/or ideology. Second, the presence of respected local leaders, families, or individuals who protect this tradition of moderation. And, third, these leaders are seen as non-corrupt, and they deliver or do something that the local community sees as valuable.

In conclusion, the fact that extremist beliefs are not most individuals' primary motivation for joining violent insurgencies has significant implications and challenges the dominant academic perspective. It suggests that these conflicts are more materially based, pointing to a more widespread presence of moderate religious views in these societies than previously recognised. For policymakers, this emphasises the importance of addressing underlying material issues such as state repression, poverty, unemployment, and lack of education. It also underscores the potential effectiveness of supporting the inherent resilience of local communities against extremist ideologies. To do so, we need to understand the context of the case in question, and we need to support and strengthen local community leaders so that they can continue to pro-

THE SAHEL—AN ENABLING ENVIRONMENT?

vide valuable contributions to their communities. To do so, and to avoid delegitimising these actors of resilience, outside actors must have the lightest possible footprint. Local authorities must be their own agents, not the agents of any outside actor. Thus, to prevent violent extremism from happening, we need to understand not only why it happens but also why it fails to happen in enabling environments.

5

HYBRIDITY IN THE SAHEL

VIOLENT ENTREPRENEURS AND BIG MEN

To make sense of the current state of Mali and its neighbouring Sahel states Burkina Faso and Niger, we need to understand the type of hybrid rule that currently characterises these states and their state–society relations. Lately, hybridity or hybrid rule have become increasingly topical concepts in political analysis. However, this concept does not originate in political science but in the life sciences, and it was first used in the social sciences in Lynn's (1995) seminal study of political systems in Central America. Today, the term 'hybridity' is widely used in political science, sociology, and criminology to account for complex political environments where the well-established categories of social science fail to describe patterns of social organisation, practices, and identities (Voltmer et al. 2021).

For example, this could be applied to cases where rulers may have come to power through the ballot box, but electoral outcomes are regularly disputed, and election violence and unrest are common, institutions work haphazardly, and outcomes cannot easily be predicted through formal means. Consequently, such a state would struggle with an undefined or contested definition of its polity, making institutional reform both difficult and threatening to the regime, as it may entail a complete loss of power and privilege, as well as a loss of basic rights. Hybrid regimes therefore tend to combine some aspects of democratic rule, authoritarian tendencies, and the instability of a conflict-prone state (see Wigell 2008). For any observer of Mali, this should sound familiar as this is very much what we have witnessed during the years that have passed since the crisis erupted in 2012.

The question is therefore how Big Men and what we defined previously in this book as violent entrepreneurs come into play in such circumstances. While Big Men appear in several guises, and the use of force is certainly not a defining feature of Big Man status, the argument is that violent entrepreneurs, as we have defined them elsewhere (Bøås et al. 2020), resemble Big Men who utilise violence and force as one of their main strategic devices.

To elaborate this argument, we start by showcasing how recent interpretations from African conflict studies (see Utas 2012; Bøås 2012, 2015b) of the classical Big Man literature by Sahlins (1963) can be useful for our thinking about events and the actors associated with them in these kind of crises in an unsettled and sparsely institutionalised state such as Mali.[1]

We start by agreeing with Driscoll (2020) that, as time as passed since Sahlins' (1963) classical study, the Big Man concept has moved away from its original meaning. Sahlins' Big Man was powerful, but as this power was based on those who recognised Big Man status, the Big Man was also indebted to them. It is a relationship based on reciprocity, and while what Driscoll (2020) calls 'Big Man Governance' is informal, it also must have a clear degree of predictability and thus be rule-bound. The Big Man is therefore by definition not the despotic, unpredictable ruler associated with Jackson and Rosberg's (1982) personal rule. As Utas (2012: 8) reminds us, 'Big Men do not generally control followers. Quite the opposite: it is in the interest of followers to maintain ties with a Big Man.'

In his foundational study from 1963, Sahlins used the terms 'developed' to conceptualise Polynesian political systems and 'underdeveloped' to describe its Melanesian counterparts. These are not words we would use today, but still it points to something important—how the polity is organised. In Polynesia the political geometry was pyramidal—smaller units integrated into larger ones through a system of intergroup ranking—and the network of representative chiefs of the subdivisions amounted to a co-ordinated political structure. In Melanesia, however, what Sahlins found was autonomous kinship–residential groups (a small village or a local cluster of hamlets), each a copy of others, where each tended to be economically self-governing and equal to the others in political status. Within these large differences in political scale, structure, and performance lies also a more personal contrast in leadership—the Big Man who appears in what Sahlins calls the 'underdeveloped' settings of Melanesia, versus the 'chief' associated with the Polynesian systems.

The argument is that, whereas the pyramidal political geometry of Polynesia shares similarities with the regulatory neopatrimonial system that existed in Mali when the country was supposedly a showcase for neoliberal reforms (Bergamaschi 2014), what the Malian state has become is more like the Melanesian model, where the space of manoeuvring for aspiring Big Men is much larger (Bøås & Strazzari 2020). The reason for this is the permanent crisis that has been in place since 2012, which illustrates how a crisis of such a magnitude—and the social insecurity, confusion, and angst that ensues when a state deteriorates—opens new social, political, and economic spaces for entrepreneurial activity and risk-taking.

Big Man authority is therefore very much based on personal power that is made and being made. Big Men can come to office—and they can succeed to or be installed in existing positions in political groups or institutions—but, even if this is the case, it is not the essence of their authority (Englebert & Dunn 2019). If the Big Man takes office, it is by his or her choice only and not out of necessity, as the status of Big Man is office enough. The attainment of Big Man status is therefore the outcome of a series of individual entrepreneurial acts, often based on actions that illustrate the Big Man's wits or willingness to take risks that elevate them above the common herd and attract an entourage of loyal lesser individuals (see Sahlins 1963). The authority of the Big Man is therefore not based on political title, as such, but on the person's acknowledged standing in the community, which is something that must be made and maintained and that followers sees value in attaching themselves to. If the value of this attachment disappears, one's status as Big Man will also evaporate. In this regard, we see the Big Man as a thoroughly bourgeois character; an enterprising individual who engages in displays of public action designed to himself as a show himself as cut above the common man and potential rivals.

The violent entrepreneur—criminal, insurgent, or social bandit?

Our violent entrepreneurs are closely connected to the Big Man conceptualisation elaborated above. They operate in a space between criminality and politically motivated violence, and while opportunism is an integral part of their repertoire, they also operate either according to political motivations or they co-operate with groups whose overall motivation is political.

While the militias and insurgencies in Mali depend on low-cost strategies of asymmetrical warfare and an ideology that promises benefits and well-being in the afterlife as the jihadi theology does, they still need to mobilise resources (Bøås 2022). Thus, even if the religious dimension suggests that insurgencies operating in Mali may be less dependent on giving their fighters money to stay loyal and continue the struggle, they still must provide their rank and file with weapons, ammunition, vehicles for transport, food, and water. While some of what the insurgencies need is stolen from national armies—for example, when they attack remote army posts and fortifications—they also need to buy supplies. The resource mobilisation of the jihadi insurgents has therefore led to much speculation and is at times presented as a mystery. The local forces of global jihad in the Sahel are supposedly mobilising resources through kidnappings, smuggling drugs and other types of contraband in alliance with transnational criminal actors (the narco-terrorism theory), or gaining control of illegal gold mines in the region.

First, what should be clear is that what is currently taking place regarding insurgent resource mobilisation is nothing new in the long history of civil war and insurgencies (see Metz 2007). Illicit activities to mobilise resources for armed struggles have always been part and parcel of insurgent strategies. Just like their predecessors, the insurgents of Mali are generally pragmatic and opportunistic about how they position themselves with regard to illicit activities. The justification for exploiting the vulnerabilities of local communities or plundering state assets can always be framed in the light of the struggle they seek to advance. This has been the case previously for secular insurgencies as well, as for example the Red Army Faction (RAF) in West Germany (see Vague 2001) during the Cold War. Robbery, thuggish behaviour, and exploitation of whatever they could lay their hands on were all justified in the name of the struggle and the long-term benefits it would bring the population at large.

Entrepreneurial illicit economic activity is thus nothing new in the global history of insurgencies, but it is played out differently within the context of an extremely weak hybrid state such as Mali. The impunity given to the strong and powerful in a weak hybrid state such as Mali has opened the gates for a blend of illicit economic activities that all bear the hallmark of entrepreneurial behaviour, where motivations as well as positions are in flux. This makes it difficult to get a proper sense of what activities are based on criminal intent and what are done to serve the larger struggle. It could be intellectually interesting to bring back Donald Crummey's (1986) adaptation of Hobsbawm's (1974) concept of social banditry. Is the violent entrepreneur that we see operating in the Sahel's landscape of violence and confusion a contemporary version of the social bandit?

The volume that Crummey edited in 1986 involves a careful analysis of Hobsbawm's concept of social banditry in an African context and includes the much-cited work by Terence Ranger on the meaning of banditry in Zimbabwe's guerrilla war for independence, as well as Crummey's own take on the Ethiopian shefta as a 'primitive' rebel. The point is that in rural areas or hinterland towns experiencing the consequences of violent conflict in a weak hybrid state as Mali, the reality of life for ordinary people quickly becomes a fog of confusion and chaos. Amid the sentiment of powerlessness that this gives rise to, criminal activity can also be interpreted as a form of resistance. This is the type of situation, Hobsbawm (1974) argued, in which banditry is a primitive form of organised social protest. Operating in the space between the myth created by the bandits themselves, popular folklore of the bandit, and the reality of violence,[2] the social bandit is very much a violent entrepreneur who encapsulates Big Man status in that followers attach themselves to this persona and remain loyal over time because the violent entrepreneur as a Big Man not only uses force, but also contributes something which his followers see as useful. This can be a political struggle that harbours some hope for a better future, but it can also be material benefits or the provision of certain modalities of order. In a case like rural Mali, the Big Man does not need to contribute much, because the weakness and corruption of the state means that it is often more a source of trouble in people's daily struggle for a livelihood than it is beneficial. The empirical examples below from the conflict in Mali will illustrate this argument.

The contours of criminality, coping, and resistance

Access to financial resources is essential for the establishment and maintenance of any insurgent group, and if a rich sponsor is not available these resources must be sought through involvement in illicit economic activities. In the case of Mali, these have ranged from high-end economic activities such as hostage-taking and drugs smuggling to more mundane practices such as cattle rustling, poaching, the smuggling and sale of motorbikes and fuel, and lately also artisanal gold-mining.

While illegal by law, the definitional problem in practice is that these activities are conducted mainly in areas where the local economy is predominantly informal. Yes, hostage-taking, drugs smuggling, and cattle rustling are illegal and should be considered illicit even in the most informal economic setting. Much more difficult to define are the activities connected to cross-border transportation and sale of motorbikes and fuel, artisanal gold-mining, and poaching. Local people at times poach to get meat on their tables, they may also buy and sell motorbikes and fuel that has avoided tariffs and taxes, and they can be involved in artisanal gold-mining. What this means is that in local economies licit and illicit goods can be so interwoven in networks of commerce and trade that it is almost impossible to discern a legal commodity from an illicit commodity or what has been part of an organised criminal activity. This is therefore another hallmark of the hybridity that exists not only in Mali but also in Burkina Faso and parts of Niger, and it must be reflected in any sober assessment of the contours of criminality, coping, and resistance in these types of countries.

The following example from the late 1990s/early 2000s illustrates not only some of these definitional challenges[3] but also that the practices discussed above have been an integral part of the Malian state and economy since before the current crisis exploded in 2012. During the Tuareg conflict of the early 1990s, Ibrahim Ag Bahanga was only a junior commander, but a popular one both among the men he commanded and in some local communities. After the conflict of the 1990s officially ended in 1996, Ag Bahanga managed to acquire formal control of a commune in the border area between Gao and Kidal. This was achieved through a combination of popular support and his ability to use force—the combined hallmarks of a Sahel-born and bred violent entrepreneur.

However, apart from Ag Bahanga and a few other younger commanders who used force to fight their way into the decentralisation process of the north, what happened can best be described as a relatively carefully designed process of co-optation. Tuareg senior commanders and other leaders, originating almost exclusively from noble and royal families, were given access to power and economic resources on the local level as well as in the national government and administration, demonstrating that it is almost impossible to draw a distinct line between the state and various projects of crime, coping, and resistance. Actors and their 'projects' can conflict with the state, but there may also be periods of collusion and collaboration. This strategy of co-optation worked for several years, but, as the benefits of the 1996 peace agreement never materialised beyond a few regional Big Men coming to dominate the political landscape of northern Mali, tensions increased, and in 2006 a group of former Tuareg fighters took to arms once more and formed the ADC. This group was organised by former fighters in the Kidal region, led by a trio who was introduced in Chapter 2, namely Ibrahim Ag Bahanga, Hassan Ag Fagaga, and Iyad Ag Ghaly, the latter the leader of Ansar ed-Dine and JNIM.

Formally, the ADC only lasted a couple of months, as a peace agreement was signed in Algiers on 4 July 2006, but it never really went away. Ag Bahanga and some of his men would occasionally continue to engage the Malian army in battle until the events of 2012 turned what had been a minor insurgency into a sandstorm that dramatically transformed not only the conflict in northern Mali, but also the country at large along with neighbouring states Burkina Faso and

Niger. This would not have happened the way it did if it were not for another group and the resources it had at its disposal.

AQIM and Belmokhtar—hostage taking, drugs, and cigarettes

We start by dipping once more back in history to the time before 2012 when the group known as AQIM started to emerge in northern Mali. AQIM fighters may have lost the civil war in Algeria, but they still had a substantial war chest that they used to smooth their integration into poor local host communities at the very margins of the Malian state. Most likely, a substantial part of AQIM's war chest came from the kidnapping of thirty-two German tourists in 2003. These tourists were travelling through the Sahara when they were captured and held hostage for several months before being released. While this never has been confirmed by the German government, credible sources claim that a ransom of €5 million was paid to secure their release (Bøås & Torheim 2013). One of the violent entrepreneurs who played a vital role in this affair was Mokhtar Belmokhtar, a veteran and a legend among the jihadi insurgents of the Sahel.

It was not always evident that this would be his destiny, as Belmokhtar had a long series of events behind him before he reached his current mythological status. Of Algerian origin, he left his birth country in 1991 to join the mujahedeen in Afghanistan. He remained there for about two years, receiving military training, combat experience, and making useful contacts. When he returned to Algeria in 1993, the country had been thrown into a bloody civil war, as the country's military leadership had annulled an election that the Islamic Salvation Front (FIS) was about to win. Belmokhtar therefore joined the GIA. When the Algerian civil war came to its close in 1996, Belmokhtar had already left the country along with others like him who did wanted neither peace nor an amnesty from the government.

Taking refuge in the border areas between Algeria, Mali, and Niger, he reorganised his unit and contributed to the establishment of the GSPC that later morphed into AQIM, also embarking on several illicit economic activities. Hostage taking was one of them, cigarette smuggling another, both highly profitable. Based on his involvement in the clandestine transborder cigarette economy, Belmokhtar earned the nickname 'Mr Marlboro'. Through his involvement in these affairs, he came to meet Iyad Ag Ghaly who at that time was working for the Malian government as a liaison officer involved in the negotiations to secure the release of the German tourists. This was not the last time that these men would meet. As events have unfolded, both men have reached an almost mythological status as violent entrepreneurs and Big Men of the Sahel jihad, Belmokhtar as the one who vanished after the spectacular attacks at In Aménas, Bamako, and Ouagadougou, and Ag Ghaly as the Salafi desert warrior that not even Operation Barkhane could kill or subdue.

Kidnapping for ransom has therefore been an important strategy of resource mobilisation for the insurgents, but most kidnappings took place prior to 2012 even if some of the hostages were released thereafter. While we will never know for certain how much money the insurgents made from this, it was probably quite a lot but not so much that it would last for more than a decade. Thus, while during the first year of the Sahel crisis there was a good deal of focus and speculation on how many resources the jihadi insurgents had mobilised with ransom money, this focus shifted elsewhere as the number of high-profile kidnappings—here meaning foreigners from countries with the capacity to pay high ransom fees—fell sharply. It was therefore no coincidence that the presumed nexus between narco-trafficking and jihadi insurgencies gained considerable attention from policymakers, security analysts, and researchers.

However, it is also well worth pointing out that a dimension of social banditry was an integral part of the insurgents' original toolbox. AQIM's approach, which as also been utilised by Ag Ghaly and others, was to introduce themselves to local populations as honest and well-intentioned traders. For example, when they wanted to buy a goat from the local population, they asked the price, and when the owner said CFA 25,000 they offered to pay 50,000. They bought themselves goodwill, friendship, and networks among poor and alienated rural communities by distributing money, handing out medicine, treating the sick, and buying SIM cards and airtime for people (Bøås & Torheim 2013). They also married locally, not into powerful families but into poor local lineages, deliberately taking the side of the poor. Thus, in many ways AQIM's strategy had clear similarities to the social banditry of Crummy (1986) and Hobsbawm (1974).

SAHEL

Shipments of cigarettes and drugs through the desert?

While the peripheries of the Sahel may seem far away, located on a lost highway far from the main routes of the global economy, these areas are well connected to the world through the trans-Saharan trade. The ancient trade routes through the Sahara never disappeared and have regained some of their old importance. Cigarettes are smuggled through this area, and Latin American drug cartels have increasingly been using West Africa and the Sahel as an important transit point in smuggling cocaine to markets in Western and Eastern Europe. Important transit countries include those on the West African coast—such as Ghana, Guinea-Bissau, Mauritania, Senegal—and in the Sahel, such as Mali and Niger. For example, an important cocaine route has been operated from coastal waters through northern Mali and Kidal across the border to Algeria, or through Niger to Libya.

Even if cigarettes are the oldest contraband and remain an important one, since around 2006 the trafficking of drugs and people has become increasingly important in terms of cross-border smuggling, offering new economic opportunities as well as establishing new networks and nodal points for governance and control. The increased popularity of these old trade and commerce routes is, however, also related to recent technological advances that have made desert travelling much easier. GPS, satellite phones, cell phones, and four-wheel-drive cars are currently standard equipment for desert travellers. The number of different routes and modern means of communication also means that it is possible to drive from, for example, Kidal in northern Mali to Tamanrasset in southern Algeria in about a day, running up and down dry riverbeds without ever travelling on a marked road (to the degree that they exist at all).

Contraband cigarettes are trafficked in this direction. They are almost exclusively Marlboro, mainly coming from Zerouate in Mauritania on trucks in large containers to Kidal. Here, the shipment is split into smaller lots and taken across the border to Algeria (mainly Tamanrasset) on four-by-four pickups. Some of these cigarettes are sold in Algeria, whereas others make their way across the Mediterranean to the European market—where they are still cheaper than the legal ones, even if a considerable number of middlemen have taken their cut since the cigarettes left North Carolina in the United States (see OCCRP 2021). Parts of the previous AQIM structure in northern Mali, and particularly Mokhtar Belmokhtar, were deeply involved in these operations and earned considerable amounts of money from them. However, after Belmokhtar took responsibility for the 2013 attack against the oil and gas installation at In Aménas in Algeria, this ruptured his involvement in cigarette contraband as well as other of his illegal economic activities. Why? Simply because it became too dangerous for the solely profit-motivated portion of his network to do business with him. Insurgents that the international community defines as global terrorists may at times—as the Belmokhtar case above illustrates—become engaged in income-generating activities with smugglers, but they are not necessarily anything more than ad hoc economic alliances.

Thus, while smugglers' activities may benefit from a weak state and uncontrolled borders, as is the case in Mali, they prefer tranquillity and to avoid international attention. This is completely the opposite of what jihadi insurgents tend to generate, whose main motivation—despite being pragmatic and not above acquiring funding wherever it can be found—is political and not profit-seeking. This is not in the interests of those who smuggle narcotics or traffic people through the Sahel to Europe for profit alone. They want to continue their clandestine activities in the shadows without receiving international attention and presence on the ground. However, this does not mean that pragmatic co-habitation is impossible. While the very idea of a crime and terror nexus in the Sahel is based on flawed assumptions, this does not mean that there are no economic relationships between those who smuggle, for example, narcotics like cocaine and the jihadi insurgents. Such relationships exist, but they tend both to be more ad hoc than long-term, and the extent to which they are negotiated and established also depends on how much the insurgents need money.

In the old days of Belmokhtar—that is, before 2013 and the In Aménas attack—he was at times ridiculed by fellow AQIM leaders for his involvement in the contraband of cigarettes. The nickname 'Mr Marlboro' was not necessarily one he was particularly fond of or one that was given to him in affection. It certainly did not fit with the image that AQIM tried to cultivate of themselves as pious men of faith and scripture.

AQIM, but also the Tuareg-led Salafi insurgency Ansar ed-Dine, has issued several fatwas condemning drug trafficking, and it has at times confiscated and burned relatively large amounts of cigarettes and drugs. However, this has not prevented them when their purses were close to empty to seek short-term arrangements with smugglers, either in the form of the traditional Sahel rite in which those with authority over a certain area or route allow goods to pass untouched in exchange for a fee that has been negotiated, or through other more business-like short-term marriages of convenience. In fact, the only jihadi insurgent leader we know of who sustained a deep, long-term involvement in narcotics smuggling was Chérif Ould Tahar, when he was one of the leaders of MOJWA. However, Ould Tahar had been involved in the narcotics trade before. Still, one might question whether he joined MOJWA in 2012 for ideological reasons or just because it suited his business operations at the time when this insurgency controlled the town of Gao, which is strategically situated at the bend of the Niger River in northern Mali (see Raineri & Strazzari 2021).

In sum, it seems reasonable to suggest that, yes, the jihadi insurgents have mobilised resources through ad hoc opportunistic arrangements with smugglers when their purses have been tight, but there is little systematic evidence that this has made them rich or that their ability to sustain and increase their area of influence in Mali and neighbouring countries is based on their involvement in the trafficking of illegal substances. Rather, their relationship with the global forces of transnational crime seems much more ambiguous, as would be suggested by their issuing fatwas against drugs, while at the same time collaborating with these same forces when they were in need of monetary resources to fund their struggle.

Artisanal gold-mining—the new pool of jihadi income?

Lately, the international focus on how the jihadi insurgents' mobilise resources for their struggle has started to focus on their presumed involvement in artisanal gold-mining (see UN 2020). The reason for this is that artisanal gold-mining has been booming in the Sahel in recent years (Raineri 2020), and large amounts of gold are being smuggled out of the region every year, most of it heading towards the Persian Gulf and the United Arab Emirates (UAE). While artisanal gold-mining is an activity that insurgents could benefit from, either by mining themselves or through coercive informal taxation of miners, it is also an activity that creates opportunities for alternative employment and income-generating activities were few such exist.

The question is therefore whether artisanal gold is about to become a new pool of income for jihadi insurgents. The evidence so far is scattered and inconclusive, but artisanal gold-mining could give the insurgents not only access to a new source of income, but potentially also a new means of local integration, as youthful populations of artisanal miners are likely to be sympathetic to anybody who protects them from agents of the state who usually either chase them away or pressure them for informal fees in order to be allowed to continue mining. However, the physical bulk of gold complicates gold smuggling, and to make a profit the insurgents would need to control more of the global parts of the value chain. Even if it has been argued that some of the insurgents have contacts among gold traders in the UAE, there is little evidence that substantiate this claim to the extent that it would suggest an involvement in the higher levels of the value chain.

In Mali, the main gold deposits are also in the south of the country, in an area that is still firmly under government control and thereby outside the area of jihadi insurgency operation. However, there are other areas in the Sahel where one can find evidence, although scattered, of an increase in jihadi insurgent activities in areas of artisanal gold-mining. Recent satellite imagery surveys by the Burkinabè government have revealed the existence of more than 220 informal gold mines in the country, and about half of these were around 25 kilometres from areas where militant groups had conducted attacks. This does not automatically mean that these attacks had anything to do with gold-mining or about attempting to control gold mines. However, they do point to a pattern of insurgents' possible geographical interests, and there are examples from the tri-border area of Liptaka-Gourma in Mali where insurgents have taken over the control of some mining sites, generating income but also substantiating an alliance with artisanal miners who come to rely on the insurgents' protection to continue to mine to sustain themselves and their families. The escalation of hostilities that started around 2020 in the tri-border area between three different armed groups—the then state-affiliated *Groupe autodéfense touareg Imghad et alliés* (GATIA), the nominally al-Qaeda-affiliated JNIM, and ISGS—could be linked to control over mining sites. ISGS used to have a certain control of some of them, but after the violent conflict started between JNIM and ISGS in the Mopti region, the former clearly has an interest in removing ISGS from Gourma and in the process taking over its control of informal mines. For GATIA, on the other hand, protecting its influence in Doro is to some extent a necessity, as this area remains its last substantial stronghold in this part of Mali.

The near future may therefore be one where the jihadi insurgents in the Sahel, at least in some places, will become more involved in natural resource extraction in the form of gold-mining as one of their most important ways of mobilising resources. What influence this will have on their strategies of warfare and their credibility as pious men of faith and scripture remains to be seen.

While the resource mobilisation of the jihadi insurgencies in the Sahel is not an enigma, but rather a long history of combining ideology and pragmatism, where insurgents have opportunistically sought resources wherever they can find them, but at no time getting too deeply involved. Gold-mining may be the game changer, but this is not a given, as larger mobilisation of resources through gold-mining requires a level of territorial control that the insurgents do not currently have, and if they did have it, this would make it easier to target them, as this kind of territorial control would make them less mobile.

What we do know is that in a situation like the one that prevails in the Sahel, money matters a lot. The traditional role of the *chef du village* has diminished rapidly, but new modern systems of governance have not replaced traditional rule. The history of AQIM's mission creep in northern Mali is therefore still instructive. They began by approaching the local population as honest, pious, and well-intentioned traders—that is, social bandits—and thus far in this history of violence, the jihadi insurgents have sought resources pragmatically and used them to acquire weapons, ammunitions, and other logistical tools needed for combat. However, they have also wisely spent resources among local communities. It is more their entrepreneurship than their acquired weaponry that has been their main comparative advantage in the asymmetrical war that they are involved in.

This means that compared to their opponents they have spent meagre resources quite wisely and operated an insurgency on what is for the most part a shoestring budget. The depth, reach, and success of their involvement in gold-mining may bring about changes to this. How, why, and in what ways this might occur remains to be seen, but many secular-minded insurgencies have throughout history lost their initial reason for rebellion in the face of valuable natural resource extraction. It remains to be seen whether Islamic insurgencies and the violent entrepreneurs who lead them are inoculated through their ideological conviction against this effect, or whether they could also fall prey to the corruption that gold so often brings.

The fine line between criminality, coping, and resistance?

Much has been written about transnational crime and so-called terrorist groups in Mali and the Sahel. Many of these reports and articles present us with interesting empirical information, but we still need to rethink how we conceptually understand the lines of division between criminality, coping, and resistance.

The reason why is that we first must take into consideration what type of state this is taking place in. It is happening in an immensely hybridised version of the ideal type of the Weberian state, where the state may be very present and controlling in capital areas but in other locations very absent and just one among many contenders for authority. Second, the places where most of these activities take place exist in a context of informality where the lines between what is licit, illicit, and solely criminal activity are already completely blurred. Third, this should open our eyes to alternative analytical lenses, as opposed to thinking about this as an either/or question between political resistance or criminal intent.

Just like their predecessors, secular or religious, Sahel insurgents are pragmatic and politically motivated at the same time. And, due to the hybrid nature of the state in which they operate, there are numerous spaces for what we have called violent entrepreneurs to operate. These personas are Big Men who operate through the use of force with some sort of political–religious intent, while they simultaneously may also have a profit motive in sight for themselves or the organisation that they lead, belong to, or collude with.

This has been the case also of one of the most famous warriors of the Sahel Jihad, Mokhtar Belmokhtar. Seeking profit through illicit activities has been part and parcel of his activities, but this has always been conducted in tandem with strategies of local integration resembling the repertoire of social banditry. Thus, while we should continue to ponder the strategies and activities of the Salafi-inspired insurgents in Mali and beyond, we should also keep in mind that the contours between criminality, coping, and resistance have always been blurred in these and similar landscapes of war.

As there is nothing new in this, we should revisit previous attempts at theorising hybrid states, rural uprisings, and Big Men politics. Here, we may find sources of inspiration to fine-tune our analyses of the relationships between politics and criminality with regard to the Sahel violent entrepreneurs to a better way of coming to a conceptual understanding of what these people represent as figures of authority locally as well as nationally.

This is even more important in a period when artisanal gold-mining has become a new source of resource mobilisation for violent entrepreneurs. Whether or not it will corrupt them in the eyes of their followers remains to be seen, but we should keep in mind that their marketing of themselves as pious men of God needs constant rebranding. And while gold can be a new pool of resources, it can also potentially tarnish their image as men incorruptible by worldly desires.

PART II

EVERYTHING GOES BACK TO THE BEGINNING

In Part II—'Everything goes back to the beginning'—we start by locating the background for the crisis that has engulfed Mali, Niger, and Burkina Faso with the decisions taken to end the conflict in northern Mali in the 1990s. This will show how the making of a new conflict was built into the peace agreement of the mid-1990s. Here, we pay particular attention to the role of the decentralisation programme that was an integral part of the National Pact that was supposed to bring lasting peace to Mali. We argue that decentralising a state as weak as Mali was at that time will not in itself lead to increased state capacity, only to more and weaker state units. This will be followed by a short and concise history of the states of the Sahel, underscoring how the unsettledness of these states has deep historical roots. History also plays a role for the jihadi insurgents, and to illustrate this a section here will delve into the Macina Empire of central Mali, illustrating how Hamadoun Kouffa's Katiba Macina has strategically made use of this history, but also how the narrative of the Macina Empire as a theological Fulani state is a double-edged sword for an insurgency that aspires to build a larger national agenda. It gave Kouffa's men a narrative of belonging which they could use to further their integration among local Fulani communities, but, as this and similar narratives are very much based on the politics of place, it also shows that while they can form a basis for local integration, they can also be a barrier to building larger alliances.

6

MALI

THE LONG ROAD TO 2012

Modern Mali is based on the ancient civilisations of vast empires like the Wagadou, Mande, and Songhay, and kingdoms such as the Fulani of Macina, Kenedougou, Khassonke, and Kaarta. Islam arrived in Mali around the ninth century, and the great cities of ancient Mali—like Timbuktu, Gao, and Djenne—became famous throughout the Islamic world for their wealth and scholarship. However, these empires eventually fractured into various smaller states, and not much was left of their former glory when the French colonial powers arrived in the late nineteenth century.

In the 1990s, Mali was portrayed as the beacon of neoliberal democratisation in West Africa. However, behind what was presented as a showcase of democracy, good governance, and peace and reconciliation, there was institutional weakness, mismanagement, and collusion involving national and regional elite interests who paid scant attention to human security and development. When the current crisis started in 2012, Mali was a weak and fragile state with hardly any formal institutions or networks capable of working out sustainable compromises on the local level. It was a multi-party democracy, but as every political party was sustained by a vertical hierarchy of patronage networks the resilience of the political system was very low, as shown by the March 2012 coup. This weakness and fragility were evident in the capital region, but even more predominantly in the peripheral border regions of northern and central Mali. It is a long way from Bamako in the south-west to Kidal in the northeast, and the implications of this centre–periphery relationship need to be recognised. Further, it is important to acknowledge that Mali shares with the other francophone countries of West Africa a tradition of centralised government that is not easily reformed or altered. This is a tradition that tends to prevail despite the weakness of the state.

The first decades

When Mali gained independence in 1960, President Modibo Keita established a series of state corporations. However, apart from those in the cotton sector, all proved to be inefficient, money-wasting enterprises. Other ambitious efforts to create a state-centred economy also failed, and in 1968 Keita was overthrown in an army coup led by Moussa Traoré. Under his rule, Mali continued to experiment with Soviet-style socialism, but economic benefits failed to materialise—aside from the spoils that the new elite kept for themselves. Aid funding disappeared into the pockets of military officers, high-ranking civil servants, and politicians, with the president himself one of the main offenders. The country was marked by corruption and impunity for the elite and the well-connected few (see Bratton et al. 2002; Hesseling and van Dijk 2005).

When the economy fell into serious recession in the 1980s, a process of economic liberalisation was finally initiated. However, it was too late to save the old regime: it was increasingly clear that Traoré's system of patronage could no longer be financed, and voices of political opposition in favour of deeper political reforms came forward. Opposition to the regime of General Moussa Traoré grew during the 1980s. Ordinary people's living conditions deteriorated while the elite lived in affluence and luxury. In 1990, a more organised opposition began to emerge, which led to peaceful student protests being brutally suppressed in January 1991. From 22–26 March 1991, mass pro-democracy rallies and a nationwide strike were held in both urban and rural communities, which became known as '*Les Évenements*'

MALI: THE LONG ROAD TO 2012

('The Events') or the March Revolution. In Bamako, in response to mass demonstrations organised by university students and later joined by trade unionists and others, soldiers opened fire indiscriminately on the nonviolent demonstrators. Despite an estimated loss of 300 lives, nonviolent protesters continued to return to Bamako each day demanding the resignation of the president. 26 March 1991 marks the clashes between soldiers and demonstrating students that led to the massacre of dozens under Traoré's orders. By 26 March, the growing number of soldiers who refused to fire into the largely nonviolent crowds of protesters turned into a full-scale tumult and resulted in thousands of soldiers putting down their arms and joining the pro-democracy movement. After three days of unrest, the army, led by General Amadou Toumani Touré (a.k.a. ATT) overthrew Moussa Traoré and assumed power. However, although this led to a political transformation of the state to a multi-party democracy, it failed to change the logic of neopatrimonial politics in any fundamental way.

One year later, General Touré resigned, in line with his pledge to arrange multi-party elections. These were held in June 1992 and were won by Alpha Oumar Konaré and his party the Alliance for Democracy in Mali (ADEMA). In 1997, Konaré was re-elected for a second term, but this time the elections were marred by irregularities and the withdrawal of opposition parties from the electoral process. Voter turnout was also very low: only 21.6 per cent in the general elections and 28.4 per cent in the presidential election. In 2002, Konaré, in deference to the new constitution established during his administration, stepped down, as he had served as president for two terms. Touré (ATT) was then duly elected president in April 2002.

These important changes were largely a process initiated and driven from Bamako. Even during the peace process and the integration that was supposed to follow, most of the Tuareg population remained on the margins. This was evident in all three Tuareg regions—Timbuktu, Gao, and Kidal—but was most explicitly felt in Kidal due to its isolation from the rest of the country. Even though Mali's territorial integrity was not seriously challenged, as it has been since 2012, the state's reach ended where the road stopped in Gao. Kidal is someplace else entirely—it is not Mali, though not another country either: it is something in between, a hinterland in the limbo between Algeria and Mali.

The Tuareg minority: a history of withdrawal, resistance, and separatism as an alias

Mali is an ethnically diverse country. The majority ethnic groups belonging to the Mande superstructure are the Bambara, Malinke, and Soninke, which comprise about half of the population. Another 17 per cent are Fulani (or Peul), 12 per cent Voltaic, 6 per cent Songhay, about 3 per cent Tuareg, and a further 5 per cent are classified as 'other'—these include the Arab or Moorish population living in the north. All these groups have their own traditions, politics, and language, but the main dividing line has historically been between the Tuareg and Arab populations living in the northernmost part of the country, and the black majority groups, most of whom live south of the Niger River.

Northern Mali, the home of the country's Tuareg minority, comprises the broad part of the Sahara that borders Algeria, Burkina Faso, Mauritania, and Niger. Resisting external intervention in their traditional livelihood of nomadic pastoralism, the Tuareg have fought several wars for autonomy, both during and after colonialism. Today, northern Mali may seem like an isolated and forlorn place at the end of the universe, but it was once an important frontier region, well integrated into the global economy. In fact, it has somewhat been restored to this status in recent decades, now through the economic power of the illicit world of trafficking in contraband, migrants, and narcotics. Thus, to a certain extent, the current increase in informal and illicit trade can be likened to a revitalisation of the ancient routes of trade, commerce, and pilgrimage that passed through this area, connecting West Africa to the Mediterranean and to the Middle East and the Persian Gulf (see Bøås 2012).

The position of the Tuareg in the northern region was turned upside-down by French colonialism, this upheaval made permanent by the postcolonial state system. The Tuareg, who had once seen themselves as the 'masters of the desert', had now suddenly become a tiny minority ruled by the black population against whom they had previously directed their slave raids. Of Mali's eleven regions, today it is only Kidal in which the Tuareg constitute a majority.[1] The Tuareg are generally seen as 'different' in Mali, and indeed they consider themselves distinct from the other groups that constitute the Malian polity, differing from them in language, lifestyle, and heritage (Seely 2001). The Tuareg 'problem', like the Kurdish 'issue', since Malian independence has been something of a Gordian knot for the state (Bøås 2015b).

Ever since Mali became an independent state, the Tuaregs have been rebelling against it. The first Tuareg rebellion took place in the early 1960s and the second in the early 1990s (Berge 2002). As the National Pact of 1992 failed to produce tangible results on the ground, a new rebellion emerged in 2006 (Bøås 2012). This one was relatively small until Tuaregs started to return from post-Gaddafi Libya with a lot of arms. This brought new momentum to the idea of rebellion, and, as we already as discussed, the MNLA was established. Whereas in previous revolutions Tuareg independence and nationalism had been more rhetoric than a real demand, the MNLA declared full independence of Azawad from Mali.[2] The issue was no longer just about breaking into the Malian state to secure positions of power and privilege for Tuareg leaders and leading lineages, but breaking away from it entirely.

However, what little that may have existed of Tuareg unity quickly disappeared. As MNLA fighters looted and plundered in the north and the Malian army ran away and launched the 21 March 2012 coup in Bamako, other forces stepped in and effectively sidelined MNLA. These forces were the Tuareg Islamist organisation Ansar ed-Din, led by Iyad Ag Ghaly, a veteran Tuareg fighter from the 1990s, as well as AQIM and MOJWA (see Chapter 2). At the outbreak of the current crisis, the international community made the key error of viewing the jihadi insurgents as alien invading forces, thereby repeating the mistake of their failure to constructively with the Democratic Forces for the Liberation of Rwanda (FDLR) in the Democratic Republic of Congo. Due to their longevity in the area, and the local alliances they had made, AQIM and MOJWA were already integral parts of the conflict mosaic of northern Mali.

Cleavages, fissures, and fragmentation in the north

Northern Mali has never constituted a coherent polity. Yes, the area is mainly inhabited by Tuaregs, but there are also minority Arab populations and further south towards the Niger River there are populations of Songhay and Fulani origin. Few of these have agreed to Tuareg demands for autonomy and independence for northern Mali.

Pre-colonial Tuareg society was constructed as a pyramid, with nobles on the top and various levels of dependents and servile groups below, stratified into the *imushar* (warriors), *inslemen* (Muslim scholars), *inhaden* (artisans), and *ikan/Bella* (slaves).[3] This hierarchy was based on race as well as descent, with noble families being fair-skinned lineages of Berber origin, whereas the Bella—or the Daoussahak, as they call themselves—are black-skinned people of slave origin. Well-protected restrictions on intermarriage reinforced these distinctions (for example, making certain that the descendants of *inhaden* (e.g. blacksmiths) only married within their own group). In what hindsight tells us was a mistake, the Tuareg strategy of resistance to French rule was one of withdrawal. Suspecting that external forces wanted to pacify them by transforming them into a sedentary population, the Tuareg sought to evade not only paying taxes, but also the secular system of education established by the colonial state (Lecocq 2004). Noble families sent the children of dependent lineages to the state schools, while sending their own children to traditional Koranic schools. The consequence was a Tuareg elite much less equipped to assume positions in government (local and national) than other Malian elites.

In 1960, Mali became independent, but for the Tuaregs this meant little. The government of Modibo Keita was just as much an external invading force as the French had been. The first Tuareg rebellion against the Malian state started in 1962 and lasted until 1964. It began pretty much the same way as it did in 2012, with small hit-and-run attacks against government targets in the Kidal area. It escalated throughout 1963, resulting in extremely volatile conditions in northern Mali. In that regard, the rebellion was successful, but it did not reflect a unified leadership, a well-co-ordinated strategy, or a coherent political programme. It even failed to mobilise the majority of the Tuareg population. It was also short on arms, ammunition, and means of transportation. The insurgency depended upon camels for transportation, and its fighters—no more than about 1,500—relied almost exclusively on small and old weapons (Keita 1998) In the end, the

MALI: THE LONG ROAD TO 2012

Malian army harshly crushed this rebellion, and the Tuareg provinces were placed under military administration. Consequently, thousands of Tuaregs fled to neighbouring Algeria and Libya.

The droughts of the 1970s and 1980s also affected the Tuaregs badly. Some scholars have therefore used the Tuareg rebellion of the 1990s as a primary example of a resource conflict caused by environmental degradation (see, for example Baechler 1998 or Kahl 2006). However, as more grounded analyses have pointed out, the rebellion was mainly a reaction to state politics and not to the drought as such (Benjaminsen 2008). First and foremost, the lack of resources and the conflict forced many Tuaregs to leave northern Mali. Some migrated to Algeria, others to Libya, and some of the latter received military training from the Libyan regime and fought in Colonel Gaddafi's Islamic Legion in Chad and elsewhere (some as far away as Lebanon). Some of these men came to constitute the vanguard of the Tuareg rebellion in the 1990s and some of their sons the rank and file of the MNLA in 2012.

Another consequence of the drought of the 1980s was that many Tuaregs also moved out of the desert and went south to the more fertile land of the river Niger. Here, the sedentary populations (mainly Songhay) did not necessarily extend them a warm welcome. Their problem initially was not with the Tuaregs as such, because some Tuareg communities already lived among the Songhay, but with the huge number that suddenly arrived. This caused local rights-based conflict over land and pasture. Thus, when the next Tuareg rebellion started in 1990, it eventually also came to pit pastoralist Tuaregs against the sedentary population (mainly, but not exclusively, Songhay). The result was the birth of the Songhay militia, *Ghanda Koy*, in 1994. *Ghanda Koy*, which means 'master of the soil', countered the Tuaregs' claim of an independent homeland, Azawad, with a different story about people, place, and belonging (see Bøås & Dunn 2013). However, even if *Ghanda Koy* fought against the Tuareg rebels, it also included some Tuaregs. The reason for this was that, as mentioned above, there were Tuareg communities who lived among the Songhay, some of whom saw their situation—their security concerns as well as economic interests—as better served by backing *Ghanda Koy* than the Tuareg rebellion. This shows how Tuareg interest is tied to geography and relative isolation. The Tuaregs who joined *Ghanda Koy* saw themselves as citizens of the Malian state, which was not necessarily the case for those living in Kidal and other peripheral places.

Thus, even if the leaders of the rebellion in the 1990s appealed to the Tuaregs to unite under the identity of a common language as much as an ethnic banner, this rebellion was diverse in social origin as well as interests. This is illustrated by the fact that the Tuareg rebels of the 1990s were split among four factions: the Popular Movement of Azawad (MPA); the Popular Front for the Liberation of Azawad (FPLA); the Revolutionary Army for the Liberation of Azawad (ARLA); and the Islamic Front of Azawad (FIAA).

These four movements represented different family and geographical lines, as well as different political alignments and economic interests. For example, the FIAA drew its members mainly from Mali's north-west Hassani Arab minority, a group that is closely related through tribal connections, dialect, and culture to the Moorish population of Mauritania and the Sahrawi of Western Sahara. Even if the Tuaregs dominated the other three groups, there were also significant differences between them. The MPA was, for instance, initially formed among Tuareg refugees and exiles in Algeria and Libya. Thus, references to the Tuareg as *Kel Tamacheq* (i.e. 'the people who speak Tamacheq') apart, the Tuaregs have never constituted one coherent community. Historically, they have been divided between several sultanates, ruled by different royal families, sometimes in co-operation with each other but also undergoing times of violent conflict. It is important to keep this aspect of the Tuareg social structure in mind, as it continues to inform this society and influence processes of social change.

The rebellion of the 1990s officially ended on 26 March 1996, and the peace agreement allowed for 7,000 Tuareg rebels to be incorporated into the national army and other public institutions. The 120,000 Tuareg refugees living in neighbouring countries were also repatriated, and the 4 rebel movements now functioning under the umbrella of the United Movements and Fronts of Azawad (MFUA) agreed to disarm and demobilise (Berge 2002). It is this agreement that made Mali into a West African showcase of conflict resolution.

However, as the benefits of the 1996 peace agreement never materialised for anyone beyond a few regional Big Men who had come to dominate the political landscape of northern Mali, tensions increased, and in 2006 a group of Tuaregs took up arms once more. In a situation of intensified discontent, the ADC was organised around former MPA fighters in Kidal. The main leaders were Ibrahim Ag Bahanga, Hassan Ag Fagaga, and Iyad Ag Ghaly (the latter would form Ansar ed-Din in 2012). Formally, the ADC only lasted a couple of months, as a peace agreement was signed in Algiers on 4 July 2006, calling for peace, security, and development in the region of Kidal. However, it never totally ceased to exist, as fighters such Ag Bahanga continued to occasionally fight the Malian state. This was the situation until events in 2012 turned what had been a minor insurgency into a sandstorm that dramatically transformed the conflict in northern Mali.

The National Pact of 1992

The rebellion in the 1960s had one thing in common with the one that occurred in the early 1990s: they related, albeit in different ways, to the issue of control of local administration in northern Mali. Should it be under the auspices of the central state or should governance in the northern territory be decentralised?

The National Pact of 1992, signed by MFUA and the transitional government of President Touré on 11 April 1992, was an attempt to deal with this issue. It laid out new administrative boundaries and established local assemblies to permit a degree of self-governance of the northern regions (Seely 2001). When President Alpha Oumar Konaré was inaugurated in June 1992, he followed up the decentralisation process laid out in the National Pact. This was not something he could choose to ignore, as the concessions made to the Tuareg rebels by his predecessor were deeply resented in the southern parts of Mali. Thus, to keep the north in the state of Mali while at the same time containing the south's discontent with the concessions made, his only possible option was to embark on a process of administrative decentralisation across the entire country (Seely 2001; Hesseling & van Dijk 2005).

To achieve this, the Decentralisation Commission (DC) was established. The DC created new administrative boundaries, not only by renaming existing ones but also by giving villages the opportunity to group themselves into communes of their own choosing. This might seem like a genuine attempt to empower local communities, but it also became a tool for local aspiring Big Men to organise their own communities as they saw fit.

Controlling a commune not only gave aspiring Big Men a political constituency, it also represented the opportunity for extraction of resources. In short, it constituted the possibility of building new small 'political castles', but these would unfortunately prove to be 'castles in the sand'. One example is Ibrahim Ag Bahanga, who after the end of the second Tuareg Rebellion managed to acquire his own commune in the area between Gao and Kidal. He achieved this through a combination of popular support and the use of force. Ag Bahanga and some other younger Tuareg commanders were not satisfied with their re-integration packages, and as such they did not disarm after the peace agreement. After a month of raiding and creating instability, Ag Bahanga was given his commune (see Bøås 2012).

Apart from Ag Bahanga and a few other younger commanders who used force to fight their way into the decentralisation process, what happened in the Tuareg regions (i.e. Gao, Kidal, and Timbuktu) was a relatively carefully designed process of co-optation. Tuareg senior commanders and other leaders, almost exclusively originating from noble and royal families, were given access to power and economic resources at the local level as well as in the national government and administration. This strategy of co-optation worked quite well for several years, but as other peace dividends failed to materialise, a new undercurrent of discontent started to emerge among those who saw no real improvements to their living conditions.

This happened first and foremost in Kidal, the most isolated of the three Tuareg regions. The main reason for this is that control over civil services and local administration remained unchanged. The quality of administrative supervision continued to be poor, and those involved in rent-seeking and other corrupt practices were neither punished nor removed, but rather encouraged. However, as time moved on, not everybody was prepared to accept this order anymore. Emerging leaders from non-ruling lineages wanted access to state power at the level of local government, both for the purpose of reform and to take advantage of this for their own personal benefit.

MALI: THE LONG ROAD TO 2012

The events in Kidal from May 2006 and onwards to 2012 are thus a combination of increased local discontent with the results of the decentralisation process of the National Pact, showing that decentralisation is not necessarily the answer when it comes to creating peace and reconciliation in a weak and fragile state. Mali was weak and fragile when the DC process was initiated, and it is quite strange that the international community that assisted this process believed that a state as fragmented as Mali would become any more coherent and better placed to respond to people's needs if it was cut up into even smaller pieces.

What is wrong with Kidal?

The traditional divisions across lineages and levels of nobility and ethnicity in northern Mali as described above were exacerbated after the implementation of the National Pact. The implementation not only created a new local state administration, but it also paved the way for more informal trade and even narco-trafficking and the regional Islamic rebels. Nowhere is this more evident than in the most traditional Tuareg settlement, the town and region of Kidal.

Here a power struggle broke out after the implementation of the 1996 peace agreement between traditional leaders and a generation of emerging leaders. The latter were not from the traditional ruling lineages but were a mixture of ex-rebels and drug traffickers. Thus, the Kidal predicament is just as much about intra-Tuareg tensions as it is a conflict with the Malian state. The implementation of the National Pact after the peace agreement enabled some regional Big Men to gain positions of power and privilege, which enabled them to extract handsome rents from the state and pay rents in turn to the Bamako political elite who allowed this to happen (Bøås 2012). Large amounts of money have been deployed to northern Mali, but with few tangible results on the ground. However, these processes have created and exacerbated tensions among the Tuaregs that have torn the social fabric apart.

After 1996, two main actors were competing for power and influence in Kidal. These were the traditional rulers of the Ifoghas clan and the rebel leader Iyad Ag Ghaly, who belongs to a lesser branch of the

Ifoghas. The Ifoghas are the dominant Tuareg clan in the Kidal region and have ruled this vast area since the arrival of the French in the early 1900s. This family has also taken part in all Tuareg rebellions. In late 2011, Alghabass Ag Intalla, the son of the chief of the Ifoghas, Intalla Ag Attaher, was nominated as the heir to his position. When the new rebellion broke out in January 2012, Ag Attaher denounced Ag Ghaly as its leader, which was most likely what initially propelled Ag Ghaly to establish Ansar ed-Din. The reason why Ag Intalla later joined Ag Ghaly in Ansar ed-Din is still unclear. Some informants claim that it was due to Ag Ghaly's ability to organise the rebellion and the failure of MNLA. Others suggest that Ag Intalla's father placed him there to prevent Ag Ghaly from leading the Ifoghas and the people of the Kidal area into an alliance with the Islamist forces, fearing that it would render any future negotiated settlement with the Malian state impossible.

In this regard, it is interesting to note that, after the In Aménas attack, a group under Ag Intalla's leadership broke away from Ansar ed-Din and formed a new group, the Islamic Movement for Azawad (IMA), claiming that they were denouncing terrorism and ready for dialogue.

All of this suggests that a significant part of the background to the current crisis was located in an internal power struggle. The heart of the matter was who should be the main focal point for the connection between the Malian state and the northern periphery and thereby also control the flow of state resources from Bamako. Thus, whereas the National Pact from 1990 was formulated to solve a national problem, it created a local problem that eventually hit back at a national level. Islamists and narco-traffickers used this internal conflict and the tensions it created to their own advantage. For these groups, Kidal's marginality, completely off the beaten track of any real government interests or surveillance, was a comparative advantage. The area has informal and illicit connections to the world of globalisation through the new economic opportunities provided by the trans-Saharan trade. The violent discontent that emerged was thus also related to the fact that the ancient trade routes through the Sahara have regained some of their old importance. Since 2006, the trafficking of contraband across borders has become increasingly important, offering new economic opportunities and new networks and nodal points for governance and control. Parts of the AQIM structure in northern Mali and in particular Mokthar Belmokhtar have been deeply involved in these operations and earned considerable amounts of money from it.

The trafficking of people across the Sahara has also increased, and the town of Gao, located at the bend of the river Niger, was becoming an important hub along this route for Congolese, Cameroonians, Liberians, Nigerians, and others who sought to leave the African continent. At Gao they were picked up for a Sahara crossing into Algeria.

Latin American drug cartels have increasingly used the Sahel as an important transit point in their smuggling of cocaine to markets in Western and Eastern Europe. Successfully making a trip across the border with this kind of drug could earn the driver as much as €3,000.

The trans-Saharan trafficking of these kinds of contraband is profitable, and for some of the Tuaregs it became an integral part of their livelihood. Most of the population were not directly involved, but, even if most of the Kidal inhabitants did not participate, they knew about it. They did not necessarily support it but saw it as just another type of trade that has come and gone across the Sahara ever since the first traders crossed this border area (see Keenan 2007). This sudden influx of cash weakened the traditional power configurations of the Tuareg society, leading to competing informal regimes of power, both locally and regionally.

This set-up was, however, unsustainable, and the initial chaos of the MNLA rebellion severely weakened this platform of informal and illicit governance. The initial MNLA combatants were all Tuareg in origin. A good number of them had stayed in Algeria and Libya for a considerable length of time and had to return to Mali after the fall of Gaddafi. This may help explain the chaos, and the looting, killings, and sexual violence they committed among those who should have been their own kin. Thus, not only Ansar ed-Din but also AQIM and MOJWA may have been deeper integrated into local communities than the members of the MNLA. The political leaders of MNLA may have had an agenda of Tuareg nationalism, but for many among the rank-and-file the main interest may have been opportunism.

Bamako 2012—a political landscape of deep cleavages

In 2012, fragmentation did not plague Mali's northern periphery alone; it was just as much of a challenge in Bamako and the south.

After the short-lived coup, Captain Sanogo reluctantly returned power to a handpicked civilian interim government. However, this government was also fragmented between different civilian and military groups. The issue of the Malian army's inability to deal with the insurgency was therefore a problem that went much deeper than just the lack of training that the establishment of EUTM in Mali suggested (BBC 2013). The army may have needed better training and more up-to-date equipment, but the structural problem was the lack of a unified national moral compass to underwrite its military operations. The army was also deeply divided between the 'red berets'—the paratroopers and presidential guard who still had some degree of loyalty to the previous president, Amadou Toumani Touré—and the 'green berets' who appointed Captain Sanogo as their leader during the 2012 coup. This was not a new conflict, but one that erupted during Touré's rule: he was a former paratrooper himself and was seen as giving privileges to the 'red berets' (Whitehouse 2012).

The March 2012 coup transformed the political landscape, resulting in divergent positions on the coup, the transition, and the question of negotiations with the north, all of which would continue to inform Bamako politics until the events of August 2020 turned the political landscape upside down (see Chapter 9). There were several coalitions of political parties and views taking different positions, but the three presented here were the most important. These are (1) the United Front to Safeguard Democracy and the Republic (FDR); (2) the Alliance Ibrahim Boubacar Keita (A-IBK); and (3) the Co-ordination of Patriotic Organisations in Mali (COPAM).

The FDR consisted of several parties and civilian organisations, including the largest party, ADEMA. The FDR was opposed to the coup and Captain Sanogo, and it called for the resignation of Interim Prime Minister Diarra. On the issue of the north, the FDR did not rule out dialogue, but not with armed actors, and it stated that the territorial integrity and secular nature of the Malian state were non-negotiable. The FDR also took the position that numerically the north and the Tuaregs were well integrated into the political system, as the last National Assembly had nineteen representatives from the north, eleven of whom were of Tuareg or Arab ethnic origin. The FDR supported the international interventions as the only means of ending the transition and the insurgencies and returning the country to democratic rule.

The A-IBK was a coalition of different groups that supported former Prime Minister Ibrahim Boubacar Keita, who at this time was a leading presidential candidate. Originally a part of the FDR, the A-IBK broke away in April 2012 but continued to share the FDR's opposition to the coup and to Captain Sanogo and his allies, arguing for a swift return to democracy. Apart from Keita's political ambitions, what separated this group from the FDR was its position on negotiations with the north and its views on the international intervention. It was absolutely against any negotiations with armed groups, claiming that people involved with the MNLA and IMA should not be eligible to stand for election. The A-IBK's position on the international intervention was more ambiguous. It supported it but also expressed concerns, the major fear being that France and ECOWAS would use MINUSMA to force through negotiations with the MNLA as an exit strategy.

Of the major political coalitions, COPAM was the one most closely affiliated to Captain Sanogo and his allies in the military. COPAM organised large demonstrations in Bamako calling for the resignation of Interim President Dioncounda Traoré, and opposed the international intervention. It was not against a military solution but argued that it had to be a Malian one, because it feared that France would force through an agreement which would lead to the 'balkanisation' of the country. This group was a strange mix of former student activists from the 1990s, including the old radical leader Oumar Mariko, and various populist groups arguing for a Malian nationalism based on the black population's autochthonous claim to its right to control the state, with the unifying factor being a common anti-neocolonial rhetoric. Elements of the former Songhay militia *Ghanda Koy*, which fought against the Tuareg rebels in the 1990s, was if not formally a part of COPAM at least associated with it. While the strength of COPAM would fade away as the international intervention seemed to succeed at first and Mali moved towards elections in 2013, the narrative of nationalism, anti-colonialism, and the suspicion of French motives—including the fear that France sought to 'balkanise' Mali to steal its national resources—never disappeared. COPAM would then return with a vengeance during the summer of

2020, when the people of Bamako exploded in anger and frustration over the shortcomings of the second Keita government.

COPAM supported the 2012 coup, arguing that it opened an opportunity for a political reconfiguration of the country's political landscape and a way to cleanse it of all representatives of what it considers the criminal Touré regime. As some COPAM members explained to the author during a meeting in Bamako in early 2013, 'the coup failed, but only because it failed to constitute a clear break with the past'. COPAM was critical of the transitional government and repeatedly called for its resignation. It did not recognise the 'Roadmap to Democracy' and argued that elections should not be held before conducting an extensive process of national consultations. COPAM ruled out including the north in these consultations; the only options were either military victory or that the northern-based rebels surrender.

As a mix of leftist political radicals and populists with a nationalist agenda, in 2013 COPAM was a strange chimera in the Malian political landscape, and it was hard to estimate the strength and size of its support base. However, while COPAM eventually ceased to exist as a political coalition, its ideas would return in full force in the neo-patriotism currently on display, not only on the streets of Bamako but also in Niamey and Ouagadougou. Lessons learned from Côte d'Ivoire and Laurent Gbagbo's political rhetoric should have warned us even back in 2013 that such a cocktail of ethnic nationalism and patriotism can not only constitute a real political force but can also potentially be quite destructive (see McGovern 2011; Bøås & Dunn 2013). There was always the possibility that COPAM's radical discourse would have an impact on other political movements, and this certainly turned out to be the case as people got tired of a democracy that gave them only hardship, endless conflict, and corrupt leaders, assisted by an international intervention that increasingly failed to either communicate with its supposed beneficiaries (the Malian population) or prevent the jihadi insurgencies of gaining ground.

Some concluding comments

The events of 2012 unmasked Mali. What had been presenting itself as a showcase of democracy, good governance, and peace and reconciliation proved to be a mire of institutional weakness, mismanagement, and collusion between regional and national Big Men interests that paid little if any respect to the security and development of its population.

In the north there was little, if any, agreement on a common position among the inhabitants, because the area was far from being a coherent polity but fragmented along numbers of lines. This was also the case in Bamako and the south. The various political groups had different views on the coup, dialogue with the north, and the international intervention. This made it challenging to find a platform for negotiations and should at that point have suggested that the National Pact of the 1990s could not serve as a blueprint for a solution to the crisis.

It was hard for the external stakeholders to envision how the militant Islamist groups could be part of a national dialogue on peace and reconciliation, but what they failed to realise was that these groups, far from being an alien element in northern Mali, had relatively successfully integrated themselves into local communities. The Malian army might have needed both training and new equipment, but its main problem was that it was not under better political control. The consequence was that it would continue to be part of the problem and not the solution.

Mali had received considerable foreign assistance in the past. Unfortunately, this did not prevent the crisis that materialised in 2012. This crisis constituted a deep challenge, but it was also a window of opportunity that could have helped Mali break with its troubled past. However, this opportunity could only be realised if the international response to the trouble in Mali had understood the complexity on the ground: the relationships between collusion, corruption, and resistance, and the way Big Men's political games opened northern Mali to the influence of armed Salafist forces. As events have showed, this was not the case, and the potential for opportunity instead became a prolonged mission without any clear endgame or exist strategy, that limped along until it was shown the exit by the Goïta government.

7

THE GRAND EMPIRES OF THE SAHEL

GOLD, TRADE, AND RELIGION

While the very early history of the Sahel is shrouded in uncertainty, what we do know is that this area of the world has contained consecutive empires whose might was formidable (see Cooper 2010). Their might was built on gold and control of the lucrative trans-Saharan trade routes. While it is hard to verify this, several sources claim that during the heyday of the ancient Sahel empires, about two-thirds of the world's gold came from this part of the world. This made these empires rich and powerful, but also entities of contestation as controlling them meant easy access to wealth. Trade and gold extraction means the possibility of accumulating riches and resources, but as this type of resource extraction is built on controlling hubs and spokes in trade networks and mining, the wealth these empires amassed was based not so much on production, but on extraction and rent-seeking from controlling access points along the trans-Saharan trade routes.

The Ghana Empire was the first state of this kind in in the Sahel. It was established in the third century CE, with its capital in Koumbi Saleh in what today is Mauritania (about 200 kilometres north of modern Bamako). By the eighth century, this empire covered much of Mali and the eastern parts of Senegal. Albeit smaller in geographical size than some of the empires that would follow, its rulers were very rich and powerful, controlling both the trans-Saharan routes as well as massive deposits of gold (see Cooper 2010). In the same period, Islam started to reach the Sahel, arriving with the trans-Saharan caravan routes. It was first the religion of trade and commerce, but it spread relatively quickly throughout the Sahel as the dominant religion. It was useful for rulers, but also for their opponents, as it created codes of government and trade that were applicable far beyond rulers' courts. It also, as we will see, could be utilised symbolically as the justification for war against 'states' and rulers that political entrepreneurs could accuse of being 'unbelievers', 'infidels', or simply of having deviated from the true version of Islam.

In this regard, there is a line of continuity between what happened here centuries ago and the current call to war by jihadi-Salafi insurgents against 'unbelief' and infidelity. In the Sahel there is a long tradition of religious radicalisation and the use of religion as a justification for war. These ideas have been there all along, and when the current crisis started in 2012 the idea expressed by both spokespersons from the Malian state and the international community, that jihad in its violent form was alien to Mali, simply does not hold up to historical facts.

As rich and mighty as the Ghana Empire may have been, it was not to last. While it had the coercive force to control trade routes through the Sahara for a long time, it did not evolve as quickly in the development of military equipment and tactics as some of the more warlike empires to its north, whose rulers must have asked themselves why the Ghana Empire should control so much trade and gold when they themselves had more military might. Thus, in the eleventh century, the better-armed Muslim Berber warriors of the Almoravid Empire (in present-day Morocco and Mauritania) attacked and destroyed the Ghana Empire. The justification was religious, claiming that the war was legitimate as the Ghana Empire was not a true Islamic empire, but their desire for gold and control of trade routes was probably just as important. This established a precedent of declaring jihad against rulers who they claimed were un-Islamic or too half-hearted in their implementation of Islamic rule that would characterise this region for centuries to come (see Lovejoy 2016).

THE GRAND EMPIRES OF THE SAHEL

The legendary empires of Mali and Songhay

While the Ghana Empire was destroyed by the Almoravid forces, it was not the end of the era of grand empires in the Sahel. Around 1240, the Mali Empire was established by Sundiata Keita, the leader of the Malinke people. This was an empire of legendary proportions that reached such levels of wealth and prestige that it sparked the outside world's interests in the African continent, and whose tales—most notably the Epic of Sundiata—have remained a part of the popular imagination in Mali ever since (see Chapter 10).

In the fourteenth century, the Mali Empire controlled not only the trans-Saharan trade routes and the gold mines that had enriched the previous Ghana Empire, but also a much broader territory than its predecessor (see Davidson 2014). The kings of the Mali Empire ruled from Senegal in the west to Niger in the east. Legends tell of a king—Abubakari II—who sent expeditions far into the Atlantic Ocean to discover new land, and his successor Kankan Musa is thought to have been the richest man who ever has lived (measured in gold). Islam was now well-established as the hegemonic religion, and Musa like his predecessors was a devoted Muslim. When he embarked on his pilgrimage to Mecca in 1324, he allegedly travelled with an entourage of 60,000 followers and needed 500 slaves to carry all the gold he brought with him (see Davidson 2014). What is fact and what is legend is a matter of debate, but it is true that he was enormously rich, and it has been established that the gifts of gold that he distributed along his route to Mecca lowered the price of gold for a decade if not more. This attracted the interests of emerging powers in Europe, where European merchants returning from Cairo brought news about an enormously rich country in the middle of the desert. It would still take a long time for European interests to reach this part of Africa, but the legend of cities of gold, wealth, and knowledge had been planted, and the myth of Timbuktu was in the making.

Timbuktu was much more than a myth. Under the Mali Empire, the trans-Sahara trade reached its peak, and the wealth created by trade and gold turned the Mali Empire's main cities into important centres of finance, trade, and culture. The most notable of these was Timbuktu. Here, two Islamic universities were established, and Arab architects from as far away as Granada in Spain designed the new mosques that were being built, one example being the Dyingerey Ber Mosque (see Hunwick & Boye 2008).

When the Mali Empire reached its peak of wealth and glory, another empire was established on its eastern perimeter. This was the state of Songhay, formed around the city of Gao. When the Mali Empire eventually crumbled due to royal decadence and conflicts over both the throne and tributaries, Gao became more powerful and better organised than the Mali Empire had been. At its height, the Songhay Empire stretched from almost Lake Chad to the proximity of the Atlantic Ocean. It had a professional army and a civil service with provincial governors, and the state subsidised Muslim scholars, judges, and doctors (see Loimeier 2013). However, like the Mali Empire, also the Songhay kings wanted to display their wealth to the rest of the world. One of its kings supposedly travelled to Mecca, bringing with him 300,000 pieces of gold, and, once more, better-organised warrior states wanted to have their share of the wealth. In 1549, large Berber armies that managed to cross the desert brought an end not only to the Songhay Empire but also to the era of great empires in the Sahel. Prior to the arrival of the colonial powers, more states would follow, but they would be smaller in size, less rich and powerful, and most would not last long, as wars and endless calls for jihad by political entrepreneurs against a rule for being un-Islamic would lead to long periods of what we may define as 'rolling wars' throughout the Sahel (see Cooper 2010). This is the period that Paul Lovejoy (2016) defines as the 'age of revolutions', lasting from about 1670 to 1850, at which point European powers, and France in particular, placed their mark on the Sahel as the dominant colonial power.

The end of the grand empires of Mali

The power of the grand empires of Mali was not just based on gold but equally on their ability to control the trans-Saharan trade. Thus, it was not very likely that a new one should emerge from the ruins of the Songhay Empire once European ships started to arrive at the West African coast in the fifteenth century. The monopoly that the empires of Mali had enjoyed on trade with the outside world was broken, and as time passed and the French colonisers came to control not only Mali but most of the Sahel, the trans-Saharan routes and the importance that they once had were forgotten. They were obviously still remembered in historical records and studies, but as a concern for practical politics they were seen as something that belonged to the archives of history. As previous chapters have shown, this is no longer the case. These routes, forgotten by Europe after their ships broke the monopoly that local rulers had on trade with the outside world, have re-emerged as transit routes for people moving northwards and for ordinary goods, but also for weapons and contraband ranging from cigarettes and soft drugs to hard drugs such as cocaine. Thus, the Sahel once again finds itself positioned as a centre of global trade and commerce.

After the fall of the Songhay Empire and the French conquest of the Sahel, several smaller kingdoms emerged, and among the latter of these was Macina, which we will return to at the end of this chapter. The largest was the Bambara Kingdom of Segou that for a short while controlled large parts of contemporary Mali. However, its power was overthrown by at least two waves of Fula-led jihadi wars. It took some time, but by the late 1890s France controlled most of what is now Mali (Mann 2021).

Just like neighbouring Burkina Faso and Niger, Mali was never a central component of the French colonial project. The most valuable assets of French colonialism in West Africa were Côte d'Ivoire and Senegal. Remaining colonies such as the trio of Mali, Niger, and Burkina Faso were given specific secondary roles, with Mali seen as the most important of them. Mali was 'developed' as a source of cash crop production—cotton and rice, and remnants of this part of the French colonial project include the large-scale irrigation scheme in Segou (the Office du Niger project) and the 1,200-kilometre Dakar–Bamako railway, both built by forced labour. Niger did not have much importance at all before uranium was discovered in the north, and Burkina Faso's role was mainly as a reserve pool of labour for the French attempt to commercially develop cocoa production in Côte d'Ivoire (see Mann 2021).

To say that these states were well prepared with an adequate infrastructure and a common political polity as nation–states when independence arrived in the early 1960s would be an exaggeration. The cards they received at independence did not make up a good hand, to put it mildly. However, the argument can also be made that the rulers who succeeded the colonial power did not play this very wisely, regarding either national development and unity.

What about Islam and jihad?

The barrier of the Sahara Desert meant that it took longer for Islam to trickle down to the Sahel and West Africa than elsewhere. It first reached the Sahel around the year 900 CE through trans-Saharan traders coming from places in present-day Morocco and Algeria. As in other cases where a religion takes root in a new place, most people probably preferred to maintain their original beliefs, but the kings and emperors of the Sahel quickly embraced the new faith, skilfully combing aspects of Islam with traditional beliefs in the administration of the states that they ruled.

Sufi Islam, which emphasises mystical and spiritual attributes, quickly gained ground as it mirrored existing beliefs and social norms and structures. Travel guides like Lonely Planet and similar popular outlets often portray Sufi Islam as the 'traditional' Islam of the Sahel and West Africa, but that view fails to give credit to the tradition of jihad in the Sahel, which is equally anchored in the local context. In the seventeenth and eighteenth centuries, when none of the contestants that emerged after the end of the grand empires were able to gain a hegemonic position, rulers were repeatedly declaring jihad against one another. Or, as was even more often the case, an entrepreneur—very much like the contemporary violent entrepreneur—would declare jihad against a leader who was accused of unbelief or of deviating too far from what their opponent defined as the true path of Islam. The main difference between the historical jihad of the Sahel and that of the present day is that in the past jihad was associated with Sufi brotherhoods, and particularly the Qadiriyya, whereas the current jihadis are Salafi and advocate a literal, strict, and puritanical approach to Islam in line with the anti-Sufi tradition of Wahhabism (see Lovejoy 2016).

The spread of jihad in the Sahel started after the collapse of the Muslim Songhay Empire in around 1591. The period that followed was seen by many Muslim scholars of the time as one of decay, where Islam was corrupted by the new military elites who came to dominate the many small states that followed the fall of the empire. In the commercial diaspora of Muslim merchants and the centres of Islamic learning now dispersed through the Sahel, a new conversation and narrative came about which articulated a yearning for a unified Islamic community. It was this vision that would bring forward jihad as a political movement in the Sahel in the seventeenth century. The history of jihadi movements in the Sahel thus spans a period of about 200 years, from the late seventeenth century to the end of the nineteenth century. It began in 1673 in the Senegal Valley and would roll through various parts of the Sahal until its last installations before being subdued by the forces of French colonialism was the Macina Empire in Mali, whose capital was near present day Mopti, and the Tukulor Empire, which started in Senegal but whose principal event was the establishment of fortresses near Kayes (present-day Mali) (see Lovejoy 2016). For a long time, this was seen as a period of interest only to those studying the history of this area, but for anyone who cares to see, it is obvious that the history of state and statehood—and of gold, trade, and jihad—also has implications for the contemporary instalment of jihad in the Sahel. This also becomes obvious when we consider the Katiba Macina's use of the history of the Macina Empire.

History and insurgency: the Macina Empire and the Katiba Macina

Mopti and the Inner Delta of the Niger River has historically been a contested space. It is rich in resources, but competing systems of governance challenge each other, and those who generally lose out are the common people of the region. Communal conflict over access to land and water is not new, but is currently being exacerbated by population growth, effects of climate change, and armed jihadi groups, that have developed strategies for appropriating conflicts that a vanishing and dysfunctional state is not able to deal with in a credible and trustworthy manner.

At the forefront of the armed conflict is the Katiba Macina, which we already discussed in Chapter 2. The group rose to prominence in 2015 and has remained the dominant insurgency in the Mopti region of central Mali. In fact, in most of the Inner Niger Delta it is the de facto authority. The Inner Niger Delta comprises the flood-prone and vegetation-rich wetlands in the west of the Mopti region and the east of the Segou region. In the north–south direction, the area is situated along the Niger River, between the cities of Timbuktu and Segou. The Katiba Macina are a jihadi-Salafi insurgency, but through Hamadoun Kouffa's rhetorical narrative of people, place, and belonging in the Inner Niger Delta it has also become a representation of Fulani pastoralist grievances against the state, but also against Bambara and Dogon farmers, as well as the Fulani aristocracy, the Jowros (Lyammouri 2021). These groups, Kouffa argues, have gained both from the French colonisers and later from the postcolonial state, which has privileged farming communities and the Fulani aristocracy at the expense of ordinary Fulani pastoralists.

Kouffa's claims are not necessarily completely accurate, but neither are they entirely false. When the colonial power started to arrive in this part of Mali sometime after the fall of the Macina Empire in 1864, the French accepted part of the original management system of natural resources. However, the new French rulers soon undermined it by establishing a parallel form of land tenure. Customary chiefs managed land under continuous cultivation, whereas the colonial administration controlled so-called 'unoccupied land' and could grant private property titles. Water and forests were placed under the control of the Water and Forest Agency—the current *Direction Nationale des Eaux et Forêts* (see Ursu 2018). This created a series of contradictions and problems for pastoralist communities (but also for farmers and fishermen) that successive postcolonial governments in Mali have done little if anything to unpack. In this regard, it is not difficult to argue that Mopti and the Inner Niger Delta constitute an enabling environment for violent entrepreneurs such as Hamadoun Kouffa (see Chapter 4). While primarily portraying his group as a jihadi-Salafi insurgency, Kouffa has shifted between foregrounding a jihadi and a Fulani identity in both his actions and his discourse. At times he has refuted claims that the Katiba Macina is a Fulani group, but he also narrates his men as defenders of the true Fulani community, and the very name of the insurgency—the Katiba Macina—promises a return to a golden age of Fulani rule of the Inner Niger Delta.

THE GRAND EMPIRES OF THE SAHEL

What was the Macina?

The Macina Empire, or more precisely the state of Hamdullahi, came into being after the death of Uthman dan Fodio in 1817 when Sekou Amadou started a jihad and established a capital for the Macina of Hamdullahi near present-day Mopti a few years later (see Brown 1968). In 1848, Hamdullahi fell to the forces of a new jihad declared by al-Haji Umar Tall under the banner of the Tijaniyya. However, while its rulers changed the state remained one of several entities at that time ruled by a Fulani aristocracy (see Lovejoy 2016). This remained the case until it swayed and crumbled when confronted with French forces in 1864. The question is yet again, what makes this important for our understanding of the current situation?

The Macina, as Kouffa mostly refers to the empire, was a Fulani state, and the use of the name thus points back to a golden age for the Fulani people when they were rulers of their own state. This is not to argue that Kouffa has any separatist ambitions, but there is a collective memory here that he makes use of.

While the Mopti of today is a place of violence and disorder, with hardly any working institutions and where those that still exist are dysfunctional and corrupted, this stands in stark contrast to the history of the Macina when the Fulani ruled. At the height of its power, a 10,000-man army was supposedly stationed in the city, and 600 madrasas were constructed throughout the empire to further the spread of Islam. Alcohol, tobacco, music, and dancing were banned in accordance with Islamic law, while a social welfare system provided for widows and orphans (Brown 1968). There was also a strong police presence that enforced social norms and rules of conduct, such as hygiene. Education was prioritised by the empire and played an important part in every citizen's life. Both boys and girls between the ages of seven to twenty-one would learn the basics of the Quran and the tradition of the Prophet, advanced theology, and mysticism, and, in some cases, more secular subjects such as grammar and rhetoric. All school fees were fixed, and teachers were subsidised by the central government (see Hopkins 1973; Moorehead 1997). This is a history that an insurgency such as the Katiba Macina can draw heavily on, as it reminds people of a time of order and welfare provision organised by pious and benevolent leaders who cared for their population. This was how it once was when the area was ruled according to Islamic principles rather than by a corrupt system imported from abroad.

The Macina also established a code regulating the use of the natural resources of the Inner Niger Delta by Fulani pastoralists, the ethnically diverse farming communities, and the Bozo fishing communities (Bruijn & van Dijk 2001). Kouffa and the Katiba Macina have several times referred to what they call the 'Macina principles' for resource management, claiming that they want to re-establish these principles as the main governing mechanism for the Inner Niger Delta. For young Fulani herders who have experienced the corrupt excesses of the *Direction Nationale des Eaux et Forêts*, this may sound much better than what they are used to. The key to Kouffa's use of history is therefore to blend certain parts that point to a bygone golden age, contrast this with people's experiences with the current state, and mix this with a promise that the future could become like it once was if the population follows Kouffa's path of Islam.

But Kouffa leaves two important factors out of his tale of the past. First, while his narrative praises certain aspects of the Macina, like its code of resource management, he for the most part leaves out the fact that the Macina Empire was one of the most sophisticated governments in Africa at the time. As a state, it operated with a system of checks and balances and a well-established tax system. It was organised as an Islamic state, but had certain democratic tendencies. The Macina Empire was governed by the king and a forty-member Grand Council, appointed for their wisdom and creativity, and sixty judges who were prominent marabouts. The Grand Council acted as the legislative, executive, and judicial branches of the empire and could make their own decisions based on strict observance of the Maliki interpretation of Sharia law. If the Grand Council and the king ever came to a disagreement, forty of the sixty judges would be selected randomly to make the final decision (Hopkins 1973). While the Shura Council of the Katiba Macina do hold power and rule on several issues of importance, there is also little doubt that the Big Man of the insurgency and the organisation is Hamadoun Kouffa. Thus, while he presents the 'Macina principles' (as Kouffa calls them) as the ideal way to run a state, while decrying the dysfunctional democracy of the Malian state, bringing such a sophisticated governing system in full into his narrative is not in his interests.

Second, and most likely a result of his alliance with Iyad Ag Ghaly through JNIM, Kouffa also skips over another important part of the history of the Macina, which is its persistent violent conflict with Tuareg groups. After the Macina's first conquest of the north-eastern regions between Timbuktu and Gao in 1818–26, the Tuareg who had previously controlled the region rebelled several times. Their aim was to escape the imposition of direct rule by the Macina-appointed Governor Abd al-Qādir residing in Timbuktu. A Tuareg force drove off the Macina garrison in 1840, but the following year they were defeated and expelled. The Tuareg then regrouped in 1842–4 and managed to defeat the Macina forces and drive them from Timbuktu. But the city was later besieged by the Macina, and its inhabitants were starved into resubmitting to Macina rule by 1846 (see Roberts 1987).

This part of the Macina history is not one that Kouffa seems to be fond of. The reason for this is not just because it points to a troubled past between the Fulani and the Tuareg in this part of Mali, but more importantly because the issues fought over back then have never been completely resolved. The Fulani and the Tuareg still compete over resources for their pastoral practices, over access to transhumance routes, and over trade rights and networks. These issues still loom over the alliance between the Katiba Macina and Ansar ed-Dine via JNIM, and they make the JNIM alliance seem less solid than it would appear from afar. JNIM is the last in a series of attempts to build an organisational superstructure that can transcend local conflicts, and it has organised so much of the insurgency mobilisation and its local integration in Mali and the Sahel at large. Kouffa is obviously aware of this, and like any skilled violent entrepreneur he carefully selects the bits and pieces of history that he can make use of here and now. Kouffa's reading of the history of the Macina is clearly opportunistic, but so far it has served him well. How this may look like in the future remains to be seen. However, if the jihadi project of JNIM should ever become more than it is today and be a serious contender for state power in Mali, it needs to establish a broader basis for its governing principles than those used by the Macina, because sophisticated as they may have been, they also point to a history, not yet forgotten, of violent conflict between key groups in the JNIM alliance.

Conclusion

The current crisis in the Sahel—which, even if it has not yet broken the existing state, has certainly rattled it to its very bones—is not the first time dramatic upheavals have taken place in this part of the world. The contemporary spread of jihadism in the Sahel is a consequence of state failure and as such is quite like what Lovejoy (2016) calls the 'jihad of the age of revolutions', which occurred between the late sixteenth century and the end of the nineteenth century. In a period of sustained civil strife, confusion, and what some scholars and imams saw as a period of corruption of true Islamic practices, several calls for jihad were made. None of them succeeded, as none achieved enough of a hegemony to subdue or kill other contenders for the jihadi throne, and the process was also interrupted by the arrival of French colonial forces. Nonetheless, they have made a mark on the social landscape of the Sahel, and, while this history may not be much known elsewhere, here in the Sahel it is still a living memory as the case of the Katiba Macina testifies to.

Similarly, the trans-Saharan routes of commerce, contraband, and people that have caused much attention and concern on the part of European policymakers is not a new phenomenon but points back to a time when those who controlled these routes were among the richest people in the world. And their wealth was not only built on trade and commerce, but also on gold. Not that long ago, gold in the Sahel was not much of a global concern. But this is no longer the case. The extraction of gold in the Sahel is currently intertwined with both global geopolitical contestation, due to increased Russian presence on the ground (see Chapter 9), and the fear that new gold fields will come under the control of jihadi-Salafi insurgents. While we should be careful in stating that history repeats itself, we certainly need an understanding of the history of the Sahel in order to account for the present.

PART III

THE PERFECT STORM

While a perfect storm in the Sahel can still be prevented, it has come much closer than what had been the case when this book was first planned. The demographic trends look unsustainable as every year masses of young men and women enter a job market that has nothing to offer them. While we should be extremely careful concerning the relationship between climate change and conflict in this part of the world, that does not mean that climate change is not real. It is, and it will have detrimental effects on the Sahel in the future. If nothing else, climatic variability will increase, meaning that, while the level of rainfall may not necessarily become less—there may even be more of it—it will come out of sync when local people need it, thereby making existing seasonal calendars obsolete, with the consequences this may have for even further communal violence connected to the relationship between pastoralists and farmers. The jihadi-Salafi insurgents are far from defeated. The external interventions of France, the UN, and the EU have failed miserably, and have by and large been asked to leave.

New military governments have come in place in Mali, Burkina Faso, and Niger, and they have turned to Russia for assistance. This means that yet another component to the 'storm' has been added, as the Sahel has now also become part of the new geopolitical contestation that increasingly looks like Cold War 2.0. Not only is Russia providing military assistance, but the Russian-based and backed private security company the Wagner Group is present on the ground as advisors, protecting the regimes, offering coup proofing, and taking part in the battles against the jihadi-Salafi insurgents. The international politics of the Sahel are therefore increasingly complicated and volatile, as illustrated by the joint decisions of Mali, Niger, and Burkina Faso to leave ECOWAS and set up their own regional organisation, the Alliance of Sahel States (AoSS).

The new external dynamics need serious attention, but we should also be very careful with analysis that fails to consider the agency of the African actors involved. As Chapter 10 will seek to show, we are dealing with a government in Mali that is very strategic. It knows what it is doing, and so far it has played its card very well internally. There are also other important religious actors on the ground, and Chapter 8 charts Imam Dicko's rise to prominence in Mali as a new type of religious Big Man. We must, however, also ponder the three military coups that have taken plaec in the central Sahel, what this means and what kind of consequences it can have, and what we can expect from these states' collective turn to Russia. This is what Chapters 9 and 10 will offer, whereas Chapter 11 will bring together the elements of the perfect storm in a concise analysis of what may be about to break out in the Sahel.

8

POLITICS IN HARD TIMES

RELIGION AND PROTEST

Mali is, by an overwhelmingly majority, a Muslim country. Nonetheless, it is also written in its constitution that it is a secular state that explicitly forbids religious political parties. Religious actors have therefore rarely been openly involved in party politics and electoral campaigns. Before the current conflict started in 2012, Mali was considered a typical West African country wherein more liberal versions of Sunni Islam were expected to dominate the religious sphere through important Sufi brotherhoods (Coulon 1983).[1] There is, however, as previous chapters have indicated, another history of Islam in Mali. In this tradition, leaders from both the Qadiriyya and Tijaniyya Sufi brotherhoods expressed ideas of reform and renewal of Islam and Islamic practices that should take place under the guidance of a state that governed in accordance with Sharia (see Lebovich 2019). Today, while most of the population still practise a form of Islam in accordance with Sunni persuasions, Salafism and various other Wahhabi-inspired congregations have remained present in the country since the 1930s (Cruise O'Brien 2009).

Throughout the twentieth century, there has been fierce competition between these interpretations of Islam, but this rarely factored in the political contestations of electoral campaigns and public protests. This changed when the country descended into violent conflict and near collapse in 2012 after a secular Tuareg rebellion in the north was followed by a coup d'état and the subsequent infiltration of large parts of the country by jihadi insurgents (see Bøås 2015a). Based on a call for support from the transitional Malian government, France launched the military intervention Operation Serval in early 2013. The French intervention halted the advance of the jihadi insurgents and facilitated the deployment of the UN peacekeeping mission, MINUSMA, later the same year. In 2015, a peace accord was also signed between a coalition of separatist Tuareg rebels, pro-government militias, and the Malian state (Bøås 2019).

Despite these efforts, as well as those of several other large international missions deployed to stabilise the country, no real improvements have materialised on the ground. The security situation has instead deteriorated, especially in the central regions of the country where jihadist insurgents were able to regroup while international attention was focused on implementing the fragile peace deal and stabilising the north. Since 2015, a locally based jihadist group, the Katiba Macina, led by the Fulani preacher Hamadoun Kouffa, has gained a substantial foothold in the important Mopti region of central Mali. Kouffa and his group are also formally partnered with the al-Qaeda-affiliated JNIM, led by the Tuareg leader Iyad Ag Ghaly. The Katiba Macina and JNIM's combined campaign of violence against the state and international forces, and their coercion and killing of non-collaborators in this part of Mali, has accelerated the retreat of the state and facilitated the insurgents' expansion (Bøås 2019). Consequently, many Malians have lost the little faith they had left in the modern state, as it does not present credible answers to their livelihood challenges (Ba & Bøås 2018; see also Schulz 2021).[2]

Several actors, including religious leaders, have attempted to take advantage of the anxiety and social confusion created by this turmoil. Although assisting their country and its population in times of precarity is certainly one function of religious leaders, they are also not above strategic manoeuvres to gain more followers. Religious leaders in Mali are largely considered to be pious, honest and non-corrupt. This is in stark contrast to how most Malians view politics, which they consider a dirty practice of shady deals and patron–client relations where Big Men seek the favour of the electorate in order to reap the spoils.³ Entering the ongoing struggle thus afforded religious leaders the opportunity to gain material support from the political class, which suddenly more than ever needed to be backed up by one of the few sources of authority left largely untainted by the crisis.

Religious leaders have since had to grapple with preserving their symbolic capital while participating more openly in the formal matters of politics, such as electoral campaigns.⁴ To achieve this, they must demonstrate their ability to manage their appetite for the various benefits that Malian politics is known to produce.⁵ However, as it is commonly said in Mali, 'appetite comes with eating'. This chapter will thus explore how, after the 2012 crisis, religious actors were drawn into the political game, what effects this had during the 2013 and 2018 elections, and how they have since tried to convince their congregations that they still can 'manage their appetite' by focusing on socially conservative issues, such as the family law code and the question of homosexuality. The latter had never been much debated in Mali before, but it enabled religious leaders to bring down the prime minister in 2019. This event, and what followed, led almost directly to the August 2020 military coup that brought down the elected government of President Ibrahim Boubacar Keita, commonly known as IBK.

Although this chapter discusses the role and involvement of several religious leaders, the main person of interest in this chapter is Imam Mahmoud Dicko. Born in the mid-1950s in the Timbuktu region of Mali, Dicko's social and political influence has grown steadily since he first gained national attention as the head of the Haut Conseil Islamique Malien (HCIM) in 2009. From this position he led a popular campaign of mass protests in 2009 that forced then President Amadou Toumani Touré to significantly weaken proposed reforms of the family law code that would have increased the rights of women in Mali. Dicko is clearly a social conservative, but his outspokenness against inequality, corruption, and state mismanagement has also made him a champion of the masses on several secular political issues. But how did a religious leader who at times self-identifies as a Wahhabi manage to get so deeply involved in politics in a country that considers politics to be a dirty game?⁶

The intention of this chapter is certainly not to signal any alarm regarding the increased involvement and influence of religious leaders in Malian politics, but rather to show that this represents a new development in the history of religion in Mali. This could signal a new pathway of political involvement for Salafi actors who navigate the straits between resistance and collaboration with the state. To achieve this analysis, the question to ask is if a religious actor such as Imam Dicko could be understood as a Big Man in the making.

As already discussed (see Chapter 4), we agree with Driscoll (2020) that the concept has moved away from its original meaning in Sahlins' study. What is important to keep in mind is that the status of Big Man is a tacit recognition, not a designated formal title, and this is what Dicko gained during the events leading up to the August 2020 coup and which enabled him to contribute to the downfall of the president.

Although in hindsight Dicko made some mistakes in 2013 and 2018, in the lead-up to the August 2020 coup he became a social hero capable of capturing the imagination of large audiences. His public performances played to a popular imagining of the hero as a 'destabilising force in society, someone who strikes against and sometimes overturns the prevailing regime' (Whitehouse 2012: 97). Seen in this light, what Dicko became was an agent of disequilibrium. This may sound dangerous, but what is often needed in a state of exception is a man of exception who can lead his followers into new social terrain (see also Hellweg 2011).

Although most cases of Big Men analysed in the new conflict literature based on anthropology and African Studies (see Utas 2012) have been secular actors, we argue that what characterises Big Man status is not a secular inclination or any other social, economic, or political position. Rather, it is entrepreneurship and the ability to craft, manage, and utilise political authority based on accumulated capital. This capital can come in many forms but is ultimately based on mutually acknowledged recognition and respect. We argue that in a context of crisis and social confusion, as is the case in Mali, an image of piety combined with strong religious credentials is a form of symbolic capital that can be co-opted and utilised as almost perfect Big Man capital.

POLITICS IN HARD TIMES: RELIGION AND PROTEST

In what follows, the chapter outlines the political career of Imam Dicko and other religious leaders leading up to the August 2020 military coup. The chapter documents both failures and setbacks, as well as how Dicko and some other religious leaders learned to play politics without tarnishing their image as pious men of God. The argument here is that Dicko's hybrid mix of theology and politics is key to his popularity—it illustrates his ability to keep his finger on the pulse of the politics of the street, leading his followers into a new landscape of politics, religion, and resistance that both his religious supporters and parts of the secular opposition can abide by. At the least, this suggests that a new pathway of resistance and collaboration for Salafi actors may be about to emerge underneath the international headlines of Mali being caught between traditional Sufi Islam and violent Salafi insurgencies.

Politics as dirty—Dicko's reinterpretation of the traditional political Big Man

Consistently ranked near the bottom of the UNDP's Human Development Index, Mali is one of the poorest countries in the world. Outside of the bigger cities, most people make a living from farming or herding, traditional livelihoods that are threatened both by violent conflict and by demographic trends.[7] State institutions are weak, administrative capacity is low, and the country is caught in a vicious cycle of violence and fragmentation which international community partners have done little to improve (Bøås 2019).

The fragile condition of contemporary Mali stands in stark contrast to its heritage of ancient civilisations with vast empires (such as the Mande and the Songhay) and kingdoms (like the Fulani of Macina). Islam arrived in Mali around the ninth century, and the cities of ancient Mali—like Timbuktu, Gao, and Djenne—became known in the Islamic world for their wealth and scholarship. However, these empires eventually fractured into smaller entities. Little was left of the ancient glory when the French colonial powers arrived in the late nineteenth century (Ba & Bøås 2018).

In the 1990s, Mali was often presented as an example of successful liberal economic and democratic reform in West Africa.[8] However, behind what was presented as a showcase of democracy, good governance, peace, and reconciliation lay institutional weakness, mismanagement, and collusion involving regional and national elite interests that paid scant attention to human security and development (Bøås & Torheim 2013). Thus, when the current crisis broke in 2012, Mali was already a weak and fragile state with hardly any formal institutions or networks capable of working out sustainable compromises at the local level. It was a multiparty democracy, but as every political party was sustained by a vertical hierarchy of patronage networks, the resilience of the political system was very low, as shown by the March 2012 coup (Bøås 2019). Most ordinary Malians are therefore deeply disillusioned by the political class and tend to believe that politicians are only there to make money. As one key informant put it: 'If they are not corrupt on entering office, they quickly learn how to use their new position to fill their pockets.'9 Malians see politics as dirty, but at the same time they fear and respect the political Big Men, whom they need.

As the crisis of 2012 has unfolded for more than a decade with no endgame in sight, the political system has deteriorated even further. What used to be a neopatrimonial state of regulatory, hierarchical patron–client relations (Murray 2016; Mkandawire 2015) has been weakened in the capital of Bamako, and has almost vanished entirely in some peripheral areas (Bøås 2015a). What it has been replaced by is a much less hierarchical Big Man type of politics, not unlike what Sahlins (1963) identified on the Melanesian Islands (Bøås 2012).

The 2013 and 2018 elections

In the beginning, Operation Serval seemed as though it would be successful, as it managed to stop the advances of the jihadi insurgents south of the Niger River. The international community expressed a strong desire to return the country to ordinary parliamentary and presidential rule as quickly as possible. National elections were hastily organised in the autumn of 2013, with the next round of elections taking place in 2018 in accordance with the schedule designed by the Malian constitution.

While religious leaders of national importance did not openly campaign for any candidate in the 2013 and 2018 elections, it was well known who their preferred candidate was. IBK won the presidency by a huge majority in August 2013 on a campaign platform to restore Mali's territorial integrity and tackle the massive corruption and economic mismanagement of the country (Ba & Bøås 2013). During the presidential elections in 2013, there was a clear consensus among religious leaders that IBK was the man who could steer Mali out of crisis. Most of them, Dicko included, therefore openly, although informally, supported IBK's candidacy. While religious leaders becoming involved in electoral politics and supporting candidates was somewhat novel, IBK's broad popularity among the Malian population meant this transition wasn't considered particularly controversial.

However, despite IBK's 2013 electoral campaign promises, the crisis deepened during his first period in power. By 2018, the conflict seemed to have become almost chronic, and the insurgents' area of operation had also come much closer to the capital of Bamako. In addition, the 'good governance' approach on which IBK had promised to base his rule had not only failed, but in effect never even materialised at all. Both citizens and international observers viewed the Malian state as just as corrupt in 2018 as it had been when IBK had assumed office in 2013. In short, none of IBK's campaign promises were fulfilled (Bøås 2019).

One would think that it would be difficult for IBK to inspire enough confidence among the Malian electorate to gain him a second term in office. His track record was undoubtedly an embarrassment, even for some of his most faithful supporters. Religious leaders were also clearly more careful in how they talked about IBK during the 2018 elections than had been the case in 2013. Despite this, IBK was re-elected after a run-off against main opposition rival Soumaila Cissé.

The 2018 presidential elections[10]

The first round of the presidential election took place on 29 July 2018, when twenty-four candidates competed for the favour of the electorate. However, only IBK (Rally for Mali), Soumaila Cissé (Union for the Republic and Democracy), Aliou Diallo (Democratic Alliance for Peace), and Cheick Modibo Diarra (The Movement for Development in Mali) were considered serious contenders. As no candidate received more than 50 per cent of the votes, a run-off had to be held on 12 August between the two top candidates, IBK and Cissé, as had been the case in 2013. In the end, IBK was re-elected with 67 per cent of the votes. The result in 2018 was thus much the same as in 2013, but for the first time in Malian history an incumbent had been forced into a run-off.

It would be wrong to explain the outcome as being solely due to the involvement of religious leaders, but it is of considerable interest to understand how they impacted the election result, how they managed this, and why this was important to them. As previously noted, religious leaders are not supposed to be openly political figures in Mali, but this did not prevent the electoral candidates from eagerly seeking the support and blessing from religious leaders, nor did it prevent the religious leaders themselves from actively and even cunningly negotiating the game of electoral politics in Mali.

In contrast to the 2013 campaign, in 2018 the religious leaders were far from united in their informal support for candidates. In fact, until the very last day of voting in the second round, they remained far more divided than civil society actors or political parties with candidates who had lost in the first round of voting. The only significant exception was Chérif Ousmane Madani Haidara (one of Mali's most influential imams in the Maliki branch of Sunni Islam and the current chairman of the HCIM), who kept his opinion well hidden from the public eye.[11] The question is why support from religious leaders was so important for the candidates, and what was in it for the religious leaders themselves?

The involvement of religious leaders in the 2013 elections must have born some fruit, as all of them (except for Haidara) were ready to do the same in 2018, even though some of those who had stood by IBK in 2013 lost credibility. The political candidates were not unaware of this, but they also knew that they still needed the religious leaders' support to strengthen their failing image as pious, legitimate leaders who sought the best for their country rather than for themselves. It was obvious when the 2018 campaign started that many Malians were deeply dissatisfied with the political class and politics in general. This was also evident in the low voter turnout in both the first and second rounds of the presidential elections (respectively 43 and 35 per cent). It is thus fair to say that these two groups of elites needed each other. The political candidates needed the blessing of religious leaders to protect their crumbling popular legitimacy, whereas the religious leaders needed to show their influence and thereby also show the politicians that they could not be ignored. In short, their appetite had grown from eating.

What has taken place in Mali since 2013 can thus be considered a slow but steady fusion of politics and religion (see also Schulz 2021). This is also clearly expressed in the political discourse, where one increasingly finds references to religious subjects such as Sharia. This fusion has opened the political space in Mali for religious actors and leaders to seek influence, but it is important to note that there are significant exceptions to this trend, with Haidara being the most important—but not the only—one.

One of Mali's most respected and venerable religious leaders is Muhammadu, the Chérif Bouyé of the town of Nioro. Muhammadu belongs to a lineage that can be traced to the Prophet Muhammed. As the only surviving son of Cheik Hamallah (1883–1943) who founded the Hamawiyya Sufi brotherhood, a branch of Tijaniyya, Chérif Bouyé sits at the top of the Sufi hierarchy in Mali (see Soares 1996). In 2018, he chose Aliou Diallo of the Democratic Alliance for Peace as his preferred candidate. This came as a surprise both because Diallo was seen as a minor candidate with little national name recognition and because Chérif Bouyé had supported IBK in 2013. Nonetheless, this was a significant decision. as Chérif Bouyé carries great symbolic weight due to the role his father and his hometown of Nioro played in the history of Islam in Mali, even if today the town is located at the very periphery of the Malian state, along the border to Mauritania. It was in Nioro that Cheik Hamallah—perhaps the most important Sufi mystic in Mali—established his Sufi order before being deported by French colonial powers, apparently for his opposition to their rule, to France where he died in 1943. It was thus a decision of national significance when Chérif Bouyé, as an important religious leader, openly expressed support for a presidential candidate in 2018. Moreover, as Chérif Bouyé had been considered something of a king-maker due to his vocal support for IBK in 2013, his switch of allegiance to Diallo in 2018 was clear evidence of the weakening of support for IBK among religious leaders. With hindsight, this was also a sign of what would come in 2020.

Why did Chérif Bouyé abandon IBK? Was he, like many other Malians, just disappointed with IBK's balance sheet and wanted to show his disapproval by trying to play the role of kingmaker once more? Or did this have less to do with IBK's track record and more with the fact that the Democratic Alliance for Peace candidate was a rich businessman? Or was it perhaps that Diallo promised more, in combination with the fact that he originated from the same area of Mali as Chérif Bouyé? Either way, Bouyé stated his support by publicly calling on his followers to cast their ballot for Diallo. Obviously, Bouyé failed as a kingmaker in 2018. His preferred candidate received few votes and did not make it to the second round. However, this had little negative impact on his legitimacy as a traditional religious leader. After all, he had chosen to support a fresh, new candidate, not yet polluted by the dirty game of politics, as general Malian sentiment considered it. As such, one could say that what looked like a very bold move by Bouyé did not actually come with a high risk.

Whereas Bouyé escaped without any harm to his legitimacy, Imam Dicko's involvement in the 2018 campaign ended in personal embarrassment and an association with 'dirty politics'. Dicko had initially announced that he would follow Chérif Bouyé's advice for which candidate to support, but then he hesitated and declared that he would not instruct his followers in which candidate to vote for. This alone would have posed little problem, but Dicko also made the mistake of indicating support for IBK by stating that some good programmes had been started during his first term in office. In the end, Dicko tried to get out of the mess by declaring a more neutral position, more in line with Haidara's, and he stated in a meeting of opposition leaders that 'we pray God for Mali to be led by the one who will bring peace and tranquillity to the country' (Bøås et al. 2019: 4).

Why Dicko stuck with IBK as long as he did, we can only speculate. However, 2013 was not the first time Dicko and IBK had exchanged favours—they had known each other since the early 2000s, and IBK may have helped Dicko become the chair of the HCIM. While the nature of the alliance between IBK and Dicko is uncertain, what the discussion above illuminates is the increasing political influence of Malian religious leaders. However, it also shows that even if 'appetite comes with eating', those who successfully navigate this game are those able to manage their appetite for politics. What we mean by this is that religious leaders can play the political game, but that doing so can be a double-edged sword, as politics can tarnish their image as frugal men of faith. They can at certain times declare openly their support for one candidate, as the case of Chérif Bouyé shows, but it can come with a cost. And if a religious leader proves incapable of reining in his appetite, he may end up in an embarrassing situation where he has to back-track on previous commitments made.

However, as events in the aftermath of the 2018 election showed, there are several tricks that religious actors can play in the context of insecurity. One of them is to re-establish a support base by finding a popular social conservative rallying cry. Dicko did so by returning to a tried and tested topic—the family law code (see Koné 2018), this time astutely adding the issue of homosexuality.

The aftermath of the 2018 elections and the path to August 2020

Like many of Mali's important religious leaders, Dicko comes from a family of well-known Muslim leaders. However, unlike his predecessors, Dicko attended a Wahhabi Mosque in Bamako before he travelled abroad to continue his religious studies. His first port of call was Mauritania, where he enrolled in two different renowned madrasas. From Mauritania, he continued his education in Saudi Arabia, where he enrolled at the University of Medina—the centre of Wahhabi learning par excellence, where students from all over the world are educated in the Wahhabi doctrine.

Through his studies, Dicko has become an accomplished religious specialist well versed in the Wahhabi doctrine, but he is more than just another Medina candidate well trained in a strict doctrinal reading of the sacred text. Dicko has become a quietist who refuses the violent aspects of jihad and Sharia. More importantly, while most Wahhabi fundamentalists reject everything that is non-Islamic, Dicko argues that what should hold society together in Mali is Islam *and* the ancient pre-Islamic traditions—that it is both social values and traditions that guarantee social order (see Macé 2020). That he is charismatic and an elegant speaker, both in local languages and in French, just adds to his influence.

Returning to Mali from his studies abroad in the early 1980s, Dicko gained prominence in the Association pour l'Unité et le Progrès de l'Islam (AMUPI)[12] before he utilised the fall of the authoritarian Traoré regime in 1991 to claim a new position as a public figure. He began to use his AMUPI position to comment not only on religious issues, but he also blended his sermons with comments on national as well as international political questions. As he levelled above other young religious figures at that time to become a figure of national standing, when the HICM was established in 2002 it was clear that Dicko would serve on its council. Just six years later he became its leader (see Lebovich 2019). His leadership of the HICM also meant that he became increasingly familiar with Chérif Bouyé; in 2009, the two joined together in an alliance that crossed the Sufi–Wahhabi divide when they together opposed reforms to the Malian family law code. This was the first, but it would not be the last, time these two religious leaders joined forces to drum up a political storm. It was at this time that Dicko emerged as an influential power broker and key player in Malian politics.

The original family law code—the Code of Marriage and Guardianship—dates back to 1962, and by the 1990s it was seen as outdated and discriminatory to women by both important donors (including the United States and several European donors) as well as women's associations in Mali, such as the Coordination des Associations et ONG Féminines du Mali (CAFO). The process of attempting to reform the family law code started in 1995. However, nationwide consultations were not held before 2000, and a new draft was not written up until 2002. This draft remained in the drawer for years and was only submitted to the National Assembly in 2009, which approved it after an extraordinary session. The new bill was not a gigantic leap forward, but it had the support of organisations like CAFO and most international donors, who considered it 'progressive' as it favoured gender equality and respect for the rights of women and children (see Koné 2018; Schulz 2010).

However, almost immediately after the new bill was adopted by the National Assembly, it was rejected by Mali's main Islamic organisations on the grounds that the new law was alien to Malian traditions and to the common Islamic social values in the country. The leading opposing organisation was the HCIM with Dicko at its helm, but AMUPI and others also contributed, as did Chérif Bouyé. It was becoming clear that, on the issue of social conservatism, an increasing number of Wahhabi-leaning imams such as Dicko and important Sufi leaders such as Chérif Bouyé were finding common ground. This common ground would be powerful enough to force through a revision of the new legal code in line with the comments made by the religious leaders.

When the question of reforms to the family law code reappeared on the political scene after the 2018 election, Dicko took the opportunity to re-establish an alliance with Chérif Bouyé. The two of them shared similar concerns on this question, but an alliance was also fortuitous, as there were rumours in circulation in Bamako that IBK was planning to take revenge on Chérif Bouyé for opposing him during the elections (see Lebovich 2019). In the end, IBK did not exact revenge, and Dicko and Chérif Bouyé, after organising massive demonstrations, once again succeeded in forcing the government to back down on reforms to the family law code, and in particular on implementing the Dutch-funded sexual education programme. The latter was in fact a small, donor-funded workshop and had nothing to do with the family law code, but Dicko nonetheless used it to his advantage. This was not only a huge personal victory for Dicko, but also a way for him to effectively re-establish himself as a pure and pious defender of the faith and not a religious leader who dabbled in dirty politics. However, what happened next took most observers of Malian affairs by quite some surprise.

On the evening of 19 January 2019, an imam, Abdoul Aziz Yattabaré, was stabbed to death in Bamako when leaving his mosque. Yattabaré was a well-known and influential religious leader, a member of the HICM and the Director of the Islamic Institute of Missira, and as such his murder was a huge shock and a cause of widespread grief. At first nobody was arrested, nor did anyone claim responsibility for his death, precipitating much public speculation. Finally, the government arrested someone they claimed to be a misguided criminal individual. However, a spokesperson for Dicko cast doubt on this account and indicated that Yattabaré had been killed because he condemned homosexuality. This led to a mass rally of over 100,000 people in Bamako on 10 February 2019 led by Dicko and Chérif Bouyé (the latter represented by one of his closest assistants). Three key demands were put forward in this rally: 1) a new law criminalising homosexuality; 2) better governance and security; and 3) for IBK to sack his prime minister, Soumeylou Boubéye Maïga, whom many protesters accused of leading a secret homosexual lobby that was about to gain control of Malian politics.

In the end, Maïga and the government he led were forced to resign in April 2019. The combination of a strong standing on social conservative issues together with the circulation of conspiracy theories with anti-Western sentiments allowed Dicko to effectively expunge the association with dirty politics he had garnered during the 2018 elections. Dicko subsequently re-emerged as the pure and pious defender of that which is 'authentic' Malian and Muslim, and as a defender of the public will and good.

Following up on his success as a real power broker in Malian politics, Dicko continued to present himself to the public as both a charismatic pious religious leader and an ordinary concerned citizen—he claimed it was as the latter that he gave interviews and commented on political affairs. He argued that as a leader of his people he was obliged to be concerned about the situation in Mali, but when asked about political ambitions, he claimed he had none.

These claims did not end the speculations that he had ambitions for the 2023 presidential elections, and when he created his own organisation—la Coordination des Mouvements, Associations, et Sympathisants (CMAS)—in October 2019 after the conclusion of his time as leader of the HICM, this only gave more credibility to this rumour. Dicko's close advisors and assistants (but not the man himself) claimed that the CMAS would not be a political movement, but rather a socio-religious organisation focusing on the 'moralisation of public life', without giving any further indication as to what exactly that meant. Dicko himself, when speaking in public about CMAS, continued to cry out against impunity, endemic corruption, and the fatal mismanagement of the state, while always adding that he was neither a kingmaker nor a president in the making.

POLITICS IN HARD TIMES: RELIGION AND PROTEST

The summer of 2020—the imam versus the president[13]

Even if we are to believe that Dicko was not a president in the making, he proved to be a kingslayer during the summer of 2020. Amidst the backdrop of a governing system based on corruption and cronyism, weak public services, accusations of electoral fraud and mismanagement, and IBK's continued failure to bring an end to intercommunal violence and the jihadi rebellions, public rage on the streets of Bamako hit unprecedented levels when pictures circulated of the president's son (Karim) on a luxury yacht in the Mediterranean, accompanied by beautiful young women wearing tiny bikinis. While the main opposition parties of the 2018 elections tried to ride this wave of popular discontent by jointly organising demonstrations on the streets of Bamako, the voice that brought people out en masse and sustained the street protests over time was that of Dicko. Capitalising on the Friday prayers, Dicko's speeches, which combined an easy-to-understand theological argument with his worldly and catchy critique against public corruption and the regime's general mismanagement of the country, brought increasingly higher numbers out into the streets. The protests soon spread to other large cities, including Sikasso in the south, Kayes in the west, Ségou in the south-central, and even Timbuktu on the fringes of the Sahara.

Dicko's power was also revealed when the Malian opposition organised in the so-called M5 alliance sat down for talks with IBK. Two days prior to this meeting, they had consulted Dicko, as they were aware that they could not strike any ordinary political compromise without his blessing. The talks between the opposition and IBK did not amount to much, but the process further emphasised Dicko's importance. Indeed, the new opposition alliance that materialised—the 5 June Movement—Rally of the Patriotic Forces (M5-RPF)—was in many ways structured around him. The M5-RPF was a heterogenous grouping, and what glued the movement together was their common conviction that IBK had to step down; it is difficult to see anything else that would have united people as disparate as Choguel Kokalla Maïga, Oumar Mariko, and Mountaga Tall, and organisations such as Dicko's CMAS, Clement Dembéle's Platform Against Corruption and Unemployment, and Cheick Oumar Sissoko's Mali Koura Hope.[14]

Still, they felt they could not form this multivarious group without the informal but conspicuous leadership of Imam Dicko.

As Dicko was addressing ever larger and more agitated crowds of protesters in Bamako, it became obvious that a serious confrontation was imminent. This was not just another crisis that IBK could navigate out of by reshuffling the old political elite. Something was about to crack, as Dicko seemed uninterested in the ordinary Malian political compromise of positions and payment in one form or another (see also Thurston 2020b). The final episode of the IBK era came on 10 July 2020, when forceful repressions of street protests in Bamako sanctioned by IBK led to the deaths of 14 protesters, with more than 300 wounded. This came as a shock not only to ordinary citizens, but also to several of the younger military leaders in the army. IBK and his closest allies and advisors became increasingly isolated in and around the presidential palace, and when military units started marching from the garrison town of Kati (15 kilometres from Bamako) on 18 August 2020, no gunshots were fired, and nobody tried to stop them when they arrested IBK and what was left of his government. Soon after, in a speech on national television, a broken but unharmed IBK announced his immediate resignation from office.

The imam had brought down the president, underscoring his position as one of the most powerful men in the country. Our assertion here is not that Dicko played any direct role in the military coup, but that he set the stage for an unconstitutional end to IBK's reign.

Conclusion

As the saga of the Malian crisis and events following the August 2020 coup are still unfolding, concrete conclusions are hard to draw. Nonetheless, what was surprising to many was that Imam Dicko did not seek a position in the transitional government that was established after the coup. Although he never withdrew from the public view, he instead chose a more backseat role for himself, concentrating on CMAS. Is this because he doesn't want to jeopardise his status as a Big Man kingslayer who brought down the president? Or is he simply biding his time until the next presidential election? Most of his communications on this issue are ambiguous, but one key text is his manifesto of 18 February 2021. In it, Dicko (2021) states:

POLITICS IN HARD TIMES: RELIGION AND PROTEST

> Mali is heir to the great empires of Western Sudan, and no one is a prophet in his country. My deep faith in the values of an Islam of tolerance and patriotic love continues to nourish my reason for living and my public discourse. This faith obliges me to speak the truth. … Those who govern must live with the obsession of the general interest of the fight against impunity and intolerance, in favour of equality before the law and in access to public services. No being is perfect either. I have often been mistaken in supporting men who, guided by selfish and materialistic interests, have failed to embody Mali's much-desired recovery. I believed, as I did in 2013, that strong participation in an electoral project could, on its own, bring hope for the resolution of our problems of political and social governance. I was mistaken. I sincerely regret it. I want to bring here the voice of a new emancipatory impulse, of an urgency to act, to think high and true, before history for new horizons, with the hope that the Malian genius will hear the echo of this voice and will raise our destiny at my side, as a pilgrim. It is an act of hope and peace. I have no hidden agenda, no personal ambitions or partisan interests, but I am concerned about the fire that is burning in our cities and in our countryside, and which could, in the long run, destroy 'Living together' in this common home that is Mali.

Here he not only accepts responsibility for his support of IBK in 2013 (not 2018) but also presents himself as a pilgrim of hope and peace, as a concerned but ordinary citizen fearing that his beloved country may be on the brink of collapse. However, towards the end of his manifesto, he concedes ambiguity about his (political) future in Mali, stating:

> Since August 18, 2020, I have left my door wide open. I have listened and observed tirelessly, but the situation seems too serious for me to remain silent. If we do not react now, actively and collectively, the state that governs us is meaningless. The country must be saved. We must act relentlessly with the living forces of the Nation to restore the authority of the State. To do this, I commit myself, freely, to go wherever I can be useful, wherever our citizens feel abandoned. I commit myself to promote dialogue among all to reconcile us. I commit myself to build bridges of exchange between civil and armed actors, to put back at the heart of the concerns, to live together and trust between communities.

This is not the humble pilgrim that speaks, but Dicko the Big Man—a man of exception in a time of exception, the man who can heal and restore Mali. If Dicko can continue to effectively bridge the divide between politics and religion and between his secular and religious followers, he could be a serious contender in future presidential elections, either as the new king himself or as the kingmaker in a Mali of his design. This remains, as with so much else in Mali, to be seen.

Dicko's relationship with the increasingly authoritarian transitional junta has become tense. His fierce opposition to the new constitution of 2023 that passed with a wide margin in a referendum in June 2023 did not please Goïta and his associates. Dicko was opposed to the secular principles of the new constitution, but he also lambasted the military rulers by demanding, 'what kind of rule of law are we talking about in a country where the justice system us used by the military to imprison people?'[15] One week thereafter, Dicko's diplomatic passport was confiscated at the airport in Bamako, very much a sign from the new military rulers that they were not afraid to strip him of his previous privileges. One year later (6 March 2024), Dicko's association CMAS was dissolved by the government, and its co-ordinator Youssouf Daba Diawara was arrested in July that same year. Just a few months thereafter, Dicko found himself the target of a social media blizzard as influencers aligned both with the government and its new partner Russia through the so-called Africa Initiative (see Chapters 9 and 10) unleashed an orchestrated campaign against him after he visited Algeria and was received by the Algerian president. The social media campaign called Dicko a traitor, accusing him of conspiring with rebels, and was clearly meant to undermine his popular legitimacy and bring him to silence (see Monteau 2023; AFP 2024b).

However, as this chapter has shown, this is not the first time Dicko has found himself in a precarious position, and he has proven able to turn the table to his own advantage before, both maintaining and increasing his numbers of followers. This is in effect what Big Man status is all about. The Big Man is accountable to followers, and the flock of followers must be maintained. Failure to do so risks losing Big Man status, hence Dicko must constantly protect his main capital—his credibility as a pious man of faith. In the Malian context, this means he must always 'manage his appetite' for politics. He can play politics, but he must also always be above the political field. If he manages this, Dicko could still come to represent a new fusion of politics and religion in a country caught between traditional Sufi Islam and violent Salafi insurgencies, as the current military regime might not last forever.

9

THE NEW MILITARY REGIMES

ADIEU FRANCE, WELCOME RUSSIA

The military coups in Mali (August 2020), Burkina Faso (September 2022), and Niger (2023) have caused a dramatic shift in the security architecture of Sahel, representing a U-turn of how it used to be. This part of the Sahel used to be the prerogative of former colonial power France. While the relationship between France and its former colonies had been through its ups and downs prior to 2020, what has happened since is unprecedented: France has been asked to leave all three countries. However, in Mali's case this has also included the UN's peacekeeping force, while the EU is just about hanging in there, not really knowing what to do.

The former intimate security collaboration with France has been replaced with Russian military assistance, in the form of supplies of military equipment and fighters from the Wagner Group on the ground. The questions are many, and how this will end remains to be seen. However, as convenient as the new security arrangement with Russia may be for Mali's new military rulers, it is almost unthinkable that Putin's Russia can replace Europe as a trade and development partner. Russia has very little on offer in this regard. Much-needed humanitarian assistance is also not something that Putin can deliver, and certain elements in the Malian army (who understandably cannot be identified) have started to ask questions regarding military supplies from Russia (see also Faulkner et al. 2023).

The challenge for Russia in this regard is of course the war the country is currently waging in Ukraine. Russia needs all its new military hardware for the purpose of its own war. The only weapons and armoury it can spare are old equipment, much of which dates to the Cold War, and while light weapons always are useful, what the Malian army wanted was state-of-the-art heavy weaponry. Instead, Mali is forced to buy drones from Turkey and seek an arrangement with Iran for similar supplies. This suggests that what we may call 'the Russian moment' might not last forever, and it is important to keep in mind that in 2013/14 there was also a French moment in Bamako which was quite like the current show of support for Russia and President Putin.

In 2013, there were no Russian flags on the streets of Bamako. The flags were French, and people saluted President Hollande. In 2013, the French intervention had huge popular support (see Bøås & Torheim 2013), and it only started to wane when the French could not deliver on its promise of peace, security, and the territorial integrity of Mali. Thus, just as France did, Russia too might come to experience the same fall from favour, as there is little reason to believe that they will succeed where France, the UN, and the EU have failed.

Signs that this could happen to Russia just as it happened to France are already starting to emerge. Three events that took place during the autumn of 2024 suggest that Russia's credibility as a security provider has if not lost most its popular appeal, at least taken a serious beating. It started with the battle of Tinzaouaten on 25 July 2024, where a joint Malian army–Wagner Group convoy was ambushed by the new Tuareg rebel coalition called Strategic Framework for the Defence of the People of Azawad (CSP-DPA), before a JNIM battalion moved in to kill as many Malian soldiers and Wagner operatives as possible. While the numbers of deaths are hard to verify, comments on Wagner-friendly blogs suggest that over fifty Wagnerites may have fallen, with a similar number of Malian soldiers (see Meyer & Hoije 2024). This was followed by JNIM's 17 September attack on Bamako which targeted both the gendarmerie and the airport, setting fire to the so-called presidential hangar in the military part of the national airport. The attack lasted for almost 9 hours, and more than 100 people are believed to have been killed (see Lawal 2024). More importantly, it showed that JNIM could strike at the very centre of political power and the regime's Russian allies could do nothing to stop them. It is therefore very likely that the fall of the House of Assad in Syria has sent shockwaves through the new military rulers who have sought regime protection and coup proofing from Moscow. Why? Because they must be thinking, 'If Russia could not protect one of its most priced assets abroad will they be able to assist us if the rebels stand at the gates of the capital?' (see also Lefdal 2024).

In this chapter, we will first discuss the three coups and the regimes currently in power, drawing a line between the regimes in Bamako and Ouagadougou on one side, and the one in Niamey on the other. They are currently firmly in a joint alliance, but there is a generational dimension that separates them. Thereafter, we will look more closely at the Russian presence on the ground, with a particular focus on the Wagner Group, arguing that the latter is best understood as an armed private commercial trading company that operates in niche security markets to achieve mineral concessions.

The new military rulers—neo-patriotism, the Sankara legacy, and opportunism

The relationship between Mali, Niger, and Burkina Faso is more intimate than it ever has been. The new military rulers constantly refer to each other as brothers united in the struggle against both jihadi-Salafi insurgents and the forces of neocolonialism (mainly, but not exclusively, France), but there are also certain important differences between the three regimes in power. Assimi Goïta and Ibrahim Traoré are both relatively young officers who have personal experience from the battlefront, whereas the same cannot be said about the older generation of generals who committed the coup in Niger. This is an important difference, as in the case of the regimes in Bamako and Ouagadougou one can detect ideas and ideology. Both Goïta and Traoré likely see themselves as contemporary reincarnations of Thomas Sankara, while it is hard to imagine that there is a similar revolutionary fervor in the case of their peers in Niamey. The Niger coup was most likely more an internal affair between the generals and President Bazoum.

Goïta and Traoré: the young and radical officers?

Assimi Goïta is the son of an army officer from the circle of Yorosso, on the border with Burkina Faso. Growing up in Bamako's military engineering camp, he followed the path of his father. After getting into to the officers' school and graduating in the early 2000s, Goïta became a platoon commander in 2008 and was stationed in northern Mali. In charge of a mobile battle group, his first mission was to try to neutralise traffickers and armed groups. This was the beginning of nearly 15 years of combat experience in Gao, Kidal, and Timbuktu. In 2015, following the attack on the Radisson Blu in Bamako, he was placed in charge of coordinating 'special operations' within the Ministry of Defence. Just before the August 2020 coup, he was leading the Special Forces in central Mali.

Goïta is not the great communicator of the regime that he leads; the role of narrator of the story the new government in Mali wishes to tell about itself has been given to prime minister Choguel Kokalla Maïga (until he was removed) and to foreign minister Abdoulaye Diop. They are the ones who have shocked France, the UN, the EU, and ECOWAS with their statements about fighting neocolonialism and a new Mali that's prepared to say no to the former colonial power and those they accuse of acting on France's behalf. Goïta seems to prefer to remain in the shadows while his prime minister and foreign minister speak to the Malian masses about sovereignty and dignity. To what extent Goïta himself holds this ideology is uncertain, but he seems determined not to be dictated to by anybody.

Concerning Mali's turn to Russia, Goïta was already in favour of seeking the support of Moscow, but the real Russophile in the regime is the Minister of Defence Sadio Camara, who studied at the Moscow War College. It was Camara who approached the Russians and was responsible for the deal with both Moscow and Wagner.

While the turn to Moscow has not had much of an impact on the war front, Goïta's military regime is of a completely different calibre than that of Captain Sanogo in 2012. After the coup of 2012, the army basically collapsed. This was not the case this time. Command and control lines have been in operation, and even the departure of Operation Barkhane and MINUSMA has not had much of an impact. The line between territory fully controlled by the government and the terrain where the jihadi insurgents are present (although not necessarily in control) is still drawn somewhere between Mopti and Segou. Thus, while Goïta and his men cannot claim victory, they have been able to hold their ground and have a few scalps under their belts, such as the return of the Malian army to Kidal in the north in November 2023. We will focus more closely on the regime's rhetoric in Chapter 10, but with the approval of the new constitution in July 2023 which enhances the power of the president and the armed forces, Assimi Goïta is well placed to stand for election if the transition ends in 2027.

Ibrahim Traoré of Burkina Faso, who came into power in the coup that ousted President Paul-Henri Damiba, has some of the same background as Assimi Goïta. He is an officer, but not a general, and like Goïta he has also has combat experience from the battlefront against the jihadi insurgents. Traoré first studied geology before he joined the Burkinabè army in 2009, where he rose through the ranks and eventually became a captain. As one of several among a group of young officers who were becoming increasingly dissatisfied with what they saw as the mismanagement by elected government of the war against the insurgents, Traoré supported the coup in January 2022 which brought General Damiba to power. However, it did not take long before the junior officers were just as frustrated with Damiba, and in late September the same year they overthrew Damiba and Traoré was installed as the transitional president of the state.

As president, Traoré has maintained the behaviour for which he had already been known before rising to power. He keeps a tight control of his official communications, but his presidency has also increasingly spread pro-government propaganda via Burkinabè traditional media and social media. Politically, Sophie Douce of *Le Monde* (2023) describes Traoré as influenced by Marxism and Pan-Africanism, and this is also visible in the government's official communications through news and reports made public in the traditional press as well as on social media. The regime is media savvy, but the room for independent journalism has been severely constrained and several prominent journalists has been forced to leave the country.

In February 2023, Traoré's government expelled the French forces assisting in fighting the insurgency from Burkina Faso. He subsequently declared that 'we really want to look at other horizons, because we want win-win partnerships' (see France 24 2023). To replace French military support, Traoré forged closer ties with Turkey and Russia. At the same time, Traoré declared a 'general mobilisation' of the population to support the military, as rebel forces continued to increase the frequency of their attacks. The general mobilisation of the so-called Volunteers for the Defence of the Homeland (VDF) has not had much impact on the battle against the jihadi insurgents, but here as elsewhere it has added another element of insecurity. The reason for this is that weapons distributed to local militia groups are not only being used for local community protection against the jihadi insurgents, but also to settle scores between local communities—particularly between farming and pastoralist communities, with the latter at times seeking the protection of the jihadi insurgents. Still, Traoré continues to pledge in public that he will reconquer all rebel-held areas, that there will be no negotiations until the insurgency had been greatly weakened, and that elections cannot be held until the insurgents are pushed back and the security situation improved.

With little progress on the war front, Traoré found himself faced with the same frustration in army circles as he himself had once directed at the previous regime. Indeed, on 26 September 2023, elements of the military tried unsuccessfully to overthrow Traoré. While the coup failed, Traoré immediately turned to Russia and the Wagner Group for protection (see Roger 2023). Thus, while no contract seems to have been made regarding Wagner operatives joining the battle against the insurgents, President Traoré and his closest circles—which include his brother and special advisor, Inoussa Traoré—have concluded that there are elements in the army that cannot be trusted, and coup proofing by enlisting Wagner operatives responsible for the president's security is their best option. The sense of insecurity that Traoré may have sensed about elements in the army did not prevent him in May 2024 from having his movement, the Patriotic Movement for Safeguard and Restoration, extend military rule in Burkina Faso by five years (i.e. to 2029), thus allowing Traoré to contest the next presidential elections if they take place according to this timetable.

What is clear both in Mali and Burkina Faso is that the new leaders are determined to rule for a long time. Whether they succeed in this matter will depend on whether they are able to deliver on some of the promises they made to their young supporters in the streets of the capitals and some other larger cities (see Chapter 10).

Bazoum and the generals—elite preservation that had to be justified?

Not counting the most recent one, Niger has undergone four military coups since the country gained independence from France in 1960, with the fourth happening in 2010. In between, there were also several coup attempts, the most recent in 2021 when military dissidents tried to seize the presidential palace two days before the inauguration of president-elect Bazoum.

Several reasons for the July coup have been discussed, ranging from rising costs of living to government incompetence, to disagreements between Bazoum and his generals concerning ECOWAS's hard stance on the military governments in Mali and Burkina Faso and joint military operations between Niger and Mali. The latter may have played a role, but the most likely trigger were Bazoum's plans to replace the head of the presidential guard, General Abdourahmane Tchiani.

When Issoufou left the presidency, Bazoum was believed to be his chosen successor. The relationship between Bazoum and Issoufou dates to their early years as radical student activists, but towards the end of Issoufou's presidency the trust between them could not have been too solid. Issoufou left the presidency to Bazoum, but he also left him with a government, administration, and military elite more loyal to Issoufou than to Bazoum.[1]

Bazoum wanted to change this. He wanted to bring in trustworthy people who would be loyal to him. Tchiani and the other military leaders of the coup may have believed that their best bet was a preemptive strike against Bazoum. They would take him before he could take them, and they knew that they could count on support from the new military leaders in Mali and Burkina Faso. Neither Goïta nor Traoré was fond of Bazoum, as he had constantly criticised them and argued in favour of a quick return to democratic rule for Niger's neighbours. Goïta and Traoré had also showed that it was possible to get away with military coups. It was possible to withstand international pressure, and in the narratives about fighting neocolonial forces (i.e. France and its allies) and restoring the sovereignty and dignity of the people of the Sahel, Tchiani and the other generals involved in the coup had a ready-made script that they could use to justify and legitimise the coup.

That Niger had become France's hub for its military operations in the Sahel following its expulsion from Mali and Burkina Faso—and Bazoum being described in international media as the one remaining pro-Western leader in the Sahel—was an advantage for Tchiani and his compatriots. As anti-French sentiment was rising among the youths of Niamey, this only made it easier to justify the coup and gain popular traction where it mattered most, namely in the capital. Whether Tchiani and company believe in their own rhetoric is certainly questionable, as none of them showed any interest in this field of radical populist politics prior to the coup. Most likely, they felt threatened by Bazoum and used the opportunity to jump on the bandwagon of the narratives produced in Bamako.

While the sincerity of their adherence to the new ideology of neo-patriotism, with its focus on fighting neocolonialism and restoring sovereignty and dignity, can be questioned, Tchiani and his collaborators have certainly been eager to rid Niger of Western forces—and not only France, but the United States as well. Just three months after France completed the withdrawal of its forces in late December 2023, Niger's new rulers also cancelled the defence agreement with the United States that allowed the Americans drone bases in Agadez (see Turse 2024).

The road to Moscow

The military coups in Mali, Niger, and Burkina Faso were a challenge for international partners as it was. However, they soon became yet another thorn in the side of the already complicated relationship between the West and the Sahel, as the return of the military to the political arena was based on a surge in popular discontent against France and its counter-insurgency Operations Barkhane and Takouba.

THE NEW MILITARY REGIMES

Increasingly, the objectives and aims of the former colonial power France and the European military coalitions under French leadership have been critically scrutinised, while the new military rulers have not been met with the same critique. For example, Malian leaders have escaped this by accusing France of betraying Mali and fanning the flames of conflict rather than extinguishing them. France, in an attempt to maintain its security co-operation with Mali, warned that a deal between the regime in Bamako and the Wagner Group represented a red line. However, this backfired completely. Instead of bringing Mali back into the fold of French external security collaboration, verbal hostilities on both sides led to a withdrawal of Operation Barkhane, as well as economic sanctions being placed on Mali by the EU, UK, and United States. Thus, in a dramatic turnaround of events and allegiance, the last French soldier left Mali in August 2022, abandoning a military mission that it had led since 2013. In Burkina Faso, the Traoré regime announced in January 2023 that it would terminate its 2018 security arrangements with France. The French ambassador to Burkina Faso was also asked to leave the country. Following this, Burkina Faso also entered into closer co-operation with the Wagner Group (Tamkin 2023). A similar scenario soon followed in Niger, and the last French soldiers left the country by the end of December 2023.

Russian flags and pictures of Putin had already been visible on the streets of Bamako and Ouagadougou a few years prior to the French departure. After Operation Barkhane left Mali, Russian military influence via the Wagner Group increased, and so did the military deals between Moscow and Bamako. The outcome has been several claims that Putin and his chief strategists have managed to wrestle Mali, and lately also Burkina Faso and Niger, away from Western influence to become allies of Moscow.

While most of us who visited the Sahel during this period observed an increased Russian presence on the ground along with protesters carrying Russian flags and cries of slogans in support of Putin, I am also aware that the frustration and anger with the France and the West did not materialise out of nowhere. It had been growing for quite some time.

The background for this is that while international engagement with Mali had reached an all-time high between 2013 and 2020, this did not correspond with any kind of improvement on the ground. The battle against jihadi insurgents continued unabated, and living conditions were just as bad as before. The battle front moved closer to Bamako, and elite corruption reached new heights. Additionally, evidence suggests that the relationship between the Malian and French militaries may have been soured for a long time, partly due to what was locally perceived as an arrogant and paternalistic attitude by the French forces (Tull 2019).

The challenge is that much of what has been written tends to assume that, in a fragile state like Mali, external actors decide foreign policy outcomes—'France left a vacuum which was exploited by Russia'—as if the Malian regime had nothing to say, no agency. Furthermore, there are assumptions that Russia, through the Wagner Group, has actively been trying to drum up anti-French/Western sentiments. This is correct. The Wagner Group and more recently the Russia funded Africa Initiative have actively promoted alternative narratives through social media campaigns led by important African influencers such as Franco-Beninese influencer Kémi Séba. Séba has around 1.3 million followers on Facebook, 307,000 followers on Instagram, and 233,000 subscribers to his YouTube channel. Moreover, there is African Initiative's latest release, an online game called African Dawn. Inspired by the Hearts of Iron saga, the aim is to create a sovereign Sahel confederation, and players can take on the role of Captain Ibrahim Traoré of Burkina Faso, President Goïta of Mali, or even President Putin in their struggle to limit the influence and abuses of neocolonial powers (Olivier 2024).

The social media campaigns have been massive, though we do not know the extent to which they have played a significant role, and we should be careful to jump to conclusions. What we do know from previous research is that misinformation and fake news campaigns work best when they resonate with an audience (Bøås & Dunn 2013; Buzan 1983; Buzan et al. 1998). This happens either when people believe the narratives that such campaigns present because they have lost trust in their government or because they use them to achieve another objective. No matter what the case is, one should neither ignore nor underestimate that there is also an African agency at play here (see Chapter 10).

THE NEW MILITARY REGIMES

The Wagner Group in the Sahel

While there has been a lot of speculation and anecdotal evidence concerning the activities of the Wagner Group in Mali, the only thing we can say for sure is that results have been at best mixed, and at worst, a failure. But this is not shown in the 2023 Mali-Mètre survey, as this reports public opinion as being in favour of the alignment to Moscow. Measured against the regime's objective to restore the state's territorial control, Wagner's mercenaries have been unsuccessful in their military action against the jihadi insurgents. This means that, while we certainly do not deny the Wagner Group's ability to conduct human rights abuses, their real track record on the battlefield may be more hype than reality. However, the war effort may not be the only reason Bamako's regime hired Wagner. Regime survival and protection against coups and popular uprisings is another possible motive.

The main challenge is that so many of the activities of this group are shadowlike and full of secrecy, to the extent that even the number of Wagner operatives present in Mali is unknown: some say there are as many as 1,400 soldiers, others report much less. One reason for this discrepancy could be the failure to understand the way Wagner operates. It is a business that also hires locally, and in Mali people have started to separate between 'white Wagnerians' and 'black Wagnerians', where the latter come from other countries in the region where Wagner is present, such as the Central African Republic, but also from Chad, with some even recruited locally in Mali. The path to understanding Wagner may therefore be to attempt to understand its business model

The Wagner business model

If we try to cut through all the hyperbole that surrounds the Wagner Group and assume a more sober approach to its activities in Africa, we can conclude the following. In Africa, Wagner is first and foremost a private security company. In this regard, it is not that different from the similar firms from the United States, such as Blackwater or Military Personnel Resources Incorporated, or the South Africa firm Executive Outcomes that was led by Eben Barlow (see Singer 2003). Wagner in Africa is a commercial entity that works in accordance with contract and hires its men at arms in accordance with contracts. It must pay its men, and as its operations are costly it must make money. The main difference between Wagner and the other companies mentioned above is that Wagner's home base is in an authoritarian state without a free press. It is important to remember that what Blackwater did in Iraq was eventually exposed by investigative journalism, which led to Congress hearings and court cases (see Johnston 2009). This is not something that Wagner ever has to fear in Russia as a result of its activities in Africa.

Wagner operates in Africa and the Sahel through contracts with governments. The only known exception is its deal with General Haftar in Libya. The business model is, however, sophisticated. Revenue from the host government in accordance with the contract is certainly important for Wagner in Africa, but the contract is just the first step to achieve something else. What Wagner really seeks is mineral concessions. They have achieved this with considerable success in the Central African Republic, and this is clearly their ambition in Mali, Niger, and Burkina Faso as well. Wagner has its own department of geologists, and we know that they have been on the ground in Mali, but so far with limited success. The reason for this is simply that almost all the easy-to-access gold deposits in the southern parts of Mali are already under concessions given to companies from Canada, France, and Switzerland, and so far the Goïta government has not dared to withdraw these concessions or nationalise the mines. The newly discovered gold deposits that for the time being are alluvial, meaning they are explored by artisanal miners, are either under the control of the jihadi insurgents or not controlled by anybody. This means that if Wagner intends to utilise some of these, the group would have to fight its way to them and hold them. For the time being, this seems to be beyond the capacity of Wagner in Mali, and it seems also to be the case of Burkina Faso, where Wagner's main task is to offer protection and coup proofing to Traoré and his closest associates.

This is important because it means that Wagner's Sahel operations cannot be as profitable as the group had hoped when it started them. They have yet not been able to recreate the way that they operate in Central African Republic in Mali and its neighbours. It has not been able to build the same business conglomerate, where revenue from gold and diamond extraction has been reinvested into several other businesses, ranging from timber and agriculture to social media, a brewery, and a local vodka distillery. It is here we see the full scale of Wagner (ex-)leader Yevgeny Prigozhin's vision of a private military company organised as a fully armed trading company, something the world has not seen since the British East India Company. This was well beyond the dreams of even Eben Barlow of South African Executive Outcomes (see Harding 1997). He envisioned a holding company, Plaza 109 Ltd, that would sell several different services, but never that he and his men would hold mineral concessions, run social media factories, and make beer and hard liquor.

While Wagner's profit from Mali, Niger, and Burkina Faso may be relatively small compared to what they have been making elsewhere (e.g. in the Central African Republic), the group has dug in. They still have the support of Kremlin, and they have a long-term focus.

The death of Prigozhin—not the end of Wagner Africa

There was great ado and speculation made about the future of Wagner's Africa operations after the death of Prigozhin on 23 August 2023 (see, e.g., Olivier 2024). Would it end, be taken over by other figures in the Kremlin, or simply cease to exist? With hindsight, not much seems to have happened. Yes, it is now at times referred to as the Russian Africa Corps, but operations, businesses, the social media factor in Bangui, and even key personnel are all still in place.

The immediate period after the death of Prigozhin was full of rumours and confusion. Key African allies who had met Prigozhin and made deals with him were concerned, and some of the key Wagner operatives on the ground in the Sahel vanished, if not from the region, at least from visibility. This did not last very long. Russian Foreign Minister Sergey Lavrov went out of the way to assure African leaders who had made deals with Wagner that nothing had changed and operations would continue as normal. Key Wagner operatives started to make themselves visible again in Bangui and Bamako, and even if there still is some confusion about whether the name change to Russian Africa Corps has stuck, for all practical purposes it is still Wagner. This was also evident when the Malian army marched into

Kidal in mid-November 2023, and one of the first pictures that emerged displayed cloth with Wagner symbols on them.

Wagner, or at least the business model that Prigozhin established, is clearly still around. Military governments and leaders who worry about both coups and jihadist insurgencies will continue to make use of the services of Wagner and similar Russian agents and enterprises, and the group may still be able to expand their businesses in Mali, Niger, and Burkina Faso which would give them the same attachment to the local political economy as what they have achieved in the Central African Republic. Where this will end remains to be seen, but rulers' turn to Moscow and their reliance on a private security company such as Wagner adds yet another component to the storm brewing. In that regard, it is interesting to note that JNIM's Iyad Ag Ghaly used almost precisely the same words as US Foreign Minister Anthony Blinken when he denounced the Wagner Group and declared jihad against them, not as a crusader force, but as an international criminal enterprise (see Roger 2023).

10

MILITARY RULERS AND NEO-PATRIOTISM

BRANDING AND MYTHMAKING

The World Bank (2022) presents the situation in Mali as bleak, with sluggish economic growth and extreme poverty levels that continue to increase due to high inflation, and it describes the state's very social contract as 'fraying' as Mali struggles to protect its citizens and deliver services. This damning critique of the ruling regime stands in stark contrast to how most Malians seem to think about their country's situation. Survey data from the Afrobarometer (2023) indicate that the population is much more satisfied with the unelected Goïta regime that came to power unconstitutionally in August 2020 than with the previous democratically elected government of IBK that was supported by France, the UN, the EU, ECOWAS, and several other bilateral donors. Data from the Mali-Mètre (Friedrich-Ebert-Stiftung 2024) shows that Goïta has an approval rating (85 per cent) that would be the envy of any political leader in a country under democratic rule. This is a riddle that seems hard to explain, as, objectively speaking, the security situation has worsened for most people in Mali since the 2020 coup. Still, the population seem very satisfied with their leader.

The question to ask, then, is whether people in Mali simply do not understand how precarious their situation is or whether it is the opposite, that the mainstream understanding of the social contract as a fiscal arrangement between the population and the state is not able to capture what is happening in Mali. We argue that it is the latter that is the case. The sovereignty discourse that seems to be going on repeat every time the main narrators of the regime (i.e. Prime Minister Maïga and Foreign Minister Diop) speak may sound unconvincing to an international audience when it is laid out in press conferences or on a global podium, such as the UN General Assembly, but then we forget who their target audience is. It is not us or the international community at large, but Malians. And here sovereignty is not a theoretical question but translates as dignity.

This suggests that coming into power as Goïta has done on the backbone of failed international interventions can be a resource—a resource that his regime has utilised to its full potential. Mali thus exemplifies the challenges of 'liberal' international state-building and security interventions, like the challenges international interventions have faced in the Democratic Republic of Congo, Somalia, and Afghanistan, where the international community has failed to address an ever-expanding system of violence. The Malian regime did not create the public debates about fighting the forces of neocolonialism (e.g. France), MINUSMA's lack of progress, and reclaiming sovereignty in order to restore the dignity of Mali and Malians, as all of this predates the current military rulers' march to power in August 2020. However, they have used it very cleverly to the extent that they have created a new multiverse of the history of Mali as both ancient and glorified, as well as, in the contemporary era, undignified, weak, and the client of the former colonial power France. This was the case until Goïta came about to be a 'man of exception' who would lead his people into a new age for Mali. An age of dignity for which sacrifices must be made until the new Mali ultimately reconnects with the golden age of Sunjata—with Goïta standing in for the mythical lion king of the legendary Mali empire of the Malinke people in the twelfth century (see Condé & Conrad 2004). To maintain this narrative, culprits were needed, and pointing fingers in directions that would be convincing to the Malian population was not difficult. As aiming at birds on a wire, the regime focused the social frustrations that existed among the population against both France, the former colonial power and the lead country in the international intervention, as well as the UN, but perhaps more surprisingly also against ECOWAS, which the Goïta regime described as a 'puppet' of former colonial powers and an arrangement of disintegration (see Peltier 2024).

To explain how this has come about, we will in this section bring to the fore an elaboration of our conceptual argument that the symbolic resources available to rulers of what we so often define as 'fragile states' should not be underestimated.[1] These rulers may have a good grip on the multiverse of time and space that coexists in a fragmented polity where parts of the population have a nostalgia for a past, preferably one that mirrors itself in contemporary circumstances. In this section, we conduct a brief tour of the 10 years of failed international interventions in Mali, showing how this represents a huge repertoire of narrative resources that the regime can utilise to its own advantage. Based on this, we provide an analysis as to how the regime, through its own narratives and those of its supporters, has cunningly established a new social contract between itself and the population which places the primary focus on dignity and thereby the impetus to seek the 'political kingdom', as Nkrumah once claimed, arguing that the rest would follow (see Mazrui & Wondji 1993).

States of exception and men of exception—making myths in weak states

While Mali is officially one of the poorest countries in the world, as it sits close to the bottom of the UNDP's Human Development Index (2022), the country is rich in resources. It has plenty of gold and quite unnoticed it has become the second or third largest African exporter of this commodity. But Mali also has other resources of an intangible kind. Just the names of cities like Gao and Timbuktu bring to the fore the fantasy of a glorified, ancient past. Visions of the desert bring about tales of noble warriors, and the hunter guilds—the dozo—of the Bambara, Songhay, and Dogon groups (see Chapter 7) are not yet a thing of the past but part and parcel of social and economic life. As Hellweg's (2011) elegant study of the Benkadi Movement of Côte d'Ivoire shows, the hunter—the dozo, in the case of Mali—is both respected and feared. He (and the hero of these hunter myths is always a 'he') is a dual character of saviour, sacrifice, and madness.

He is an agent of disequilibrium—a man of exception, in a state of exception (Agamben 2005; Bøås 2015a), who under dire circumstances can save his community but also possibly destroy it.

This theme is modern and ancient at the same time, but as a narrative it is founded in the Sunjata—the epic story from the twelfth century that almost everybody in Mali knows and can relate to. The Sunjata in brief is an epic poem of the Malinke people that tells the story of the hero Sunjata Keita (who supposedly died in 1255), the founder of the Mali Empire. As the tale goes, Maghan Kon Fatta (Maghan 'the Handsome') was a Mandinka king who one day received a soothsaying hunter at his court. The hunter predicted that if Maghan married an ugly woman, she would give him a son who one day would become a mighty king. Maghan was already married and had a son, Dankaran. However, when two Traoré hunters from the Do kingdom presented him an ugly, hunchbacked woman named Sogolon, he remembered the prophecy and married her. She soon gave birth to a son, Sunjata Keita, who in his childhood was unable to walk. When Maghan died (around the year of 1224), his first son, Dankaran, assumed the throne despite Maghan's wishes that the prophecy should be respected. Sunjata and his mother suffered the scorn of the new king and had to escape into exile to the Mema Kingdom.

While living in the Mema Kingdom, Sundiata began to grow 'as strong as a lion', and he fought with the greatest general of the Mema people, Moussa Tounkara. Sundiata became such a great warrior that he was made heir to the Mema throne. However, his mother urged him to 'fulfil his destiny' and return home to become king. Meanwhile, another king attacked the Malinke kingdom, and as Dankaran fled in panic the desperate Malinke sent for Sunjata to return from exile. He returned, fought the enemy successfully, and was later crowned as 'king of kings'—the 'lion king'—and became the first ruler of the Mali Empire. Sunjata re-organised the empire, presenting the nobles at his coronation with a new oral constitution known as the Kouroukan Fouga, a model for rule that would guide his empire to greatness (see Condé & Conrad 2004).

The question is how is this relevant to the current situation in Mali and Goïta's surprisingly high approval ratings? We argue that acknowledging the current relevance of this foundational myth of Mali is necessary if we are to understand what type of powerful resources the Goïta regime has at its disposal. They know this history, the Malian population knows this history, and the regime's key spokespersons, such as Foreign Minister Diop, have several times referred to Sunjata's Kouroukan Fouga. Malians believe that they live in a state of exception, and for good reason. Mali is a state made up of a threatened, oppressed, and fragmented polity, much the same as the one from which the Malinke people pleaded with Sunjata to return home to be their saviour.

In an environment of chaos, war, confusion, and despair where the institutional environment of the state is decaying, what the story needs is the hunter–warrior hero, the agent of disequilibrium who can not only save but re-calibrate society in an orderly and just manner, bringing back not only sovereignty but dignity to his people, as long as they are willing to make the same necessary sacrifices as he does.

Here it is worth recalling that the dozo myth is also built on the ultimate sacrifice, such as the legend of Manimory, the mythical father of the dozo supposedly sacrificed both his first wife and the son of his second wife before he disappeared in the bush, evaporating into thin air (Hellweg 2011). Completely violating the social norms of a father and husband, the original dozo is dangerous, an agent of disequilibrium, as he operates on the very fringes of normality. But under a state of exception, a people who need to become exceptional must seek a man of exception—someone like Goïta, modern like Thomas Sankara, immortal like Sunjata—thus underlining Agamben's point that 'being outside and yet belonging is the very essence' of exceptionality (see Agamben 2005: 35). In a context of hybridity like this one, where the very nature of politics is shapeshifting in nature (see Geertz 2004), statehood is negotiated in ways that do not necessarily resemble the ideal picture of the Weberian state. As Hagmann and Peclard (2010: 5) argue, 'states are not only the product and realm of bureaucrats, policies, and institutions, but also of imageries, symbols, and discourses'. Thus, in parallel to material resources, political actors utilise symbolic resources, drawing on social and cultural repertoires to further their interest, mobilise support, and give social meaning to their actions.

The combination of material resources—such as bureaucratic capacities, access to state resources, and control over physical violence—with symbolic resources suggests that rulers of 'fragile states' may not necessarily always reign over choiceless states (see Mkandawire 1999; Hagmann & Peclard 2010) but rather have a powerful repertoire to tap into, if they can create a narrative that their people believe in, which can potentially legitimise a turn towards autocracy.

As the analysis moves forward, it aims to show that the social contract between rulers and subjects that the Goïta regime tries to establish is far from the standard social contract which a political economy textbook would conceptualise as a set of implicit or explicit agreements between individuals and a sovereign authority. Thus, an example of a 'fiscal contract' would be that citizens pay taxes in return for public services and influence over public policy (Brautigam et al. 2008). The more dependent a government is on the prosperity of its taxpayers, the stronger incentives it has to promote economic growth. In turn, taxpayers have stronger incentives to hold the government to account if it underperforms. On this basis, bargaining over taxation between taxpayers and the government is central to the development of a social contract (Fjeldstad 2014). However, this Western notion of a state–citizens social contract struggles to capture the diversity and nuances of state–society relations in non-Western contexts (see Loewe et al. 2021; Hickey & King 2016).

First, social contracts are not one size fits all, as their content can be based on diverse exchanges between government and society (Loewe et al. 2021). Second, weak states might have multiple and overlapping social contracts existing simultaneously at different levels, involving both state and non-state actors vying for influence over various societal groups (Leonard & Samantar 2011; Cloutier et al. 2022). Thus, social contracts can be shaped by alternative logics beyond fiscal exchange, drawing on various resources (material or symbolic) between the government or non-state actors and various segments of society (Makovicky & Smith 2020). In Mali, large parts of society may tolerate social and economic hardships in exchange for regaining long-lost national sovereignty and dignity.

This, social contract, built on the long-term goal of restored pride may outweigh the prospects of a more economically rational fiscal contract. After all, in Mali, as in other states in West Africa, people can often be heard saying, 'there is no progress without hardship' (see Bledsoe 1990). In sum, what this adds up to is an alternative social contract that does not necessarily have to include every group in society. It has come into being and evolved quickly through repeated discursive interaction between the regime in power and its support groups, combined with the regime's use of coercive means to supress political opponents and close civic spaces. Under this type of social contract, the ruler and the regime reclaim sovereignty while the people's part of the bargain is to show their support in the streets and on social media, and to accept the rules made by the regime. Obviously, one might ask how long a social contract made almost solely on symbolic resources and coercion can last, as opposed to one built on economic development and improving livelihoods. However, in the case of Mali, it has held firm since 2020 and shows no sign of evaporating anytime soon. Eventually it will weaken if it cannot be transformed, but the creation and scapegoating of new enemies of Mali's quest for sovereignty can most likely maintain in it for a good while.

Mali—10 years of an ill-fated international intervention

As this volume has already documented, since the Sahel crisis erupted in Mali in 2012, a plethora of various international interventions have attempted to promote security, stability, and peace in Mali. Among them have been several international security providers ranging from ECOWAS, the AU, the EU, the UN, and France (see Osland & Erstad 2020).

The fall of Gaddafi in 2011 in Libya triggered a chain reaction in Mali. An influx of weapons and fighters, primarily Tuareg soldiers returning from Libya, flared up low-intensity conflict in the north in 2012. This emboldened a mix of secessionist and jihadist groups who swiftly conquered northern cities like Gao and Timbuktu, threatening to move towards Mali's capital Bamako. At the same time, the Malian army, dissatisfied with the management of the armed forces, mutinied and toppled the government of Amadou Toumani Tourè (a.k.a. ATT).

As the security situation rapidly deteriorated, Mali became the host of several external interventions. At the request of Mali's transitional government, the international community, led by France, intervened militarily with Operation Serval. This intervention successfully recaptured rebel-held cities, but the fight against the insurgencies was far from over. To sustain the effort and stabilise the new democratically elected regime of President Ibrahim Boubacar Keita that came into power in 2013, France established Operation Barkhane in 2014, deploying a significant force of 5,100 soldiers.

Recognising a need for a broader approach, the international community also established MINUSMA. The UN peacekeeping mission, with around 15,000 personnel, became the largest of its kind globally. Additionally, the EU launched a training mission to strengthen Malian security forces (the EUTM) and another one to boost civilian capacity (the EUCAP Sahel). Regionally, the Sahelian states, with French support, formed the G5 Sahel in 2014, which from 2017 was mandated to create a force of 5,000 military personnel to coordinate and counter terrorism across the regions.

Despite these multi-faceted interventions, critical studies argued that their emphasis on state-security prioritising counter-insurgency operations—particularly against jihadist groups seen as 'global threats'—neglected underlying local grievances (see, for example, Osland & Erstad 2020; Bøås 2019). This state-centric approach has allowed these grievances to fester, contributing to renewed conflict and persistent insecurity (Raleigh et al. 2021).

The failure of FAMA and the international interventions that followed Operation Serval to contain the insurgencies baffled the Malian population. The various jihadist insurgent groups skilfully capitalised on local grievances towards the state and between different communities in the north and centre. By 2015, the jihadist group Katiba Macina had taken control of the rural areas of Mopti in central Mali (Bøås 2015a; Raleigh et al. 2021). In the next years, the insurgencies spread to Burkina Faso, which was weakened from recent internal political struggles and regime change (Haavik et al. 2022), and to Tillabéri, the western region of Niger by appropriating local grievances (Bøås et al. 2020). Raleigh, Nsaibia, and Dowd (2021) show that while French counter-insurgency operations eliminated several important jihadist commanders in 2018, which was the most successful year since 2014, the jihadist groups simultaneously greatly expanded their operations and influence in the region.

MILITARY RULERS AND NEO-PATRIOTISM

The international interventions were massive, but as the security situation continued to deteriorate and large-scale corruption continued unabated, the public mood in Bamako and other larger cities turned increasingly hostile. Large-scale demonstrations against the Keita government that had been re-elected in 2018 became a regular phenomenon. In August 2020, public anger in Bamako had a reached boiling point, and as the regime was about to fall, a group of younger officers led by Goïta took control over the situation and formed a transitional government with some civilian representatives (see Chapter 8).

Following the second coup in 2021 that strengthened the military's position in the transitional government, all but the EU interventions ceased to operate within two years. Most notable were the exit of French soldiers in 2022 and the withdrawal of MINUSMA in 2023. The junta severed Mali's ties with France and found a new security partner in the Wagner Group (now officially renamed Africa Corps under the authority of the Russian Ministry of Defence after its founder, Prigozhin, was killed), and it founded the AoSS together with Burkina Faso and Niger.

The failure of 10 years of ill-fated international interventions, and the deep-seated anger this created in many Malians, has become an essential resource for the current military rulers to mobilise political support. It is, however, important to understand that the grievances that they represent are very real, and the discourse of sovereignty and dignity that they gave rise to was not created by the military rulers nor by their newfound Russian allies. They existed beforehand, but the Goïta regime has used them well for its own purpose.

Pro-regime/anti-intervention discourses

The combination of a Malian population grown weary of many years of insecurity, failed military interventions, and Malian–Russian (dis)information campaigns that encouraged and exacerbated the social frustrations that already existed created the basis for popular support to challenge President Keita and his regime's external supporters (ICG 2023). As democracy in Mali has failed to deliver not only security and development, but also a renewal of the political system to make it more transparent and less corrupt, the young officers around Goïta saw the opportunity to promote the need for 'strong men' to deal with security threats and reclaim Mali's sovereignty and dignity. It is this discourse of reconquering a national sovereignty hitherto undermined by insurgents, previous security partners, and regional organisations influenced by what the regime calls 'hostile countries' that has contributed to the remarkably robust and long-lasting political support for the military rulers. They have been in power for three and a half years and the situation has not improved, but their approval rating remains extremely high, indicating the development of a social contract legitimising the junta's rule among large segments of the Malian population.

Reclaiming Mali's dignity through the platform of the UN

Leading up to the first coup, criticism was not only directed at Keita's government, but also at France and the UN, spearheaded by the M5 alliance where the influential Imam Malam Dicko played a key role (Asala 2020). He and the M5 alliance took the lead in street-based opposition against the Keita government from which the current prime minister, Choguel Maïga, emerged. Furthermore, non-governmental organisations (NGOs) like *Urgences Panafricanistes* and smaller protest movements like *Yèrèwolo Debout sur les Remparts* aimed to expel the French and pave the way for the Russians. Likewise, Yèrèwolo perceived MINUSMA as 'an occupying force, which revives and maintains fear, ethnic divisions and mistrust between communities in Mali' (Haidara 2022). Consequently, when the palace coup in 2021 brought several already strained international relationships to their breaking point, the military regime could tap into existing discourses surrounding the increasingly unpopular foreign military interventions.

As to anti-intervention discourses, the UN has been one of the preferred venues for the Malian government to demonstrate its ambitions to restore the sovereignty of Mali and reclaim the dignity of the Malian people. This is evident in how speeches at the UN General Assembly have clearly been aimed at a domestic audience to rally support for the regime, tapping into discourses about the 'neocolonial' France, the UN's hidden agendas, and symbols of Mali as a 'state of exception'.

MILITARY RULERS AND NEO-PATRIOTISM

Following France's unilateral decision in 2021 to withdraw its troops from Mali, the regime's key spokesperson, Colonel Abdoulaye Maïga, delivered a speech to the UN General Assembly in which he accused the French authorities of having stabbed Mali in the back (Secrétariat Général du Gouvernement Mali 2022). He made further accusations against France for using 'neo-colonial, condescending, paternalistic and revanchist practices' and praised the 'exemplary and fruitful cooperative relations between Mali and Russia' (Ibid.: 9). To Malian state television, Colonel Maïga also pointed a finger at French authorities, calling them a 'junta', for allegedly 'sparing no effort to cause the MINUSMA to flee, instead of an orderly withdrawal' (Le Cam 2023). In the words of Prime Minister Choguel Maïga, 'they [the French] want to humiliate us' (Maclean 2022). In this line, the junta has put itself at the forefront of popular grievances against foreign interventions, developing a social bond between itself and its supporters using failed interventions as a symbolic resource that provides meaning to its own authority and actions.

The junta's rhetoric has successfully instrumentalised France's colonial past and later mistakes to mobilise political support, using France as a scapegoat for the current security crisis. For example, when French authorities got annoyed with Mali's lack of gratitude following the death of fifty-nine French soldiers on Malian soil, they received a damning critique by Spokesperson Maïga in the UN, who stated that Mali pays tribute to all the victims of insecurity, including the French soldiers. He then suggested that France remember the 2011 intervention in Libya, 'decried by the whole of Africa', the thousands of African soldiers who served in the world wars, and not to mention the slave trade, 'which explains the economic rise of many countries' (Secrétariat Général du Gouvernement Mali 2022). This critique aligns with pronouncements from civil society figures like Boubacar Sidiki Sylla, the national co-ordinator of *Urgences Panafricanistes* in Mali, who stated, 'They [the French] came to play fireman in Mali, but they set the fire in Libya' (Munshi 2021), which serves as an example of the interplay between the regime's rhetoric and supportive civil movements. The UN and MINUSMA would also become a scapegoat following the regime change.

The Goïta regime became increasingly critical of MINUSMA's role in the ongoing conflict, and the UN started to play a larger role in the regime's discourse about reclaiming national sovereignty. Following the events of 2020 and 2021, the UN criticised the military takeover and demanded a return to civilian rule, but nevertheless aimed to continue the stabilisation mission. However, MINUSMA faced the challenging task of mitigating the jihadist threat while lacking the authority to actively supress it, causing much frustration with the mission (ICG 2022).

Tensions between Mali and the UN gradually intensified as officials from the military regime increasingly criticised MINUSMA as being inefficient and an obstacle to FAMA's counter-insurgency operations, echoing widespread sentiment that the UN was failing to meet expectations. In a speech to the UN General Assembly in 2021, Prime Minister Choguel Maïga demanded 'a more offensive posture on the ground' from the peacekeeping mission, showcasing the difficult balancing act the UN had to keep up in Mali (Jeune Afrique 2021). At the same time, the UN was increasingly worried about security collaboration between Mali and the Wagner Group. The UN investigation of the Moura massacre in 2022 became a breaking point, as the Human Rights Office concluded that over 500 people had been killed by Malian army and Wagner personnel (OHCHR 2023). Colonel Maïga, while thanking the peacekeeping force for its sacrifices, also denounced 'negative external influences and attempts to instrumentalise certain entities legally present in Mali, to serve hidden agendas, including through the exploitation of the human rights issue for destabilisation purposes' (Secrétariat Général du Gouvernement Mali 2022). When the report was released, Colonel Maïga again accused MINUSMA of breaking the momentum of FAMA through the political use of human rights issues, and thereby indirectly trying to assist the jihadi insurgents.

These UN speeches have tapped into popular imaginations and have been welcomed by supporters of the regime. Mali's 'voice' is heard by every country in the world, demonstrating that Mali is capable of standing up to hostile countries. This is seen in how, for example, Colonel Maïga, on his return from the UN General Assembly, was welcomed by a crowd of young Malians who saw his speech as a kind of 'rediscovery of their dignity', lost through the years of conflict (Le 360 Afrique 2022). In this light, the key figures of the regime come to be contemporary versions of legendary Malian rulers (such as Sunjata) and resemble the heroes of Dozo legends who prevail in their struggle against huge odds and powerful adversaries. They are men of exception who stand firm in an age where Mali's very existence is threatened, just as Sunjata once did.

Spokesperson Maïga's accusations was followed by a speech by Foreign Minister Diop that aimed to show if not the world at large then at least its supporters in Mali and elsewhere that the regime represented a Mali that could say no: a Mali that would prioritise Malian solutions to Malian problems, finding its own path which would be rooted in ancient Malian values. Thus, in a speech to the UN General Assembly in 2023, he argued that MINUSMA is too passive, and its negligence not only fuels inter-communal tensions in Mali but also serves the agenda of hostile countries. Diop goes on to state that Mali 'does not need to be lectured on human rights', referring to Sunjata's Kouroukan Fouga, he calls Mali 'a cradle of great civilisations, where the tradition of hospitality and tolerance makes the promotion and defence of human rights a national priority' (UNGA 2023). Here, the reference is not to a mythical legend as a warrior–hero, but to Sunjata as a statesman and to the Kouroukan Fouga as part of a canon in the history of human rights. It is this historical legacy that will be Mali's way out of crisis, and not the Western model of human rights. Similar lines of argument are also visible in the conflict with ECOWAS.

The standoff with ECOWAS—'defying sanctions' as a political resource

Defying France and the international community, including ECOWAS, has become a great source of pride for many Malians, and has strengthened the social bond between the regime and the population (see Whitehouse 2022). Relations between Mali and ECOWAS deteriorated rapidly after the second coup, with the latter imposing sanctions on Mali after the Goïta regime announced a 4-year delay for a return to civilian rule in January 2022. These sanctions included closure of land and air borders, suspension of commercial and financial transactions between Mali and ECOWAS countries, and the freezing of Mali's assets in all ECOWAS banks. This added further strain to traders and families already struggling to cope with high inflation on essentials, but the military regime skilfully painted themselves as defending Mali's people against bullying neighbours, which struck a chord with many Malians (BBC News 2022). The regime called for protests, and Malian citizens gathered in large rallies across the country in January 2022 in a rare display of national unity in the face of the ECOWAS's sanctions (Al Jazeera 2022). With such a show of popular support, the regime was eventually able to negotiate a lifting of the sanctions in July 2022 in return for holding elections in 2024, a significant success for the regime.

However, the lifting of sanctions did not bring about a more compliant stance by the regime towards the international community. An opportunity for the junta to further its sovereigntist approach presented itself in July 2022, when a contingent of Ivorian soldiers that had arrived to replace another MINUSMA contingent made some administrative errors around the transfer (Gourlay 2022). Ivorian President Alassane Ouattara, a close ally of France, had consistently worked to maintain sanctions against Mali. The regime seized the opportunity and arrested forty-nine Ivorian soldiers, accusing them of being mercenaries. According to Doussouba Konaté, the country director of anti-corruption organisation Accountability Lab Mali, 'In Bamako the population agrees with the fact that they are mercenaries' (Maclean et al. 2022). It was a popular move, connecting the sovereigntist narrative with clear action.

Further escalation occurred when ECOWAS threatened military intervention following the coup in Niger in July 2023, playing into the hands of the Malian regime, which cleverly capitalised on the unpopular sanctions. As described by Bakery Fomba in the *Sahel Tribune*:

> But beyond the spectacle, millions of lives are impacted by these political decisions. Ordinary citizens suffer the consequences of power plays conducted by those who claim to represent them. Sanctions are lifted here, and imposed there, but does it really change anything for those who live with the horrors of political instability on a daily basis? (Fomba 2024)

These sanctions, and the threat by the Nigerian ECOWAS Chairman to take military action against Niger in order to restore President

Bazoum to power paved the way for the three countries' decision to leave ECOWAS in January 2024 (Maclean 2024).

While several points of contention have been brought to the fore, there are four main accusations that the Goïta regime has levelled at ECOWAS: 1) having departed from its original vision of regional integration for autonomous state-building and development; 2) being an instrument of foreign influence by countries hostile to Mali's sovereignty; 3) providing little assistance to combat insurgents and terrorists (in which the regime conveniently forgets the initial ECOWAS initiative of 2012);[2] and 4) imposing sanctions on member states. These accusations are exemplified by spokesperson Colonel Maïga's statement in February 2024: 'From an organisation of integration, ECOWAS has become an organisation of disintegration in the hands of powers hostile to the interests of the people of West Africa, notably through the illegal, illegitimate and inhumane sanctions, which are still in force against people of Niger, whose resilience we salute again' (Icimali.com 2024).

The regime's recent decision to withdraw from ECOWAS, though risky due to its landlocked nature and dependence on regional trade, aligns with its rhetoric of reclaiming Mali's sovereignty in the face of external pressure, confirming the country as a 'state of exception'. This narrative resonates with West African nationalists critical of the CFA franc, the common currency shared by Mali within the West African Economic and Monetary Union (WAEMU). Withdrawing from WAEMU and establishing a new currency could further this sovereigntist approach, though its feasibility and potential consequences remain unclear (Ahmed 2024).

However, so far, the Goïta regime's hard-line approach against France, the UN, and ECOWAS has paid off again and again. By escalating tensions—including threatening to leave ECOWAS altogether—Mali together with Niger and Burkina Faso have successfully pressured the organisation to back down, and in late February 2024 ECOWAS lifted all sanctions. The military regime in Mali could therefore claim yet another significant victory over an external actor and present itself as the defender of the sovereignty and dignity of the Malian people, further consolidating the symbolic social contract between the regime and its supporters. For now, the political base of the military regime seems content with enduring current hardships in return for a 'restoration of long-lost dignity'.

Goïta as the ultimate modern hunter

While Goïta himself is not a prolific speaker, this is of little concern in a country where the names of legends, the famous, the powerful, and the rich are not necessarily spoken by themselves, but by their griots—the storytellers and narrators who are part of a tradition that dates all the way back to Sunjata's Mali Empire. While the trio of Foreign Minister Diop, Prime Minister Maïga, and Spokesperson Maïga are certainly are not griots, part of their mandate in the regime is to fulfil precisely this function. They are the regime's key storytellers who narrate their poems of Goïta as the man of exception who has come to Mali in an age of exception. In doing so, they evoke the old legends of the return of the hunter—the agent of disequilibrium who in a time of extreme danger saves his community by making ultimate sacrifices.

This is a potent brew, particularly when it draws on the contemporary myth of Thomas Sankara, which has recently has risen in stature to an all-time high. The legacy of Thomas Sankara, the Burkinabè revolutionary leader who was killed in 1987, had been in decline for a long time. However, as frustration with France took root among the youth population, Sankara's name and story received a boost in Bamako as well as in Ouagadougou and Niamey (see Chapter 2). The hope was that once again young inspirational leaders would step forward and take on the anti-colonial/anti-imperialist mantle that was lost when Sankara was killed. The coming to power of first Goïta in Mali (2020), then Ibrahim Traoré in Burkina Faso (2022), and finally the coup in Niger (July 2023) suggested that this was in the making. For those who came into power, this idea could be utilised as the basis for a social contract, which demands resistance and sacrifice in the struggle for the new and glorious future for Africa which they promise will be their end goal. Goïta's credibility in this regard is based on three elements in our view:

- As a new broom sweeps clean, Goïta is a man of the people, unrelated to the elite and thereby not a member of the discredited political class.

MILITARY RULERS AND NEO-PATRIOTISM

- He is a military leader akin to the hunter (the dozo), who as an agent of disequilibrium defies the odds and social status, taking on whatever enemy threatens his community. He cut the umbilical cord with France, severed the ties with the UN and ECOWAS, and remade the post-Cold War regional security architecture in opposition to the West and ECOWAS heavyweights. And he delivered the final blow to the Algiers Accords by recapturing Kidal.
- As a parallel to Sunjata, he envisions a new 'constitutional' order through the implementation of the inter-Malian dialogue.

Despite profound socio-economic and security crises, most Malians admire Goïta (see Friedrich-Ebert-Stiftung 2024). The regime's supporters demonstrate a willingness to endure difficulties for now. One reason for Goïta's popularity is his perceived success in removing the established political class, whom many blame for the country's woes. From their perspective, the democracy Mali has had delivered little different from that of the post-independence authoritarian regimes of Modibo Keita and Moussa Traoré. The most visible deliverables have been corruption, lack of opportunities, and rising inequality (Whitehouse 2022). Contrary to this, Goïta's image has been projected as like that of the popular Sufi leader and imam Chérif Ousmane Madani Haidara, who has maintained a strictly neutral political position in order to avoid association with the popular view of politics as a dirty business (see Bøås & Cissé 2022).

On social media, influential Facebook groups such as the *Collectif pour le soutien de la transition malienne* portray Goïta as a champion of restoring Mali's sovereignty and dignity.[3] Inspired by the speeches of figures like Thomas Sankara and Burkina Faso's current transitional leader, Captain Ibrahima Traoré, these platforms encourage young Malians to become a bulwark against those who oppose the transition, which in this case refers to external actors—France in particular—and domestic political opponents. According to Freedom House (2024), Mali's transitional government has been cracking down on dissent and freedom of the press since the 2020 coup. Critics of the regime—including politicians, journalists, and activists—face arrest, intimidation, and legal action. This has led to self-censorship by many, with few remaining vocal critics. Media outlets are pressured to report positively on the junta while independent foreign journalists are finding it increasingly difficult to operate in the country.

It is in severing ties with France that Goïta has proved himself an 'agent of disequilibrium'. He builds on the example of Thomas Sankara, often seen as the symbol of opposition to *Françafrique*, advocating for African countries to take matters into their own hands (see Harsch 2017). Rightly or wrongly, many Malians see France, whose powerful army had operated for nine years in Mali amidst a continuously worsening security situation, as the root cause of all their country's woes. Unlike his predecessor, President Goïta cut the umbilical cord linking Mali to France and later forced the withdrawal of MINUSMA. In doing so, he shook up the regional security architecture built on external Western support, which was structured around the 'global war on terror'. FAMA, which had once fled and mutinied in 2012, would now play the main role in retaking territorial control together with the regime's Russian ally, guided by a new social contract of sacrifice, resistance, and dignity.

Perhaps the most significant symbol of Mali's reassertion of control and sovereignty is the Malian military's capture (or liberation) of the northernmost city, Kidal. The city has, since independence, been a historical stronghold and symbol of rebellion, rarely under the control of the national authorities in Bamako (Le Monde 2023). The capture of Kidal was presented as the culmination of choices made by the regime, headed by Goïta. 'Despite the hiccups, betrayals and plots … the fanciful forecasts, our valiant Armed and Security Forces have achieved their objectives, and Mali is and will remain one and indivisible,', said the spokesman for the regime, Colonel Abdoulaye Maïga. The print media were full of editorials glorifying the victory and the army. Goïta stated to the public, 'Our mission is not over,' and 'I remind you that it consists of recovering and securing the whole territory, without exception' (Monteau 2023).

Following the capture of Kidal, President Goïta set in motion plans for inclusive, inter-Malian dialogue to find an end to the conflict (Fomba 2024). In a speech on national television, Prime Minister Maïga said that peace concerns all Malians. 'When Kidal was taken, President Goïta understood that to remain in the course of history, all citizens must be brought together to build peace', he explained.

MILITARY RULERS AND NEO-PATRIOTISM

'The Dialogue inter-Malians will enable us, this time, to put our problems down amongst ourselves and settle them definitively ... I am very optimistic.' For Maïga, the path that President Goïta has just mapped out is the best one today, and, as the figures from the Afrobarometer and the Mali-Mètre show, Prime Minister Maïga is not the only person in Mali who has faith in Goïta and the path he has chosen for Mali. The results from both surveys are robust in their approval, showing that people believe in the project. They believe in it because everything else has ended in frustration and disillusionment, but also because the way this political project is narrated makes sense, including the turn towards authoritarian rule. Mali is in a stage of exceptionality, and its people were desperate for a story they could believe, and that made sense amid the dense fog they felt themselves and the entire country caught up in, with no end in sight until the 'Man' came around.

Conclusion

Fragile states and their rulers are usually seen as weak, powerless, and impotent in relation to world powers, be they countries or international organisations. Mali and Goïta are the opposite to that. Here is a ruler who can say 'no' and a country that agrees to this. If this has been the case just temporarily it would have been easier to explain, as it could have been written off as the sentiment of the day of regime change. However, at the time of writing Goïta has been in power for three and a half years, and his approval ratings are higher than ever. Goïta is popular and Malians, as poor and destitute as they may be, takes joy and comfort from the regime's confrontations with and—as they are presented to them—victories against formidable adversaries, be it France, the UN, or ECOWAS. The way they see it, their 'man', their 'hero' goes into battle and emerges victorious.

Nothing lasts for ever, and as with any other regime, this one will not last forever. But the ideational power of the current regime should not be underestimated, and the power of rulers of weak states should not be disregarded. The blending of history, myths, epic poems, contemporary revolutionary legacies, and the fallout from failed and misguided international interventions and sanctions can shape a powerful multiverse of past and present, fiction and facts, that can constitute the foundation for a strong powerbase. So far, most of the literature concerned with states defined as fragile has placed more emphasis on detailing the flaws of such regimes and everything they lack vis-á-vis the ideal model of the Weberian state than seriously considering how rulers of weak states actually rule and what constitutes the social basis for their rule. This contribution is an attempt to signal that we should stop black boxing 'fragile states' and begin to focus on their internal affairs, including what resources and repertoires of an ideational nature are available to the rulers of such states, and how some leaders leverage these tools very successfully.

This not only has huge implications for how we approach such states, but also for future interventions aiming for state-building in states defined as 'fragile'.

What does the importance of symbolic resources mean for future interventions, particularly those aiming to do state-building? Liberal state-building focusing on public service provision and improving the functioning of formal state institutions faces huge challenges under democratic but illegitimate rulers, such as IBK in the case of Mali. International interventions failing to deliver tangible results risk getting dragged down in the mud of 'dirty politics' eventually becoming a narrative resource for emerging new and more autocratic leaders.

11

THE PERFECT STORM?

Mali and neighbouring Niger and Burkina Faso are among the poorest and most fragile states in the world. When conflicts first start in such an environment, managing them and finding solutions that will achieve peace, security, and development that the population buy into is extremely difficult. We also see this elsewhere, Afghanistan and Somalia being unfortunate examples of this. When a weak state lacking in legitimacy that exists without the relative coherence of a settled polity breaks down or loses its grip on considerable parts of its territory, bringing that state back in order can be an almost impossible task. While we should be careful with arguments of path dependency, the current situation in the Sahel has historical roots that date further back than colonialism. This is not to say that French colonialism did not contribute to the current malaise. It certainly did, but in the Sahel as elsewhere it has a much deeper and richer history than the colonial period, and here as again elsewhere what matters is the totality of history.

History matters—from the tales of the Macina principles of natural resource management to the clever use of the Sundiata by the regime in Bamako—but also as a key to understand the relationship between rule and production. Due to the harshness of the environment of the Sahel, rulers have tended for their regime security to favour natural resource extraction and control over trade routes over production. This was the case for the golden-age empires of Ghana, Mali, and the

Songhay through the period of what Lovejoy (2016) calls the 'Age of Revolutions' to French colonialism and into the postcolonial regimes. This has been the way of rule, but for the rural population agricultural production and pastoralism has been the way of life—a way of life that at times has been co-operative and consensual, but that at other times has resulted in violent conflict, as this relationship needs to be either self-regulated or regulated by someone else.

Currently we are in a period of violent conflict. Self-regulation has become much harder due to population pressure. The demographic trends of Mali, Niger, and Burkina Faso constitute a perfect storm in itself—the million-dollar question is what livelihood will be available to somewhere around 40–45 million Malians in 2050, as both the labour market and the resource base are already struggling to cope with the current population size. Forthcoming climate change effects will only make this much harder. This is not necessarily because the Sahel will be dryer: it could become wetter, but rainfalls will become even more unpredictable, coming as hard rain when it is not needed by farmers and pastoralists, which will lead to soil erosion.

Facing up to these challenges will be very difficult, as it is currently happening in some of the weakest and most fragile states in the world whose ability to cope is very low, as is their capacity to absorb international assistance. Add in violent conflict and the fact that the Sahel has become a pawn in the new geopolitical contestation, and it becomes even more difficult to imagine solutions. A perfect storm in the Sahel can potentially bring about a regional collapse as governments lose what little control they have. The jihadi insurgents may be able to bring down governments in this scenario, but that is all they can do; they cannot assume government and start governing. The consequence would be chaos, and it would be a nightmarish scenario for the people of the Sahel, for its neighbours to the north and south, and for Europe as well. Unfortunately, this is not a horror story, but a real possibility. However, it does not have to happen. But for this to be avoided, something has to change.

Twelve years since 2012

Entering its twelfth year, not only is the Sahel crisis continuing unabated, but practically every year a new dimension is added to an already poisonous cocktail of poverty, fragility, and conflict. The conflict may be about to have a reach beyond Mali, Niger, and Burkina Faso, as the jihadi insurgencies are trying to gain a foothold in Atlantic states such as Benin, Ghana, and Togo. France and the UN have basically been thrown out of the Sahel, the EU is sidelined, most European countries do not know what to do while they still try to revise previous Sahel strategies, and Russia has moved in.

In rural areas, jihadi insurgencies are still standing strong, and the new military governments that promised to handle the security predicament better than their democratically elected predecessors have not made much of difference. However, they still seem to be riding a wave of youthful patriotism in capital areas, which also takes a positive stance towards increased Russian involvement and influence. These are all ingredients in the Sahel security conundrum that makes the region an enigma.

What this means becomes clear when we contrast two different perceptions about Mali. One is from a recent World Bank (2022) analysis, and the other is the public perception of the Goïta regime captured by both the Afrobarometer (2023) and the Mali-Mètre survey (Friedrich-Ebert-Stiftung 2024). The World Bank presents the situation in Mali as bleak, worrying about sluggish economic growth, extreme poverty that continues to increase due to high inflation, and describing the social contract as 'fraying' because the state is unable to protect its citizens or deliver even the most basic services. This stands in contrast to the way most Malians seem to think about their country and their lives. Survey data from the Afrobarometer (2023) indicates that the population is much more satisfied with the unelected Goïta regime that unconstitutionally came to power in August 2020 than with the previous democratically elected government of Ibrahim Boubacar Keita. Data from the Mali-Mètre (Friedrich-Ebert-Stiftung 2024) shows that Goïta has an approval rating of 85 per cent. This is remarkably high and would be the envy of any political leader in a country under democratic rule.

This is not easy to explain, but we also see similar trends in Burkina Faso and Niger. At least in major cities and capital areas there is popular support for the military regimes, the anti-French position they have taken, and their subsequent turn to Moscow for military support. Urban youth who have become extremely disenfranchised with a decade of international interventions led by France, the UN, and the EU which only led to more conflict and despair are currently pinning their aspirations for a better life on military strongmen and their new allies in Moscow.

The question is therefore how long this 'Russian moment' might last. It is worth remembering that when the current Sahel crisis started there was also a 'French moment'. Back in 2013 people were waving French flags, but that did not last; now there are Russian flags on the street, but for how long? Can Russia really deliver where France, the UN, and Europe have failed? Most likely not, and this will have consequences for how Europe should think and act in the current situation.

The jihadi insurgency and local population—most people are not radicalised

The conflict with the jihadi insurgencies represented by JNIM that are nominally aligned with al-Qaeda and ISGS and that have some ties (mainly virtual) to what is left of IS in the Middle East is serious and deadly. The security situation has objectively worsened for most people in Mali and Burkina Faso. The insurgencies control more territory, and even where they may not have fixed control of territory, they have considerable social control over rural populations. However, while they are still in a strong position, they have not made any real attempts at capturing larger cities or carrying out operations in the capitals. They either consider themselves to be not yet strong enough militarily to do this, or alternatively they do not see such attempts as serving their interests.

It is highly likely that they could capture and hold regional cities like Ménaka and Mopti in Mali, but this could also expose one of their main limitations. They have become very good at what they currently are doing, namely carrying out asymmetrical warfare implemented through highly mobile hit-and-run tactics, but their governing capacities remain low. Yes, the jihadi insurgencies do attempt to govern the rural populations that fall under their control or influence, but this governance is rudimentary, sporadic, and haphazard. It is one thing to order people to dress in certain ways, to give orders limiting women's mobility, or occasionally rule in local land disputes; governing a city—even smaller ones like those mentioned above—is something completely different. What we must keep in mind is that the type of mobile asymmetrical warfare that these groups has come to master does not fit very well with an attempt to build administrative capacity for the purpose of civilian governance. This is still their weakness. They can fight and survive against a stronger enemy, as was the case when the French forces of Operation Barkhane was still around, and they can continue to do considerable damage to the national armies of Mali, Burkina Faso, and Niger, but they cannot take over the state as the Taliban did in Afghanistan. They are very far from having this kind of administrative governance capacity.

In addition, we also need to acknowledge that even if most of the young men that these groups recruit come from rural communities, this does not mean that much of the rural population have been radicalised. This is far from being the case. Most people are not radicalised. The support for the jihadi insurgencies is more circumstantial than wholehearted. There is no doubt that radicalised leaders and cadres exist, but this is not necessarily the case for most of those involved. On the contrary, research shows (see Bøås et al. 2021) that radicalisation and mobilisation into the world of violent extremism are firmly connected to the social worlds of these young recruits. The journey into extremism is not necessarily dislodged from their ordinary lives, but a pathway to provide an alternative social order to improve their life chances. It is thus the situation of the turn to becoming a jihadi in the Sahel that we need to understand. This is well illustrated by data from the study referenced above. In this study, respondents were asked if they knew somebody who had joined one of the jihadi insurgencies inspired by extremist Salafi interpretations in the Sahel, and if they answered 'yes', they were asked why they thought this person had joined such a group.

Very few of the responses referred to religion or ideology. Instead, the main reference points were insecurity, lack of employment, education, and other economic opportunities, and not least coercion and repression by government forces. This means that becoming part of an armed movement that international society defines as a terrorist organisation may have less to do with an all-consuming devotion to extremist interpretations of religion but rather should be seen as a pragmatic pose that is determined by context. This has important ramifications not only for how we should think about the conflicts in the Sahel, but also for how we should plan for programmes in the future to bring people back from the world of violent extremism.

Foregrounding individual deradicalisation programming may have little effect if it was mainly material grievances that made jihadis embark on a journey into extremism. If many of those who have joined extremist insurgencies did this not out of religious devotion but in response to all the reasons mentioned above, this might also suggest that what they crave is not a return to a medieval state, but rather a modernity and a state that works for them, as opposed to a modernity that is not for them and a state that works against them, as they have experienced thus far. If this is the case, as this author tends to believe, the current 'security first' approach taken by the military rulers of Mali, Niger, and Burkina Faso is not likely to yield any better results than what France and the UN managed. Thus, with all likelihood, we are far from seeing an end to the violent conflicts in the Sahel.

The new military rulers—sovereignty as dignity

Mali has been under military rule since August 2020, Burkina Faso since 2022, and the coup in Niger took place during the summer of 2023. In each case, the new military rulers have lambasted the failures of international interventions and those of the former colonial power France and called for the restoration of national sovereignty and dignity. The sovereignty discourse that seems to be going on repeat every time the main narrators of the regimes (for example, former Malian Prime Minister Maïga and Foreign Minister Diop) speak may sound unconvincing to an international audience when laid out in press conferences or on a global podium as the UN General Assembly, but then we forget who their target audience is. It is not us or the international community at large, it's their own populations, and for them sovereignty is not a theoretical question but translates directly as dignity.

This suggests that coming into power during a failed international intervention is a resource that the incumbent can make use of. Mali

THE PERFECT STORM?

therefore exemplifies the challenges faced by large external interventions that aim to produce both security and state-building. What has happened in Mali, and in Burkina Faso and Niger, is similar to the challenges and problems international interventions have faced in the Democratic Republic of Congo, Somalia, and Afghanistan, all situations where the international community has also failed to address an ever-expanding system of violence.

The Goïta regime did not create the narratives about the ills of neocolonialism (e.g. France), MINUSMA's inability to deal with the conflict, or the necessity of reclaiming sovereignty. These narratives are older than the current military rulers' August 2020 march to power. Nonetheless, they have used them shrewdly to create a new multiverse of the history of Mali as ancient and glorious, and simultaneously contemporary, undignified, and weak as the client of the former colonial power France. As the regime presents the story, this was the case until Goïta arrived at the scene to serve as the 'man of exception' in a 'state of exception'. This narrative has a strong hold on the imagination of young urbanites in Mali, but we also see a similar trend in Ouagadougou and Niamey.

The new military rulers are not winning the war against the jihadi insurgents, but for the time being they are not losing it either. They control the main political castles, important forts (regional cities), and access routes to the most economically important parts of their respective countries, and they remain popular, as Goïta's high approval rating testifies to.

What is emerging is something that can best be described as a recreation of the old garrison state model. The ruler controls the 'iron throne' in the main garrison (the capital) and some key outpost and access routes that ensure that the main fortress can be replenished with resources. Given the fact that the insurgents may lack both the military strength and the administrative capacity to take on larger cities, such a state model can be sustainable for quite some time as long as the inhabitants of the main garrison still support the ruler or else are too afraid to rebel against the military rulers. Göita and his peers in Ouagadougou and Niamey may therefore be relatively secure in their respective 'castles' for the time being, and regime security is also enhanced by the coup-proofing that Russia and the Wagner Group provide.

The real losers if this situation prevails is the rural population, who for such a regime will simply become disposable and will have to negotiate their security as best as they can with jihadi insurgents, military campaigns by national armies and their new allies, and bands of community-based self-defence militias and bandit groups.

Urban patriotism—new, youthful nationalism

Previously in the text, we stated that regarding the question of the strength of the jihadi insurgents we must acknowledge that most people are not radicalised. Much of the same can be said about the new youthful nationalism that is concentrated to capital areas and key cities not yet too affected by violent conflict. It is also mainly circumstantial. It is a situational pose against President Macron and French policies, and much less an ideological stance against France and French values, ideas, and lifestyles. Instead, one could say that this is what these young urbanites who support the regime want. They aspire to access to a modernity that could work for them, that includes at the very least a chance at accessing a better life represented by the idea of Europe and France. By day, they march to the sound of neo-Marxist speeches and slogans, filling streets and squares with their protests against France and in support of their new military rulers, then they may also dance the night away to the latest club music coming out of Paris.

The protests that we have seen in Bamako, Ouagadougou, and Niamey are born out of despair and a sentiment of wasted youth, and not out of an ideological conviction that runs very deep. Russia, Russian flags, and even Putin himself become a symbol of defiance and resistance, not because of what these youth believe they are, nor because they have any aspirations of going to Moscow. The Russian flag and Putin become symbols to express anger that the youth know will be recognised, will be seen, ensuring that they themselves will be seen, and not least because they know embracing these symbols will irritate Macron and Western powers.

The question is how long this will last. In the case of Mali, it's been present since August 2020, and there are no signs that it is about to evaporate. Despite profound socio-economic and security challenges,

THE PERFECT STORM?

most Malians still admire Goïta (see Fredrich-Ebert-Stiftung 2024). The regime's supporters demonstrate a willingness to endure difficulties for now. One reason for Goïta's popularity (and much of the same could be said about his peers in Ouagadougou and Niamey) is his perceived success in removing the established political class, who many blame for the country's woes. From the perspective of his supporters, democracy in Mali delivered little difference from the post-independence regimes of Modibo Keita and Moussa Traoré. The most visible deliverables have been corruption, lack of opportunities, and rising inequality (Whitehouse 2022). In contrast to this, the image Goïta has projected has been similar to that of the popular Sufi leader and imam Chérif Ousmane Madani Haidara, who has maintained a politically neutral position to avoid being associated with the popular view of 'politics as dirty' (see Bøås & Cissé 2022). On social media, support groups portray Goïta as a champion of restoring Mali's sovereignty and dignity, and for the time being this seems to be enough to keep the young urbanities of the streets behind him. But this will not last forever, and the challenge will come when people start to demand more than just a regime that picks fights with external powers while it continues to wage an internal war against the jihadi insurgents that it is highly unlikely that it will win. Sooner or later, people will realise that sovereignty does not bring food security or jobs, and that feeling dignified does not necessarily improve your prospects in life, nor is it an answer to aspirations for a better life.

The turn to Russia—how long will the Russian moment last?

Russia is having its moment in the Sahel. Its flags are being waved on the streets, and people carry pictures in support of President Putin. France has left its former colonies, and they have sought a new security alliance with Moscow. Reports from this part of the world are most certainly received with pleasure in Kremlin. However, what Russian stakeholders also should ask themselves is how long it can last.

The answer is that it is inevitable that the Russian moment in the Sahel is temporary. Russia simply cannot replace France and Europe as a development, humanitarian, and trading partner. All Russia can do in Africa is operate in what we may call niche security markets. It can offer some weapons and armoury, but not that much and not high-tech modern military gear, as it is using its top-tier military equipment at a very rapid pace in the war in Ukraine. It can send some military advisors, and it can offer some military assistance and coup-proofing through the Wagner Group. This might consolidate the situation for some time, but it cannot solve it. Russia will not be able to give these military regimes what they really want, which is a decisive victory against the jihadi insurgents. France could not do this, the UN could not, nor could the EU, and Russia will also fail in this endeavour.

What is important, however, to ensure that the Russian moment does not last any longer than necessary, is that Europe does not fall into the trap that Putin wants it to fall into. This is to treat what is currently taking place in the Sahel as a Cold War 2.0—a game of geopolitical conflict where two value systems stand against each other: liberal democracy versus authoritarian rule.

This is not a game Europe is well positioned to win right now. Ten years of massive international interventions that failed have left a huge scar on the public perception of Europe in the Sahel. In 2013, people thought that France had come to fix their problem. However, the conflict not only continued unabated, but as the security situation deteriorated large-scale corruption increased. France and Europe are blamed for this, as they continued to support a political class unable to stop 'eating' public resources.

Europe has therefore lost much of the legitimacy it used to have, and regaining the trust of the Sahel populations will take time. Europe should therefore stay engaged where it can and await the time for a return based on a critical reflection of what went wrong. For European policymakers, it may be more convenient to continue to portray Malians and others in the Sahel as fools who have fallen for Russian fake news and disinformation campaign. However, this will play right into Putin's hands, and it will help neither the Sahel nor Europe.

Conclusion

The situation in the Sahel, dire as it was, has been further complicated by the fact that the region has become a battleground of rivalry between the West and Russia. The turn to Moscow by Bamako,

THE PERFECT STORM?

Ouagadougou, and Niamey complicates things, but the situation may not be as bleak as one might think.

In the long run, Russia cannot replace Europe in the Sahel. This means that with all likelihood the Russian moment we are currently seeing in the Sahel is not going to last. If this is handled with maturity by European stakeholders, it will not last longer than necessary, but a certain degree of patience will be needed. The Sahel needs Europe and Europe needs the Sahel, but when and if the relationship is steadied it must be based on a new partnership model anchored in an acceptance that a lot went wrong during the period of massive international interventions led by the West.

Second, while Europe might rightly be worried about the combined growth of extremist religious views as well as more secular anti-Western sentiment, it should be acknowledged that most people in the Sahel are not radicalised. They have not fully embraced any of these ideologies but rather turn towards them out of desperation and despair. People crave a state and a modernity that is for them, that includes rather than excludes. In this regard, Europe should have a comparative advantage over a player like Russia, because if what people want is a state and a modernity that work for them, then they also crave good governance and credible government. Russia cannot offer this; Europe can assist in this endeavour, but only if it gets its priorities right and realises that the answer to the Sahel crisis is not in military means alone (it is needed), but in finding agreeable pragmatic solutions based on good governance that are context and conflict sensitive.

pp. [11–46]

NOTES

1. SAHEL: ACTORS AND INGREDIENTS

1. Jean-François Bayart (1993: 325) uses the Foucauldian concept of *gouvernementalité* to investigate the power relations in sub-Saharan Africa as a complex reticulation and a mode of governing that 'surrounded the whole set of institutions and powers that operated as of the advent of modern times in Africa', but at the same time failed to incorporate the totality of the political discourse.
2. On arms flows in the Sahel, see Koné (2020).
3. We will return to the case of Mahmoud Dicko in Part III.
4. For information about this project, see https://www.prevex-balkan-mena.eu/.

2. MALI: THE EPICENTRE OF THE SAHEL CONFLICT

1. Ag Bahanga died in northern Mali under unclear circumstances. Some claim that he died in a car accident others that he was killed in a shoot-out resulting from an argument over how to share a large deposit of arms transported out of Libya.
2. The UN force, known by its French acronym MINUSMA, was first approved by the UN Security Council in April, and thereafter approved for deployment from 1 July 2013 by the Security Council on June 25. See BBC (25 June 2013) UN gives go-ahead to deployment of Mali peacekeepers.
3. We will return to this issue in Part III.
4. The term *Azawad* traditionally referred to the vast plain between Timbuktu and Gao but was gradually expanded to mean the entirety of northern Mali by the rebels fighting there in the first half of the 1990s. See Flood (2012); Bøås & Torheim (2013).
5. In communities in Mopti, this group is usually just referred to as 'Kouffa's men' or 'the men of the bush'. 'Katiba' refers to combat units, while the 'Macina' refers to the theocratic nineteenth-century Macina Empire that stretched over the floodplain areas of the Inner Niger Delta, in what today are the Malian regions of Mopti and Ségou. See Chapter 7 for more details.
6. There is some confusion concerning the relationship between IS-aligned groups in

this region. However, ISGS is distinct from the breakaway faction of Boko Haram that has taken the name 'Islamic State West Africa Province' (ISWAP). Their origin is completely different, their approach to governance and governing people differs, and they operate in separate territories: ISGS mainly in the border areas between Burkina Faso, Mali, and Niger; ISWAP mainly in Nigeria and, to much less extent, in Niger's Diffa region that borders Lake Chad and northern Nigeria (see also Berlingozzi & Stoddard 2020).

3. THE NEIGHBOURS: BURKINA FASO AND NIGER

1. Diendéré was directly involved in the 1987 coup that brought Compaoré to power. A longtime aide to Compaoré, he was the commander of the RSP—the praetorian guard of the President. Bassolé, a military officer by training, rose to prominence through several diplomatic missions that Compaoré sent him on: to Togo (1993), as mediator in the conflict in northern Niger (1994), and as Minister of Security and main interlocutor of the Ouagadougou Accord in 2007 during the conflict in Côte d'Ivoire.
2. *Zakat* is an Islamic form of taxation that is supposedly collected for the benefit of the poor. Most Islamic insurgencies in the Sahel collect *zakat* in various forms, monetary as well as material, as is the case here. While these armed groups may give some funds to poor people to gain their support, in most cases the *zakat* collected is used to provide for their fighters.
3. The term 'Bella' is here used as to refer to 'black' Tuareg pastoralists who live in Tillabéri. These people would call themselves 'Daoussahak' or 'Idaksahak', as they consider the term 'Bella' a pejorative. They are a nomadic pastoralist group that lives between Meneka in Mali and Tillabéri in Niger. Historically, the Daoussahak are a community of a lower caste in Tuareg society, as they used to be herdsmen enslaved by the noble Tuareg families. As this group have a darker skin tone, they are still commonly referred to as the Bella ('black') Tuareg.
4. The data utilised in this section is collected from the Tillabéri Regional Development Plan 2016–2020, fieldnotes from November 2018 and 2019, and interviews conducted between 29 April and 6 May 2020.
5. This section is based on information obtained from conversations with HACP representatives and civil society activists in Niamey in November 2018.
6. Transcript from author fieldnotes.
7. Interviews with 'smugglers' in Agadez (November 2019 and February 2021).
8. Intervention by Antonio Vitorino (IOM) at an Expert Roundtable in Berlin, 30 May 2023, organised by the German Federal Foreign Office.
9. Namely the Immigration and Border Management (IBM) programme, the Migration Resource and Response Mechanism (MRRM), and the Sustainable Return from Niger (SURENI) programme.
10. Interviews with migrants in IOM transit centres in Agadez and Niamey (November 2019 and February 2021).

11. From an interview with a former driver of migrants across the desert to Libya, conducted by the author in Agadez in November 2021.

5. HYBRIDITY IN THE SAHEL: VIOLENT ENTREPRENEURS AND BIG MEN

1. For more on the Malian state as unsettled and sparsely institutionalised, see Bøås and Torheim (2013) and Craven-Mathews and Englebert (2018).
2. On the myth and reality of social banditry see Kheng (1985).
3. This example is based on material from Bøås & Torheim (2013).

6. MALI: THE LONG ROAD TO 2012

1. Mali's eleven regions included the capital Bamako, which is not formally a region but is referred to as the 'Capital District'.
2. The term 'Azawad' traditionally referred to the vast plain between Timbuktu and Gao, but as it was used by the rebels fighting there in the first half of the 1990s, it gradually expanded to mean the entirety of northern Mali. See Flood (2012).
3. 'Ikan' is the Tuareg name for this group, whereas 'Bella' is the Songhay term, much more commonly used in Mali. Bella is therefore not a separate ethnic category, but a collective term for people of slave descent. See Pedersen and Benjaminsen (2008).

8. POLITICS IN HARD TIMES: RELIGION AND PROTEST

1. The most important Sufi orders of West Africa—the Qadiriyya and the Tijaniyya—are also present in Mali, with the latter being the most important (see Clark 1999; Seesemann & Soares 2009).
2. The degree to which Malians have had faith in the modern state is an open question, and Schulz (2021) is probably correct in arguing that in rural Mali state interventions are often seen as more predatory than benign.
3. In the Afrobarometer study of 2020, trust in religious leaders was high (78 per cent). The president's approval rating, on the other hand, stood at 38 per cent (the lowest recorded by the Afrobarometer in Mali), while the National Assembly only had the trust of 29 per cent of the respondents (see Afrobarometer 2020).
4. Our understanding of symbolic capital draws on Bourdieu (1989: 17)—'the form that the various species of capital assume when they are perceived and recognised as legitimate'.
5. Mali's perceived public corruption score, as evaluated by Malian citizens, is 29 out of 100, with zero being the worst possible score. See Transparency International (2021).
6. Dicko has become immensely politically savvy and, as will become clear in this chapter, presents himself differently to different audiences. This means that at times he embraces the Wahhabi label, at other times he distances himself from or even outright rejects it.

7. Mali's current population of approximately 19 million is projected to increase to over 45 million by 2050. This projection is based on the current annual population growth of over 3 per cent, where each woman in Mali gives birth to an average of 6.2 children.
8. For a review of this debate see Sears (2007).
9. Interview with Malian academic, Bamako, November 2016. See Ba & Bøås (2018).
10. This section draws on Bøås, Cissé, and Diallo (2019).
11. Haidara leads the Sufi association he himself founded in 1983 called Ansar Dine. It has grown steadily since its inauguration, and Haidara's views on Islam are seen by his many supporters as closely related to the local way of life and Bambara culture in particular (see Chappatte 2018). The Ansar Dine of Haidara must not be confused with the jihadi insurgency Ansar ed-Dine led by Iyad Ag Ghaly.
12. The AMUPI was established in 1981 by President and General Moussa Traoré to manage Islamic affairs and in particular the relationship between Sufis and those practising more scriptural versions of Sunnism. The AMUPI still exists, and it held its fourth ordinary congress in Bamako in November 2019. The current president and vice president are Issiaka Traoré and Mahmoud Dicko respectively.
13. This section is built on both our and our colleagues' observations in Bamako and analysis of several international and national media reports about the affairs of the summer of 2020. See, for example, Melly (2020) and Baudais & Chauzal (2020).
14. Maïga and Tall can best be characterised as career politicians who have been around for quite some time. Maïga has served in various governments since the late 1990s, and Tall was removed from a ministerial post as late as 2017 by IBK. Oumar Mariko is a former student activist from the early 1990s: a medical doctor by training and staunch socialist, he has always been a controversial opposition figure in Malian politics.
15. Statement by Dicko, 16 June 2023, referred to in an article in the *Africa Report* (27 June) by Flore Monteau.

9. THE NEW MILITARY REGIMES: ADIEU FRANCE, WELCOME RUSSIA

1. This analysis is based on confidential conversations with contacts in Niamey after the July coup. For obvious reasons, these interlocutors cannot be identified.

10. MILITARY RULERS AND NEO-PATRIOTISM: BRANDING AND MYTHMAKING

1. Symbolic resources can also be referred to as 'narrative resources'. We use these terms interchangeably.
2. In late 2012, the UN Security Council authorised AFISMA, a collaboration between ECOWAS and the African Union. The mission was transferred to the UN in April 2013 (see Osland & Erstad 2020).
3. Collectif pour le soutien de la transition malienne | Facebook, https://www.facebook.com/groups/819832048078841/

BIBLIOGRAPHY

ACLED (2023) ACLED Profile: Jama'at Nusrat al-Islam wal-Muslimin (JNIM), https://acleddata.com/2023/11/13/actor-profile-jamaat-nusrat-al-islam-wal-muslimin-jnim/
AFP (2024a) Going, going: Burkina Faso, Mali, Niger quit West African block ECOWAS (28 January).
AFP (2024b) Arrestation d'un proche du célèbre imam malien Mahmoud Dicko (14 July).
Afrobarometer (2020) Is democracy in Mali dying? Not if citizens' voices are heard, https://www.afrobarometer.org/articles/democracy-mali-dying-not-if-citizens-voices-are-heard/
Afrobarometer (2023) Round 9 Survey, https://www.afrobarometer.org/publication/mali-round-9-resume-des-resultats/.
Agamben, Giorgio (2005) *State of Exception*, Chicago: University of Chicago Press.
Ahmed, Lassaad Ben (2024) Retrait de trois pays sahéliens de la Cédéao: Une tension à court terme (Expert), *Anadolu Ajansi*, https://www.aa.com.tr/fr/afrique/retrait-de-trois-pays-sahéliens-de-la-cédéao-une-tension-à-court-terme-expert-/3123665.
Al Jazeera (2022) Malians rally after army calls for protests over ECOWAS sanctions, Al Jazeera (14 January), https://www.aljazeera.com/news/2022/1/14/malians-rally-after-army-calls-protests-over-ecowas-sanctions.
Al Jazeera (2024) Niger suspends military cooperation with the United States, Al Jazeera (16 March).
Al-Karjousli, Soufian (2016) *Facteurs de paix et islam sahélien*, Paris: Agence Française de développement.
Arieff, Alexis (2009) Still standing: neighbourhood wars and political stability in Guinea, *Journal of Modern African Studies*, vol. 47, no. 3, pp. 331–48.
Asala, Kizzi (2020) M5 accuse France of meddling in Malian political crisis,

BIBLIOGRAPHY

Africanews (8 March), https://www.africanews.com/2020/08/10/m5-accuse-france-of-meddling-in-malian-political-crisis/.

Assanvo, William, Baba Dakono, Lori-Anne Théroux-Bénoni & Ibrahim Maïga (2019) *Violent Extremism, Organised Crime and Local Conflicts in Liptako-Gourma*. Pretoria: Institute for Security Studies (West Africa Report 26).

Atkinson, Ronald (1994) *The Roots of Ethnicity: the Origins of the Acholi of Uganda Before 1800*, Philadelphia: University of Pennsylvania Press.

Austen, Ralph A. (2010) *Trans-Saharan Africa in World History*, Oxford: Oxford University Press.

Ba, Boubacar & Morten Bøås (2013) *The Mali Presidential Elections: Outcomes and Challenges*, Oslo: NOREF (NOREF Report October 2013).

Ba, Boubacar & Morten Bøås (2017) *Mali: a Political Economy Analysis*, Oslo: NUPI: Report Commissioned by the Norwegian Ministry of Foreign Affairs.

Bacon, Tricia & Elizabeth G. Arsenaul (2019) Al Qaeda and the Islamic State's break: strategic rift or lackluster leadership, *Studies in Conflict & Terrorism*, vol. 42, no. 3, pp. 237–8.

Baechler, Günther (1998) *Violence Through Environmental Discrimination: Causes, Arenas, and Conflict Models*, Dordrecht: Kluwer Academic.

Barak, Oren (2018) Security networks, deep states, and the democratic deficit in the Middle East, *The Middle East Journal*, vol. 72, no. 3, pp. 447–65.

Baudais, Virginie & Gregory Cahuzal (2020) *Mali's Transition: High Expectations and Little Time*, Stockholm: SIPRI.

Bayart, Jean-Francois (1993) *The State in Africa: the Politics of the Belly*, New York: Longman.

Bayart, Jean-Francois, Stephen Ellis & Béatrice Hibou (1999) *The Criminalisation of the State in Africa*, Oxford: James Currey.

BBC (2013) Mali crisis: EU troops begin training mission, BBC News (2 April).

BBC (2018) Low turnout in Mali run-off, BBC News (13 August).

BBC (2022) Mali coup: how junta got ECOWAS economic sanctions lifted, BBC News (6 July).

Benjaminsen, Tor-Arve (2008) Does supply-induced scarcity drive violent conflicts in the African Sahel? The case of the Tuareg rebellion in Northern Mali, *Journal of Peace Research*, vol. 45, no. 1, pp. 831–48.

Benjaminsen, Tor Arve & Boubacar Ba (2009) Farmer-herder conflicts, pastoral marginalisation, and corruption: a case study from inland Niger Delta of Mali. *The Geographical Journal*, vol. 175, no. 1, pp. 71–81.

Benjaminsen, Tor-Arve & Boubacar Ba (2019) Why do pastoralists in Mali join jihadist groups? A political-ecological explanation, *Journal of Peasant Studies*, vol. 46, no. 1, pp. 1–20.

BIBLIOGRAPHY

Benjaminsen, Tor Arve & Christian Lund (eds) (2001) *Politics, Property and Production in the West African Sahel: Understanding Natural Resource Management*, Uppsala: Nordic Africa Institute.

Bergamaschi, Isaline (2014) The fall of a donor darling: the role of aid in Mali's crisis, *Journal of Modern Africa Studies*, vol. 52, no. 3, pp. 347–78.

Berge, Gunvor (2002) *In Defence of Pastoralism: Form and Flux Among the Tuareg of Northern Mali*. PhD dissertation, Faculty of Social Sciences, University of Oslo.

Bertrand, Monique (2019) A cadastre for Mali? The production of land titles and the challenge of property data on the periphery of Bamako, *Land Use Policy*, vol. 81, February, pp. 371–81.

Bledsoe, Caroline (1990) No success without hardship: social mobility and hardship for Sierra Leone children, *Man* (N.S.), no. 25, pp. 70–88.

Boeke, Sergei (2022) *Pathways out of the Quagmire? Perspectives for al-Qaeda in the Sahel*, International Centre for Counter-Terrorism, https://icct.nl/publication/pathways-out-quagmire-perspectives-al-qaeda-sahel

Bonfiglioli, Angelo & Carol Watson (1992) *Pastoralists at a Crossroads: Survival and development issues in African pastoralism*, Nairobi: NOPA, UNICEF/UNSO Project for Nomadic Pastoralists in Africa.

Border Forensics (2023) *Mission Accomplished? The Deadly Effects of Border Control in Niger*, available: https://www.borderforensics.org/investigations/niger-investigation/.

Bourdieu, Pierre (1989) Social space and symbolic power, *Sociological Theory*, vol. 7, pp. 14–25.

Boyer, Florence & Harouna Mounkaila (2018) Européanisation des politiques migratoires au Sahel: le Niger dans l'imbroglio sécuritaire, in Emmanuel Grégoire (ed.) *L'État réhabilité en Afrique: Réventer les politiques publiques a l'ere néoliberale*, Paris: Karthala, pp. 267–85.

Bratton, Michael, Massa Coulibaly & Fabiana Machado (2002) Popular views on the legitimacy of the state in Mali, *Canadian Journal of African Studies*, vol. 36, no. 2, pp. 197–238.

Brautigam, Deborah, Odd-Helge Fjeldstad & Mick Moore (2008) *Taxation and State-Building in Developing Countries: Capacity and Consent*, Cambridge: Cambridge University Press.

Brown, William A. (1968) Towards a chronology for the caliphate of Hadullahi (Masina), *Cahiers d'etudes africaines*, vol. 8, no. 31, pp. 428–34.

Bruijn, de Mirjam & Han van Dijk (2001) Ecology and power in the periphery of the Masina: the case of the Hayre in the 19th century, *Journal of African History*, vol. 42, no. 2, pp. 217–38.

Buhaug, Håvard & Kristian S. Gleditsch (2008) Contagion or confusion? Why conflicts cluster in space, *International Studies Quarterly*, vol. 52, no. 2, pp. 215–33.

BIBLIOGRAPHY

Buzan, Barry (1983) *People, States and Fear: the National Security Problem in International Relations*, Brighton: Wheatsheaf Books.

Buzan, Barry, Ole Wæver & Jaap de Wilde (1998) *Security: a New Framework for Analysis*, Boulder: Lynne Rienner.

Bøås, Morten (2000) Nigeria and West Africa: From a Regional Security Complex to a Regional Security Community?, in Einar Braathen, Morten Bøås & Gjermund Sæther (eds) *Ethnicity Kills? The Politics of War, Peace and Ethnicity in Sub-Saharan Africa*, London: Macmillan, pp. 139–62.

Bøås, Morten (2003) Weak states, strong regimes: towards a 'real' political economy of African regionalisation, in Andrew Grant & Fredrik Söderbaum (eds) *The New Regionalism in Africa*, Aldershot: Ashgate, pp. 31–46.

Bøås, Morten (2005) The Liberia civil war: new war/old war?, *Global Society*, vol. 19, no. 1, pp. 73–88.

Bøås, Morten (2012) Castles in the sand: informal networks and power brokers in the northern Mali periphery, in Mats Utas (ed.) *African Conflicts and Informal Power: Big Men and Networks*, London: Zed Books, pp. 91–136.

Bøås, Morten (2015a) *The Politics of Conflict Economies: Miners, Merchants and Warriors in the African Borderland*, London: Routledge.

Bøås, Morten (2015b) Crime, coping and resistance in the Mali-Sahel periphery, *African Security*, vol. 8, no. 4, pp. 299–319.

Bøås, Morten (2017) Fragile states as the new development agenda?, *Forum for Development Studies*, vol. 44, no. 1, pp. 149–54.

Bøås, Morten (2019) *The Sahel Crisis and the Need for International Support*, Uppsala: Nordic Africa Institute (Policy Dialogue no. 15).

Bøås, Morten (2020) EU migration management in the Sahel: unintended consequences on the ground in Niger, *Third World Quarterly*, vol. 42, no. 1, pp. 52–67.

Bøås, Morten (2022) Le mystère de la mobilisation de ressources, *Afkar*, no. 63, https://www.iemed.org/publication/le-mystere-de-la-mobilisation-de-ressources/?lang=fr, 2021.

Bøås, Morten & Abdoul Wakhab Cissé (2022) The Sheikh versus the President: the making of Imam Mahmoud Dicko as a political Big Man in the shifting landscape of Malian politics, *Third World Thematics: a TWQ Journal*, DOI: 10.1080/23802014.2022.2109993.

Bøås, Morten & Kevin C. Dunn (2013) *The Politics of Origin in Africa: Autochthony, Citizenship and Conflict*, London: Zed Books.

Bøås, Morten & Kevin C. Dunn (eds) (2017) *Africa's Insurgents: Navigating an Evolving Landscape*, Boulder: Lynne Rienner.

Bøås, Morten & Viljar Haavik (2025) Failed international interventions and the making of new social 'contracts' in Mali, *Journal of Intervention & Statebuilding* (https://doi.org/10.1080/17502977.2025.2461295).

BIBLIOGRAPHY

Bøås, Morten & Kathleen M. Jennings (2011) Luttes armées, rebelles et signeurs de la guerre: le spectre du patrimonialisme, in Daniel C. Bach & Mamadou Gazibo (eds) *L'Ètat Néopatrimonial: Genèse et Trajectoires Contemporaines*, Ottawa: Les Presses de Université d'Ottawa, pp. 175–89.

Bøås, Morten & Kari M. Osland (2025) Enabling environments, in Morten Bøås, Ulf Engel, Gilad Ben-Nun & Kari Osland (eds) *Resisting Radicalization: Exploring the Non-Occurrence of Violent Extremism*, Boulder: Lynne Rienner, pp. 22–5.

Bøås, Morten & Francesco Strazzari (2020) Governance, fragility and insurgency in the Sahel: a hybrid political order in the making, *The International Spectator*, vol. 55, no. 4, pp. 1–17.

Bøås, Morten & Liv Elin Torheim (2013) The trouble in Mali—corruption, collusion, resistance, *Third World Quarterly*, vol. 34, no. 7, pp. 1279–92.

Bøås, Morten, Abdoul Wakhab Cissé and Abubacar Diallo (2019) *Mali—Religious Leaders and the 2018 Presidential Campaign*, Oslo: NUPI.

Bøås, Morten, Abdoul Wakhab Cissé & Laouali Mahamane (2020) Explaining violence in Tillabéri: insurgent appropriation of local grievances?, *The International Spectator*, vol. 55, no. 4, pp. 118–32.

Bøås, Morten, Kari Osland, Alessio Iocchi, Viljar Haavik, Abdoul Wakhab Cissé, Luca Raineri, Laouali Mahamane, Djallil Lounnas & Akram Benmrahar (2021) *Working Paper on Enabling Environments, Drivers and Occurrence/Non-Occurrence of Violent Extremism in the Sahel and the Maghreb Regions*, Oslo: PREVEX (PREVEX Worling Paper D6.2).

Carayol, Rémi (2019) What happened when the EU moved its fight to stop migration to Niger? *The Nation* (5 July).

Carbonnel, Alissa de & Robin Emmott (2018) Donors pledge $500 more for troops in West Africa's Sahel, Paris: Reuters (23 February).

Chappatte, André (2018) Crowd, sensationalism, and power: the yearly Ansar Dine 'pilgrimage' of Maouloud in Bamako, *Journal of Religion in Africa*, vol. 48, pp. 3–34.

Cissé, Abdoul W., Ambroise Dakouo, Morten Bøås & Frida Kvamme (2017) *Perceptions About the EU Crisis Reponses in Mali—a Summary of Perception Studies*, Brussels: EUNPACK Policy Brief 7.7.

Clapham, Christopher (ed.) (1998) *African Guerrillas*, Oxford: James Currey.

Clark, Andrew F. (1999) Imperialism, independence and Islam in Senegal and Mali, *Africa Today*, vol. 46, no. 3–4, pp. 149–67.

Cloutier, Mathieu, Bernard Harborne, Deborah Isser, Indhira Santos & Michel Watts (2022) *Social Contracts for Development: Bargaining, Contention, and Social Inclusion in Sub-Saharan Africa*, Washington, DC: The World Bank, https://doi.org/10.1596/978–1–4648–1662–8.

CNN (2024) Niger ends military agreement with US, calls it 'profoundly unfair' (16 March).

BIBLIOGRAPHY

Cockayne, James & Adam Lupel (2009) Introduction: rethinking the relationship between peace operations and organized crime, *International Peacekeeping*, vol. 16, no. 1, pp. 4–19.

Cold-Ravnkilde, Signe M. & Boubacar Ba (2022) Jihadist ideological conflict and local governance in Mali, *Studies in Conflict & Terrorism*, https://doi.org/10.1080/1057610X.2022.2058360.

Compaoré, Ismael & Heidi Bojsen (2020) Security from below in Burkina Faso: Koglweogo, guardians of the bush, guardians of society?, *Cahiers d'etudes africaines*, no. 239, pp. 671–97.

Condé, Djanka Tassay & David C. Conrad (eds) (2004) *Sunjata: a West African Epic of the Mande Peoples*, Indianapolis: Hackett Publishing Company.

Cooper, Barbara (2010) The Sahel in West African history, in *Oxford Research Encyclopaedias—African History*, Oxford: Oxford University Press.

Coulibaly, Brahima & Shixiang Li (2020) Impact of agricultural land loss on rural livelihoods in peri-urban areas: empirical evidence from Sebougou, Mali, *Land*, vol. 9, no. 12, article 470.

Coulon, Christian (1983) *Les Musulmans et le Pouvoir en Afrique Noire, Religion et Contre-Culture*, Paris: Karthala.

Council on Foreign Relations (2023) Violent extremism in the Sahel, *Global Conflict Tracker*, Centre for Preventive Action, 10 August.

Craven-Matthews, Catriona & Pierre Englebert (2018) A Potemkin state in the Sahel? The empirical and the fictional in Malian state reconstruction, *African Security*, vol. 11, no. 1, pp. 1–31.

Croix, Kevin, Jérôme Marie, Luc Ferry & Frédéric Landy (2011) De nouvelles dynamiques de mécanisation agricole: commerce, usages et spatialisation au sein de la région de Ségou (Mali), *Annales de géographie*, no. 678, pp. 174–92.

Cruise O'Brien, Donal (2009) *Symbolic Confrontations: Muslims Imagining the State in Africa*, Basingstoke: Palgrave Macmillan.

Crummey, Donald (ed.) (1986) *Banditry, Rebellion and Social Protest in Africa*, Oxford: James Currey.

Danish De-Mining Group (2014) *Evaluations des Risques Sécuritaires aux Frontiérs: Région du Liptako-Gourma: Mali, Burkina Faso et Niger*, Copenhagen: DDG.

Davidson, Basil (2014) *West Africa Before the Colonial Era: a History to 1850*, London: Routledge.

Debos, Marielle (2009) *Porous Borders and Fluid Loyalties: Patterns of Conflict in Darfur, Chad, and the CAR*. New York: Center for Strategic and International Studies (CSIS).

Demuynck, Méryl & Mathis Böhm (2023) *Unravelling the Niger Coup and Its Implications for Violent Extremism in the Sahel*, International Centre for Counter-terrorism, 4 August.

BIBLIOGRAPHY

Dicko, Mahmoud (2021) *Manifesto for the Refoundation of Mali*, Bamako (18 February).

Dixon, Jeffrey (2009) What causes civil wars? Integrating research findings, *International Studies Review*, vol. 11, no. 4, pp. 707–35.

Dokken, Karin (2008) *African Security Politics Redefined*, New York: Palgrave.

Douce, Sofie (2023) Au Burkina Faso, le capitaine Ibrahim Traoré, le president enigmatique qui defie la France, *Le Monde* (29 September).

Driscoll, Barry (2020) Big man or boogey man? The concept of the Big Man in political science, *Journal of Modern African Studies*, vol. 58, no. 4, pp. 521–50.

Dwyer, Maggie (2017) Situating soldiers demands: mutinies and protests in Burkina Faso, *Third World Quarterly*, vol. 38, no. 1, pp. 219–34.

The Economist (2021) How not to lose the war on terror in Africa, *The Economist* (20 November).

Eizenga, Daniel (2019) Long-term trends across security and development in the Sahel, *West African Papers*, vol. 25, Paris: OECD Publishing.

Emerson, Stephen (2011) Desert insurgency: lessons from the third Tuareg rebellion, *Small Wars & Insurgencies*, vol. 22, no. 4, pp. 669–87.

Englebert, Pierre (1996) *Burkina Faso: Unsteady Statehood in West Africa*, New York: Westview Press.

Englebert, Pierre & Kevin C. Dunn (2019) *Inside African Politics*, Boulder: Lynne Rienner.

Erdmann, Gero & Ulf Engel (2007) Neopatrimonialism reconsidered: critical review and elaboration of an elusive concept, *Commonwealth and Comparative Politics*, vol. 45, no. 1, pp. 95–119.

Eriksen, Stein Sundstøl (2011) State failure in theory and practice: the idea of the state and contradiction of state formation, *Review of International Studies*, vol. 37, no. 1, pp 229–47.

FAO (2020) *Niger Response Overview*, Rome: FAO.

Faulkner, Christopher, Raphael Parsens & Marcel Plichta (2023) The West needs to prepare for the 'next Wagner' in Africa, *World Policy Review*, 20 July.

Fjeldstad, Odd-Helge (2014) Tax and development: donor support to strengthen tax systems in developing countries, *Public Administration and Development*, vol. 34, no. 3, pp. 182–93.

Fjeldstad, Odd-Helge, Morten Bøås, Julie B. Bjørkheim & Frida M. Kvamme (2018) *Building Tax Systems in Fragile States: Challenges, Achievements and Policy Recommendations*, Bergen: CMI (Report 3, March 2018).

Flood, Derek Henry (2012) Between Islamization and secession: the contest for Northern Mali, *CTC Sentinel*, vol. 5, no. 7, pp. 1–5.

Fomba, Bakery (2024) Assimi Goïta, la nouvelle figure du panafricanisme?, *Sahel Tribune*, (15 January) https://saheltribune.com/assimi-goita-la-nouvelle-figure-du-panafricanisme/.

BIBLIOGRAPHY

France 24 (2023) French army ends operations in Burkina Faso, Paris: France 24.

Freedom House (2024) Mali: Freedom in the World 2024 Country Report. Freedom House: https://freedomhouse.org/country/mali/freedom-world/2024.

Friedrich-Ebert-Stiftung (2024) *Mali-Mètre 2024*, Berlin: Friedrich-Eberhart-Stiftung.

Fröhlich, Silja (2024) The struggle for control in Mali's restive north. *Deutsche Welle*, (29 February), https://www.dw.com/en/malis-military-in-the-north-the-struggle-for-control/a-68387109.

FRONTEX (2017) *Central Mediterranean Route*, http://frontex.europe.eu/trends-and-routes/central-mediterranean-route/.

Gatt, Leah & Oliver Owen (2018) Direct taxation and state–society relations in Lagos, Nigeria, *Development and Change*, vol. 49, no. 5, pp. 1195–222.

Geertz, Clifford (2004) What is a state if it is not a sovereign? Reflections on politics in complicated places, *Current Anthropology*, vol. 45, no. 5, pp. 577–93.

Gingeras, Ryan (2011) In the hunt for the 'Sultans of Smack': dope, gangsters, and the construction of the Turkish deep state, *The Middle East Journal*, vol. 65, no. 3, pp. 426–41.

Gourlay, Youenn (2022) Indictment of 49 soldiers in Mali complicates negotiations with Côte d'Ivoire, *Le Monde* (17 August), https://www.lemonde.fr/en/international/article/2022/08/17/indictment-of-49-soldiers-in-mali-complicates-negotiations-with-cote-d-ivoire_5993846_4.html.

Government of Mali (2011) *Cadre Stratégique pour la Croissance et la Réduction de la Pauvreté, CSCRP 2012–2018*, Bamako, Republique du Mali.

Gramsci, Antonio (2005) *Selections From the Prison Notebooks*, Quintin Hoare & Geoffrey Nowell-Smith (eds), London: Lawrence & Wishart Ltd.

Guichaoua, Yvan (2011) Circumstantial alliances and loose loyalties in rebellion making: the case of Tuareg insurgency in Northern Niger (2007–2009), in Yvan Guichaoua (ed.), *Understanding Collective Political Violence*. Basingstoke: Palgrave Macmillan, pp. 246–66.

Guichaoua, Yvan & Mathieu Pellerin (2017) *Faire la paix et construire l'Etat: Les Relations entre pouvoir central et périphéries sahéliennes au Niger et au Mali*, Pris: IRSEM.

Haavik, Viljar, Morten Bøås & Alessio Iocchi (2022) The end of stability—how Burkina Faso fell apart, *African Security*, vol. 15, no. 4, pp. 1–24.

Hafez, Mohammed K. (2017) Fratricidal rebels: ideological extremity and warring factionalism in civil wars, *Terrorism and Political Violence*, vol. 32, no. 3, pp. 604–29.

BIBLIOGRAPHY

Hagberg, Sten (2019) Performing tradition while doing politics: a comparative study of the Dozo and Koglweogos self-defence movements in Burkina Faso, *African Studies Review*, vol. 62, no. 1, pp. 179–93.

Hagberg, Sten, Ludovic Kibora, Sidi Barry, Siaka Gnessi & Adjara Konkobo (2018) *Nothing Will Be as Before! Anthropological Perspectives on Political Practices and Democratic Culture in a 'new' Burkina Faso*, Uppsala: Upsala University Press.

Hagmann, Tobias & Daniel Péclard (2010) Negotiating statehood: dynamics of power and domination in Africa, *Development and Change*, vol. 41, no. 4, pp. 539–62.

Haidara, Boubacar (2022) Amid popular opposition, is the UN's peacekeeping mission in Mali doomed?, *The Conversation*, http://theconversation.com/amid-popular-opposition-is-the-uns-peacekeeping-mission-in-mali-doomed-189005.

Hansen, Eva (2023) Farmer-herder relations, land governance, and the national conflict in Mali, *Journal of Peasant Studies*, vol. 51, no. 4, pp. 1046–71.

Harding, Jeremy (1997) 'The mercenary business: 'executive outcomes', *Review of African Political Economy*, vol. 24, no. 71, pp. 87–97.

Harsch, Ernest (2014) *Thomas Sankara—An African Revolutionary*, Athens: Ohio University Press.

Harsch, Ernest (2017) *Burkina Faso: a History of Power, Protests, and Revolution*, London: Zed Books.

Hellweg, Joseph (2011) *Hunting the Ethical State: the Benkadi Movement of Côte d'Ivoire*, Chicago: University of Chicago Press.

Hesseling, Gerti & Han van Dijk (2005) Administrative decentralisation and political conflict in Mali, in Patrick Chabal, Ulf Engel & Anna-Maria Gentili (eds), *Is Violence Inevitable in Africa? Theories of Conflict and Approaches to Conflict Prevention*, Leiden: Brill, pp. 171–92.

Hibou, Béatrice (ed.) (2004) *Privatising the State*, London: Hurst & Company.

Hickey, Sam & Sophie King (2016) Understanding social accountability: politics, power and building new social contracts, *The Journal of Development Studies*, vol. 52, no. 8, pp. 1225–40.

Hobsbawm, Eric (1974) Social banditry, in Henry A. Landsberger (ed.) *Rural Protest: Peasant Movements and Social Change*, London: Macmillan, pp. 142–57.

Holder, Gilles (2012) Chérif Ousmane Madani Haïdara et l'association islamique Ansar Dine: un réformisme malien populaire en quête d'autonomie, *Cahiers d'études africaines*, no. 206–2007, pp. 389–425.

Hopkins, Anthony G. (1973) *An Economic History of West Africa*, New York: Longman.

Hunwick, John O. & Alida Jay Boye (2008) *The Hidden Treasures of Timbuktu: Historic City of Islamic Africa*, London: Thames & Hudson.

BIBLIOGRAPHY

Hüsken, Thomas & Georg Klute (2017) Heterarchie, Konnektivität, Lokale Politik und die Neuaushandlung der postkolonialen Ordnung von Libyen bis nach Mali, in T. Demmelhuber, A.T. Paul, M. Reinkowski (eds), *Arabellion, Vom Aufbruch zum Zerfall einer Region*, Baden-Baden: Nomos, pp. 155–79.

Ibrahim, Ibrahim Yahaya (2017) *The Wave of Jihadist Insurgency in West Africa: Global Ideology, Local Context, Individual Motivations*, Paris: OECD (West Africa Papers).

ICG (2013) *Burkina Faso: With Our Without Compaoré, Times of Uncertainty*, Brussels: ICG.

ICG (2016) *Central Mali: an Uprising in the Making*, Brussels: ICG.

ICG (2017) *The Social Roots of Jihadist Violence in Burkina Faso's North*, Brussels: ICG.

ICG (2020a) *Burkina Faso: Stopping the Spiral of Violence*, Brussels: ICG.

ICG (2020b) *Side-lining the Islamic State in Niger's Tillabery*, Brussels: ICG.

ICG (2022) *MINUSMA at a Crossroads*, Brussels: ICG.

ICG (2023) *Mali: Avoiding the Trap of Isolation*, Brussels: Crisis Group Africa Briefing No. 185.

ICIMALI (2024) ECOWAS has become an organization of disintegration, Colonel Abdoulaye Maïga from Ouagadougou—Icimali.com, (February 18). https://icimali.com/la-cedeao-est-devenue-une-organisation-de-desintegration-colonel-abdoulaye-maiga-depuis-ouagadougou/.

ICRC (2011) *Niger: North Tillabéri in the Grip of Violence and Drought*, Geneva: ICRC.

IISS (International Institute for Strategic Studies) (2017) Ansar Dine Ansar al-Din, https://acd.iiss.org/en/nonstatearmedgroups/ansar-dine-ansar-al-din-1803.

INSD (2019) *Les Comptes Nationaux Annuels de 2019*, Ouagadougou: INSD.

Jackson, Robert (2016) Regime security, in Alan Collins (ed.), *Contemporary Security Studies*, 4th edition, Oxford: Oxford University Press, pp. 200–14.

Jackson, Robert H. & Carl G. Rosberg (1982) *Personal Rule in Black Africa: Prince, Autocrat, Prophet, Tyrant*, Berkeley: University of California Press.

Jeune Afrique (2021) Mali: Le Premier ministre Choguel Maïga accuse la France d'«abandon» (26 September), https://www.jeuneafrique.com/1240113/politique/mali-le-premier-ministre-choguel-maiga-accuse-la-france-d-abandon/.

Jeune Afrique (2023) Rokia Doumbia, l'influenceuse qui a taclé Assimi Goïta, placée sous mandat de dépôt (16 March), https://www.jeuneafrique.com/1427695/politique/au-mali-une-influenceuse-tacle-assimi-goita-et-se-retrouve-en-garde-a-vue/.

Johnston, Karli (2009) Private military contractors: lessons learned in Iraq

BIBLIOGRAPHY

and increased accountability in Afghanistan, *Georgetown Journal of International Affairs*, vol. 10, no. 2, pp. 93–9.

Joscelyn, Thomas & Caleb Weiss (2016) Islamic State recognizes oath of allegiance from jihadists in Mali, *FDD's Long War Journal*, 31 October, https://www.longwarjournal.org/archives/2016/10/islamic-state-recognizes-oath-of-allegiance-from-jihadists-in-west-africa.php.

Kadivar, Jamileh (2020) Exploring takfir, its origins and contemporary use: the case of takfiri approach in Daesh's media, *Contemporary Review of the Middle East*, vol. 7, no. 3, pp. 259–85.

Kahl, Colin H. (2006) *States, Scarcity and Civil Strife in the Developing World*, Princeton: Princeton University Press.

Keegan, John (2011) *War and Our World*, New York: Knopf Doubleday.

Keen, David (2006) *Conflict and Collusion in Sierra Leone*, Oxford: James Currey.

Keenan, Jeremy (2007) The banana boat theory of terrorism: alternative truths and the collapse of the second (Sahara) front in the war on terror, *Journal of Contemporary African Studies*, vol. 25, no. 1, pp. 32–58.

Keenan, Jeremy (2008) Uranium goes critical in Niger: Tuareg rebellions threaten Sahelian conflagration, *Review of African Political Economy*, vol. 35, no. 117, pp. 449–66.

Keenan, Jeremy (2014) Interview, *Middle East Eye*, 30 June.

Keita, Kalifa (1998) *Conflict and Conflict Resolution in the Sahel: the Tuareg Insurgency in Mali*, Carlisle: US Army War College Press.

Kheng, Cheah Boon (1985) Hobsbawm's social banditry, myth and reality: a case in the Malaysian state of Kedah, 1915–1920, *Bulletin of Concerned Asian Scholars*, vol. 17, no. 4, pp. 34–51.

Koné, Hassane (2020) *Where Do Sahel Terrorists Take Their Heavy Weapons?* Pretoria: ISS.

Koné, Ousmane (2018) L'influence des organisations Islamique dans le processus d'élaboration du code des personnes et de la famille au Mali autopsie d'une victorie, in Anne Calves, Fatou Binetou & Richard Marcoux (eds) *Nouvelles dynamiques familiales en Afrique*, Québec: University of Québec Press, pp. 329–47.

Laub, Zachary & Jonathan Masters (2015) Al-Qaeda in the Islamic Maghreb (AQIM), Council on Foreign Relations, 27 March, https://www.cfr.org/backgrounder/al-qaeda-islamic-maghreb.

Lawal, Shola (2024) More than 70 killed in Mali attack. What happened, and why it matters, Al Jazeera, 20 September.

Le 360 Afrique (2022) Mali: Après son discours devant les Nations unies, Abdoulaye Maïga accueilli en héros (29 September), https://afrique.le360.ma/mali/politique/2022/09/28/39448-mali-apres-son-discours-devant-les-nations-unies-abdoulaye-maiga-accueilli-en-heros-39448/.

BIBLIOGRAPHY

Le Cam, Morgane (2023) Au Mali, Kidal, un symbole tombé aux mains de l'armée et de Wagner, *Le Monde* (27 November), https://www.lemonde.fr/afrique/article/2023/11/27/au-mali-kidal-un-symbole-tombe-aux-mains-de-l-armee-et-de-wagner_6202569_3212.html.

Le Monde (2023b) L'ONU se retire du Mali, la junte dénonce une «trahison» et accuse la France, https://www.lemonde.fr/afrique/article/2023/10/19/l-onu-se-retire-du-mali-la-junte-denonce-une-trahison-et-accuse-la-france_6195437_3212.html.

Lebovich, Andrew (2019) *Sacred Struggles—How Islam Shapes Politics in Mali*, Paris: European Council on Foreign Relations.

Lecocq, Bas (2004) Unemployed intellectuals in the Sahara: the Teshumara nationalist movement and the revolutions in Tuareg society, *International Review of Social History*, vol. 49, no. S12, pp. 87–109.

Lecocq, Bas, Gregory Mann, Bruce Whitehouse, Dida Badi, Lotte Pelckmans, Nadia Belalimat, Bruce Hall & Wolfram Laccher (2013) One hippopotamus and eight blind analysts: a multivocal analysis of the 2012 political crisis in the divided Republic of Mali, *Review of African Political Economy*, vol. 40, no. 137, pp. 343–57.

Lefdal, Kristian (2024) Regimekollaps i Syria kan få dramatiske konsekvenser for Afrika, *Panorama Nyheter*, 19 December.

Leonard, Daniel & Mohammed Samantar (2011) What does the Somali experience teach us about the social contract and the state? *Development and Change*, vol. 42, no. 2, pp. 559–84.

Loewe, Markus, Tina Zintl & Annabelle Houdret (2021) The social contract as a tool of analysis: introduction to the special issue on framing the evolution of new social contracts in Middle Eastern and North African countries, *World Development*, vol. 45, pp. 1–16.

Loimeier, Roman (2013) *Muslim Societies in Africa: a Historical Anthropology*, Bloomington: Indiana University Press.

Lounnas, Djallil (2014) Confronting Al-Qa'ida in the Islamic Maghreb in the Sahel: Algeria and the Malian crisis, *Journal of North African Studies*, vol. 190, no. 5, pp. 810–27.

Lovejoy, Paul (2016) *Jihad in West Africa During the Age of Revolutions*, Athens: Ohio University Press.

Lyammouri, Rida (2021) *Central Mali: Armed Community Mobilization in Crisis*, Washington, DC: Resolve Network.

Lynn, Terry K. (1995) The hybrid regimes of Central America, *Journal of Democracy*, vol. 6, no. 3, pp. 72–86.

Macé, C. (2020) 'Mali: Mahmoud Dicko, l'imam qui défie le président IBK', *Libération*, https://www.liberation.fr/planete/2020/06/04/mali-mahmoud-dicko-l-imam-qui-defie-le-president-ibk_1790277/.

Machesin, Philippe (1992) *Tribus, Ethnies et Pouvoir et Mauritanie*, Paris: Karthala.

BIBLIOGRAPHY

Maclean, Ruth (2022) 'Down with France': former colonies in Africa demand a reset, *The New York Times* (14 April), https://www.nytimes.com/2022/04/14/world/africa/france-macron-africa-colonies.html.

Maclean, Ruth (2024) Three African juntas leave regional bloc, accusing it of 'inhumane' sanctions, *The New York Times* (28 January), https://www.nytimes.com/2024/01/28/world/africa/west-africa-junta-leave-ecowas.html.

Maclean, Ruth, Mamadou Tapily & Loucoumane Coulibaly (2022) They said they went to Mali to keep the peace. Now they're jailed as mercenaries, *The New York Times* (December 30).

Makovicky, Nicolette & Robin Smith (2020) Introduction: tax beyond the social contract, *Social Analysis*, vol. 64, no. 2, pp. 1–17.

Mann, Gregory (2021) French colonialism and the making of the modern Sahel, in Leonardo A. Villalón (ed.), *The Oxford Handbook of the African Sahel*, Oxford: Oxford University Press, pp. 37–50.

Manning, Patrick (1998) *Francophone Sub-Saharan Africa: 1880–1995*, Cambridge: Cambridge University Press.

Marchal, Roland (2013) Une nouvelle aventure militaire au Sahara?, *Sciences Po Newsletter*, 4 February, http://www.sciencespo.fr/newsletter/show/?id=725.

Marnham, Patrick (1979) *Nomads of the Sahel*, London: Minority Rights Group.

Marotte, Adrien (2024) What's the fallout from the setback for Mali army Wagner ally, *Agence-France-Presse*.

Mazrui, Ali & Christophe Wondji (eds) (1993) *General History of Africa: Africa Since 1935*, vol. VIII, London: Heinemann Educational Books.

McDougall, Anne E. (2006) The legacy of slavery: between discourse and reality, *Cahiers d'études africaines*, vol. 45, no. 179/80, pp. 957–86.

McGovern, Mark (2011) *Making War in Côte d'Ivoire*, London: Hurst.

McGovern, Mark (2017) *A Socialist Peace? Explaining the Absence of War in an African Country*, Chicago: University of Chicago Press.

Melly, Paul (2020) Mahmoud Dicko: Mali imam challenges President Keita, BBC: London.

Metz, Steven (2007) *Rethinking Insurgency*, Carlisle: United States Army War College Press.

Meyer, Henry & Katarina Hoije (2024) Russia's Wagner suffers most casualties since deploying to Mali, *Bloomberg*, 29 July.

Migdal, Joel S. (1988) *Strong Societies and Weak States: State-Society Relations and State Capabilities in the Third World*, Princeton: Princeton University Press.

Mkandawire, Thandika (1999) Crisis management and the making of choiceless democracies, in Richard Joseph (ed.) *State, Conflict and Democracy in Africa*, Boulder: Lynne Rienner, pp. 119–36.

BIBLIOGRAPHY

Mkandawire, Thandika (2015) Neopatrimonialism and the political economy of economic performance in Africa: critical reflections, *World Politics*, vol. 67, no. 3, pp. 1–50.

Moelnaar, Fransje & Thibault Van Damme (2017) *Irregular Migration and Human Smuggling Networks in Niger*, The Hague: Clingendael Report (February).

Monteau, Flore (2023) The battle of Kidal, a triumph for Mali's Assimi Goïta (17 November), https://www.theafricareport.com/328176/the-battle-of-kidal-a-triumph-for-malis-assimi-goita/

Moorehead, Richard (1997) *Structural Chaos: Community and State Management of Common Property in Mali*, London: International Institute for Environment and Development.

Munshi, Neil (2021) How France lost Mali: failure to quell jihadi threat opens door to Russia, *Financial Times* (22 December).

Murray, Philip (2016) Human security in Mali: overcoming obstacles to economic solvency and democratic governance through external intervention, *Small Wars Journal*, https://archive.smallwarsjournal.com/index.php/jrnl/art/human-insecurity-in-mali.

Niang, Amy (2016) *Blaise Compaoré in the Resolution of the Ivorian Conflict: From Belligerent to Mediator in-Chief*, New York: Social Science Research Council.

Nigerien National Institute of Statistics (2012) *Demographic and Health Data*, Niamey: Nigerien Institute of Statistics.

Nsaibia, Héni & Caleb Weiss (2018) Ansaroul Islam and the growing terrorist insurgency in Burkina Faso, *CTC Sentinel*, vol. 11, no. 3, pp. 21–7.

Nsaibia, Héni & Caleb Weiss (2020) The end of the Sahelian anomaly: how the global conflict between the Islamic State and al-Qa'ida finally came to West Africa, *CTC Sentinel*, July, pp. 1–14.

Nugent, Paul (2010) States and social contracts in Africa, *New Left Review*, vol. 63, no. 3, pp. 426–41.

Nyadera, Israel N. & Hamani Massaoud (2019) Elusive peace and the impact of ungoverned space in the Sahel conflict, *The Journal of Security Sciences*, vol. 8, no. 2, pp. 271–88.

OCCRP (2021) *British American Tobacco Fights Dirty in West Africa*, Stanford: OCCRP, https://www.occrp.org/en/loosetobacco/british-american-tobacco-fights-dirty-in-west-africa.

OCHA (2019) *Inform Risk Index Niger 2019*, New York: OCHA.

OHCHR (2023) *Malian Troops, Foreign Military Personnel Killed Over 500 People During Military Operation in Moura in March 2022—UN Human Rights Report*, OHCHR (12 May), https://www.ohchr.org/en/press-releases/2023/05/malian-troops-foreign-military-personnel-killed-over-500-people-during.

BIBLIOGRAPHY

Olivier, Mathieu (2024) 'African Dawn', the Russian video game to fight France in Africa, *The Africa Report* (23 August), https://www.theafricareport.com/359212/african-dawn-the-russian-video-game-to-fight-france-in-africa/.

Olson, Mancur (2000) *Power and Prosperity: Outgrowing Communist and Capitalist Dictatorships*, New York: Basic Books.

Osland, Kari M. & Henriette U. Erstad (2020) The fragility dilemma and divergent security complexes in the Sahel, *The International Spectator*, vol. 4, no. 55, pp. 18–36.

Paquette, Danielle & Joby Warrick (2020) Al-Qaeda and Islamic State groups are working together in West Africa to grab large swaths of territory, *Washington Post*, 22 February.

Pedersen, Jon & Tor-Arve Benjaminsen (2008) One leg or two? Pastoralism and food security in Northern Mali, *Human Ecology*, vol. 36, no. 1, pp. 43–57.

Peltier, Elian (2024) This alliance united West Africa for decades. Now countries are backing out, *New York Times* (10 July), https://www.nytimes.com/2024/07/10/world/africa/west-african-countries-leave-ecowas.html.

Penney, Joe (2018) Drones in the Sahara: a massive US drone base could destabilize Niger—and may even be illegal under its constitution, *The Intercept* (18 February).

Penney, Joe (2019) Burkina Faso has replaced Mali at the epicentre of the Sahel's security crisis, *Quartz Africa* (27 November).

Potter, Geoff D. (2018) The renewed jihadi terror threat to Mauritania, *CTC Sentinel*, August, pp. 16–20.

Pringle, Robert (2006) *Democratisation in Mali: Putting History to Work*, Washington, DC: United States Institute of Peace.

Qutb, Sayyid (1964) *Milestones (Ma'alim fi al-Tariq)*, Cairo: Kazi Publications.

Raineri, Luca (2018) Human smuggling across Niger: state-sponsored protection rackets and contradictory security imperatives', *Journal of Modern African Studies*, vol. 56, no. 1, pp. 63–86.

Raineri, Luca (2020) Gold mining in the Sahara-Sahel: the political geography of state-making and unmaking, *The International Spectator*, vol. 55, no. 4, pp. 100–17.

Raineri, Luca & Francesco Strazzari (2015) State, secession and jihad: the micropolitical economy of conflict in Northern Mali, *African Security*, vol. 8, no. 4, pp. 249–71.

Raineri, Luca & Francesco Strazzari (2021) Drug smuggling and the stability of fragile states: the diverging trajectories of Mali and Niger, *Journal of Intervention and Statebuilding*, vol. 16, no. 2, pp. 222–39.

Raleigh, Clionadh & Caitriona Dowd (2013) Governance and conflict in the Sahel's ungoverned space, *Stability*, vol. 2, no. 2, pp. 1–17.

BIBLIOGRAPHY

Raleigh, Clionadh, Héni Nsaibia & Caitriona Dowd (2021) 'The Sahel crisis since 2012', *African Affairs*, vol. 120, no. 478, pp. 123–43.

Roberts, Richard L. (1987) *Warriors, Merchants and Slaves: the State and the Economy in the Middle Niger Valley 1700–1914*, Stanford: Stanford University Press.

Robinson, David (1988) *La guerre sainte d'al-Haji Umar: le Soudan occidental au milieu du XIXe siècle*, Paris: Karthala.

Roger, Benjamin (2023) 'Red guard? Will Russian military protect Ibrahim Traoré in Burkina Faso?, *Africa Report* (15 November).

Rupesinghe, Natasja & Morten Bøås (2018) *Local Drivers of Violent Extremism in Central Mali*, Addis Ababa: UNDP (policy brief).

Sahlins, Marshall D. (1963) Poor man, rich man, big man, chief: political types in Melanesia and Polynesia, *Comparative Studies in Society and History*, vol. 5, pp. 285–303.

Salih, Zeinab Mohammed (2023) Niger observers link coup to presidents support for EU migration policies, *The Guardian* (23 August).

Sandor, Adam & Aurélie Campana (2019) Les groups djihadistes au Mali, entre violence, recherche de légitimité et politiques locales, *Canadian Journal of African Studies*, vol. 53, no. 3, pp. 415–30.

Sangary, Boukary (2016) Le centre du Mali: epicentre du djihadisme?, *GRIP* (20 May), pp. 1–12.

Scheele, Judith (2009) 'Tribus, états et fraude: al région frontalière algéro-malienne', *Études Rurales*, vol. 184, no. 2, pp. 79–94.

Schulz, Dorothea E. (2010) Sharia and national law in Mali, in Jan Michiel Otto (ed.), *Sharia Incorporated: A Comparative Overview of the Legal Systems of Twelve Muslim Countries in Past and Present*, Amsterdam: Amsterdam University Press, pp. 529–52.

Schulz, Dorothea E. (2021) *Political Legitimacy in Postcolonial Mali*, Oxford: James Currey.

Sears, Jonathan Michel (2007) *Deepening Democracy and Cultural Context in the Republic of Mali, 1992–2002*, PhD Thesis, Kingston: Queen's University.

Secrétariat Général du Gouvernement Mali (2022) *Discours du Colonel Abdoulaye MAIGA Premier ministre p.i, Chef du Gouvernement du Mali, à l'occasion du Débat général de la 77ème Session ordinaire de l'Assemblée générale des Nations Unies*, République du Mali, https://www.un.int/mali/sites/www.un.int/files/Mali/rev_allocution_mali_agnu_24_septembre_2022_2.pdf.

Seely, Jennifer (2001) A political analysis of decentralisation: co-opting the Tuareg threat in Mali, *Journal of Modern African Studies*, vol. 39, no. 3, pp. 499–524.

Seesemann, Rüdiger & Benjamin F. Soares (2009) Being as good Muslims as Frenchmen: On Islam and colonial modernity in West Africa, *Journal of Religion in Africa*, vol. 39, no. 1, pp. 91–120.

BIBLIOGRAPHY

Shaw, Mark & Prem Mahadevan (2018) When terrorism and organized crime meet, *Policy Perspectives*, vol. 6/7, pp. 1–4.

Sikor, Thomas & Christian Lund (2009) Access and property: a question of power and authority, *Development and Change*, vol. 40, no. 1, pp. 1–22.

Singer, Peter W. (2003) *Corporate Warriors: the Rise of the Privatised Military Industry*, Ithaca: Cornell University Press.

Soares, Benjamin F. (1996) The prayer economy in a Malian town, *Cahiers d'études africaines*, vol. 36, no. 144, pp. 739–53.

Soares, Benjamin F. (2010) Rasta, Sufis, and Muslim youth culture in Mali, in Asef Bayat & Linda Herrera (eds), *Being Young and Muslim: New Cultural Politics in the Global South and North*, Oxford: Oxford University Press, pp. 241–58.

Söyler, Mehtap (2013) Informal institutions, forms of state and democracy: the Turkish deep state, *Democratization*, vol. 20, no. 2, pp. 310–34.

Strazzari, Francesco (2014) Captured or capturing? Narcotics and political instability along the African route to Europe, *European Review of Organised Crime*, vol. 1, no. 2, pp. 5–34.

Tamkin, Emily (2023) France recalls Burkina Faso ambassador ahead of troop withdrawal, *Foreign Policy Morning Brief*.

Tardy, Thierry (2016) France: the unlikely return to UN peacekeeping, *International Peacekeeping*, vol. 23, no. 5, pp. 610–29.

Théroux-Benoni, Lori-Anne (2014) The long path to MINUSMA: assessing the international response to the crisis in Mali, in Marco Wyss & Thierry Tardy (eds), *Peacekeeping in Africa: The Evolving Security Architecture*, London: Routledge, pp. 134–56.

Thomas, Dominique (2016) État Islamique vs Al-Qaida: autopsie d'une lutte fratricide, *Politique Étrangère*, vol. no. pp. 95–106.

Thurston, Alexander (2019) *Escalating Conflicts in Burkina Faso*, Berlin: Rosa Luxemburg Stiftung.

Thurston, Alexander (2020a) *Jihadists of North Africa and the Sahel: Local Politics and Rebel Groups*, Cambridge: Cambridge University Press.

Thurston, Alexander (2020b) *Could Mali's Coup Have Been Avoided?*, Sahelblog.worldpress.com.

Tillabéri Regional Development Plan (2016) *Tillabéri Regional Development Plan 2016–2020*, Niamey: Government of Niger.

Tinti, Peter & Tom Westcott (2016) *The Niger-Libya Corridor: Smugglers' Perspectives*, Dakar: ISS Paper 299.

Tønnessen, Truls H. (2015) Heirs of Zarqawi or Saddam? The relationship between al-Qaida in Iraq and the Islamic State, *Perspectives on Terrorism*, vol. 9, no. 4, pp. 49–60.

Transparency International (2021) Mali, www.transparency.org/en/countries/mali.

BIBLIOGRAPHY

Tull, Dennis (2019) Rebuilding Mali's army: the dissonant relationship between Mali and its international partners, *International Affairs*, vol. 95, no. 2, pp. 405–22.

Turse, Nick (2024) U.S. trained Niger Junta kicks out U.S. troops, drone base, *The Intercept*.

UN (2000) *Report of the Panel of Experts on Violations of Security Council Sanctions Against UNITA*, New York: United Nations (S/2000/203).

UN (2009) *Final Report of the Group of Experts on Côte d'Ivoire Pursuant to Paragraph II of Security Council Resolution 1842*, New York: United Nations (S/2009/521).

UN (2014) *Letter Dates 9 June 2014 From the Chair of the Security Council Committee Established Pursuant to Resolution 1988 (2011) Addressed to the President of the Security Council*, New York: United Nations.

UN (2020) *Mali: Panel of Experts Report to the Security Council*, New York: United Nations.

UNDP (2016) *Preventing Violent Extremism by Promoting Inclusive Development, Tolerance and Respect for Diversity*, New York: UNDP.

UNDP (2017) *Human Development Report 2016: Human Development for Everyone*, New York: UNDP.

UNDP (2022) *Human Development Report 2021–22: Uncertain Times, Unsettled Lives: Shaping our Future in a Transforming World*, New York: UNDP.

UNECA (2017) *New Fringe Pastoralism: Conflict, Insecurity and Development in the Horn of Africa and the Sahel*, Addis Ababa: UNECA.

UNGA (2023). Mali—Minister for Foreign Affairs addresses general debate, 78th session, UN Web TV [Broadcast], 23 September, https://webtv.un.org/en/asset/k15/k156s6ldbq

Ursu, Anca-Elena (2018) *Under the Gun: Resource Conflicts and Embattled Traditional Authorities in Central Mali*, The Hague: Clingendael—Netherlands Institute of International Relations (CRU Report).

Utas, Mats (ed.) (2012) *African Conflicts and Informal Power: Big Men and Networks*, London: Zed Books.

Vague, Tom (2001) *Televisionaries: The Red Army Faction Story 1963–1994*, Edinburgh: AK Press.

Van Dessel, Julia (2019) International delegation and agency in the externalization process of EU migration and asylum policy: The role of the IOM and the UNHCR in Niger, *European Journal of Migration and Law*, vol. 21, no. 4, pp. 435–58.

Vium, Christian (2013) The phantom menace: fear, rumours and the elusive presence of AQIM in south-eastern Mauritania, in Morten Bøås & Mats Utas (eds), *Post-Gaddafi Repercussions in the Sahel and West Africa*, special section of the *Strategic Review for Southern Africa*, vol. 35, no. 2, pp. 92–116.

BIBLIOGRAPHY

Voltmer, Katrin, Kjetil Selvik & Jacob Høigilt (2021) Hybrid media and hybrid politics: contesting informational uncertainty in Lebanon and Tunisia, *International Journal of Press Politics*, vol. 26, no. 4, pp. 842–60.

Wagemakers, Joas (2016) What should an Islamic state look like? Salafi debates on the war in Syria, *The Muslim World*, vol. 106, no. 3, pp. 95–106.

Weber, Max (2004) D.S. Owen & T.B. Strong (eds), *The Vocation Lectures*, Indianapolis: Hackett.

Wedel, Janine R. (2009) *Shadow Elite: How the World's New Power Brokers Undermine Democracy, Government, and the Free Market*, New York: Basic Books.

Weiss, Caleb (2017) Analysis: merger of Al Qaeda groups threatens security in West Africa, *FDD's Long War Journal*, 18 March, http://www.longwarjournal.org/archives/2017/03/analysis-merger-of-al-qaeda-groups-threatens-security-in-west-africa.php.

WFP (2020) *Conflits persistants, pertes de terres agricoles et insécurité alimentaire récurrente dans la région du Liptako-Gourma*, New York: World Food Programme.

Whitehouse, Bruce (2012) The force of action: legitimising the coup in Bamako, Mali, *Africa Spectrum*, vol. 47, no. 2–3, pp. 93–110.

Whitehouse, Bruce (2022) Betting big on sovereignty, *Bridges From Bamako*. https://bridgesfrombamako.com/2022/02/18/betting-big-on-sovereignty/.

Wigell, Mikael (2008) Mapping hybrid regimes: regime types and concepts in comparative politics, *Democratisation*, vol. 15, no. 2, pp. 230–50.

Wood, Graeme (2015) What ISIS really wants, *The Atlantic* (March).

World Bank (2022) *Mali—Systematic Country Diagnostic*, Washington, DC: World Bank.

Wright, Lawrence (2017) *The Terror Years: From al-Qaeda to the Islamic State*, New York: Penguin Random House.

Yao, M. & S. Kondo (2021) Artisanal gold mining in Mali is an economic boon and an environmental disaster, *Sahelian.com*, 6 January.

Zouhir, Yahia (2021) Why Algeria cut diplomatic ties with Morocco: and implications for the future, *The Conversation*, 14 September.

INDEX

Abd al-Qādir, 171
Abdramane, Amadou, 109–10
Abou Zeid, 32
Abubakari II, Emperor of Mali, 163
Accountability Lab Mali, 227
ADEMA, 156
Afghanistan, 132, 210, 229, 233, 235
Africa Corps, xxi, 207, 217
Africa Initiative, 192, 204
African Dawn, 204
African Union (AU), 3, 33, 34, 215
Afrobarometer, 21, 209, 227, 231
Ag Bahanga, Ibrahim, 11, 15–16, 29, 131, 151, 152
Ag Fagaga, Hassan, 131, 151
Ag Ghaly, Iyad, 11, 39–41, 47, 131, 133, 147, 153–4
    1990 rebellion, 40, 153
    2006 rebellion, 151
    2012 rebellion, 29, 36–7, 39, 44, 154
    Bassolé, meeting with (2012), 72, 76
    Islamic State, relations with, 50–51, 52
    Katiba Macina, relations with, 171, 176
    Wagner Group, views on, 208
Ag Intalla, Alghabass, 154
Agacher Strip, 55
Agadez, Niger, 24, 80, 81, 96–110, 202
agriculture, xviii, xx
    in Burkina Faso, 57, 200
    in Mali, 6–7, 26, 42–3, 46, 120, 168
    in Niger, 84, 85, 88–90
AIDS, 60
Algeria, 15, 23, 34, 37–9, 45, 52, 132, 192
    cigarette smuggling in, 134
    Civil War (1992–2002), 37–8, 132
    migration through, 98, 100, 103, 104–5
    Tuaregs in, 149, 150, 155
Algiers Agreement (2015), 4, 91, 225
Ali ibn Abi Talib, 49
Alliance for Democracy in Mali (ADEMA), 145
Alliance Ibrahim Boubacar Keita, 156–7

INDEX

Alliance of Sahel States (AoSS), 55, 174
Almoravid Empire (1050s–1147), 162
Amaq News Agency, 46
Aménas attack (2013), 133, 135, 154
Ansar Dine, 121
Ansar ed-Dine, 29, 36–7, 39–41, 50, 76, 136, 147, 154, 155
Arab people, 146, 147–8, 150
Areva NC, 96
Arlit, Niger, 96, 101, 105
Armed Forces of Mali (FAMA), 52, 109, 199, 208, 216, 220, 226
Armed Islamic Group (GIA), 38
al-Assad, Bashar, 30, 197
Assamakka, Niger, 105
Association pour l'Unité et le Progrès de l'Islam (AMUPI), 186, 187
autocratic cliques, 62–5, 71
Azawad, 28, 29, 36, 40, 147, 149

al-Baghdadi, Abu Bakr, 46–7, 90
Bamako, Mali, 4, 7, 29, 31, 155–8, 181, 196–7, 198
Bambara people, 115, 118, 146, 211
Bandiagara, Mali, 118
banditry, 73–4, 75, 76–7, 94, 102, 129–30, 133
Banibangou, Niger, 92
Bankilaré, Niger, 94
Barlow, Eben, 205, 207
Bassolé, Djibril, 64, 66, 72, 75, 76
Battle of Tinzaouaten (2024), 30, 196
Bazoum, Mohamed, xviii, 55, 79–80, 100, 101, 107, 109, 198, 201–2

Belmokhtar, Mokhtar, 46–7, 132–6, 140
Benin, xix, 5, 44, 57, 231
Benkadi Movement, 211
Berber people, 148, 162, 164
Big Men, 10, 15–16, 17, 19, 32, 126–30, 140
  in Burkina Faso, 58, 63–9, 70, 71, 72, 73, 75, 76, 78–9
  in Mali, 127, 130, 131, 150–51, 159, 178, 179–80, 192–3
  in Niger, 83, 108
Bilal, Cheick Soufi, 121
Blackwater, 205
Blinken, Anthony, 208
Boko Haram, 58, 98
Boulgou, Burkina Faso, 77
bourgoutiéres, 51
Bozo people, 115, 170
Burkina Faso, xv, xvi, xvii, xviii, 5, 20, 23, 56–79
  Agacher Strip dispute, 55
  AoSS formation (2023), 55, 174
  banditry in, 73–4, 75, 76–7
  Christianity in, 56
  Compaoré presidency (1987–2014), 57, 58–9, 61–74, 76, 77, 78–9
  constitution, 74
  coup d'état (Jan 2022), 56, 199
  coup d'état (Sep 2022), 56, 195, 202, 224, 234
  Decree 1052 (2016), 77–8
  ECOWAS withdrawal (2024), 55–6, 174
  France, relations with, xx–xxi, 3, 34, 59, 61, 195, 203, 231
  G5 Sahel project, 34–6
  inter-communal conflicts, 75–8
  Ivorian Civil War (2002–7), 70, 72, 73

INDEX

jihadist insurgency (2016–), 57, 76–9, 216, 233
Kaboré presidency (2015–22), 67, 75, 76–9
Liberian Civil War (1989–97), 70, 73
Mali War (2012–) and, xvi, 4, 25, 52, 53, 59, 79
Mali, relations with, 70, 71, 72, 197
mediation industry, 71–3
mineral production, 56, 57, 206
mutiny (2011), 73, 74
name change (1984), 60
Niger, relations with, 71, 72, 201
Operation Barkhane (2014–22), xix, 3, 4, 33, 202
patrimonial politics in, 62–9, 70, 71, 72, 73, 75, 76, 78–9
population growth, 56, 57, 230
Russia, relations with, xx–xxi, 3, 173–4, 195
Sankara presidency (1983–7), 57, 59–61, 65, 224, 225, 226
Sierra Leonean Civil War (1991–2002), 70, 73
state weakness, 24, 56–7
Traoré presidency (2022–), 55, 59, 197, 199, 206
uprising (2014), 57, 58, 59, 61, 64
Wagner Group in, 206

Caliphate, 48
Camara, Sadio, 198
Cameroon, 58, 155
Central African Republic, 205, 206, 207
Chad, 30, 33, 34, 36, 58, 101, 149, 205
Christianity, 56
cigarette smuggling, 132–3, 134–6, 165
Cissé, Soumaila, 31, 181–2
Clapham, Christopher, 13
clientelism, 12, 19, 66, 68
climate change, xvii, xviii, xx, 5–7, 18, 20, 26, 88, 96, 167, 173, 230
Co-ordination of Patriotic Organisations (COPAM), 156, 157–8
coal, 88
cocaine, 102, 134, 135, 155, 165
cocoa, 165
Code of Marriage and Guardianship, 186
colonialism, 4, 14, 61, 65, 143, 146, 165, 167, 168, 172, 179, 229, 230, 235
education and, 148
indirect rule, 65, 108
land rights and, 42, 85, 107, 168
migration and, 57
resistance to, 59, 157, 197, 198, 210
Sufism and, 183
trans-Saharan trade and, 165
Comité de Paix d'Agadez, 97
Committees for the Defence of the Revolution, 61
Communist Officers Group, 60
Compaoré, Blaise, 57, 58–74, 76, 77, 78
Compaoré, François, 67
Congrés pour la Démocratie et le Progrés (CDP), 67, 75
Constantine, Algeria, 45
Coordination des Associations Féminines (CAFO), 186
Coordination des Mouvements (CMAS), 188, 189, 190, 192

INDEX

copper, 56
corruption, 8, 12, 21, 114, 115, 122
　in Burkina Faso, 60–61, 66
　in Mali, 24, 27, 31–2, 37, 43, 181, 189, 225
　in Niger, 94, 95
Côte d'Ivoire, xix, 5, 44, 57, 58, 61, 70, 72, 158, 165, 211, 222
COVID-19 pandemic (2019–23), 26
crime, xvii, 3, 8–9, 12, 13, 16
　banditry, 73–4, 75, 76–7, 94, 129–30, 133
　cigarette smuggling, 132–3, 134–6, 165
　drug trade, 8, 12, 31, 130, 133, 134, 136, 146, 153, 154, 155, 165
　hostage taking, 40, 69, 72, 130, 132, 133
　human trafficking, 24, 63, 96, 102–3, 155
　hybridity and, 128–40
　Mali War and, 32, 130–40
　violent entrepreneurs, 128–30
Crummey, Donald, 129, 133

Dagalo, Mohamed Hamdan, 107
Damiba, Paul-Henri, 199
Dana Amassagou, 116–17
Daoussahak people, 45, 46, 47, 50, 90, 91, 93, 148
Dargol River, 88
Decentralisation Commission, xix, 32, 131, 141, 151–3
Decree 1052 (Burkina Faso, 2016), 77–8
deep state, 58, 62–9, 70, 71, 72, 73, 75, 76, 78–9
Dembéle, Clement, 189

Democratic Alliance for Change (ADC), 40, 131, 151
Democratic Alliance for Peace, 181, 184
Democratic Republic of Congo, 147, 155, 210, 235
democratisation, 12, 32, 33, 107–8, 143, 179–80, 217
Diallo, Aliou Boubacar, 31, 181, 183, 184
Diamongou River, 88
Diarra, Cheick Modibo, 31, 181
Diawara, Lassine, 68
Diawara, Youssouf Daba, 192
Dicko, Mahmoud, 19, 174, 177–9, 181, 184–93, 218
Dienderé, Gilbert, 64, 66, 67, 70, 75, 76
Diop, Abdoulaye, xvii, 198, 210, 213, 221, 224, 234
Direction de la Surveillance du Territoire, 105
Dirkou, Niger, 99, 101
disarmament, demobilisation, re-integration (DDR), 93, 150
Djenne, Mali, 143, 179
Dogon people, 56, 115, 116–17, 118, 168, 211
donor assistance, 10, 24–5, 35, 67, 80, 209
Donzos, 116–17
Douce, Sophie, 199
Dozo, 77, 211, 213, 221, 225
Driscoll, Barry, 64, 126, 178
droughts, 6, 39, 86, 88, 149
Droukdel, Abdelmalek, 38–9, 43, 52
drug trade, 8, 12, 31, 130, 133, 134, 136, 146, 153, 154, 155, 165
Dyingerey Ber Mosque, Timbuktu, 164

INDEX

Dyula, 60

economic liberalisation, 32, 144
ECOWAS, 3, 33, 34, 36, 70, 72, 84, 157, 198, 201, 211, 215
  withdrawal from (2024), 55–6, 174, 221–3, 225
education, 60, 87, 88, 111, 113, 115, 119, 148
Emergency Transit Mechanism (ETM), 105
employment, 57, 87, 89, 96, 111, 115, 119, 122, 173
enabling environments, 46, 81, 87–90, 111–23
  corruption and, 114, 115, 116, 122
  education and, 87, 88, 111, 113, 115, 119
  employment and, 87, 115, 118, 119, 122
  land conflicts and, 115–23
  non-occurrence in, 119–22
  social mobility and, 114, 115, 122
  state weakness and, 114, 115, 117, 122
Epic of Sundiata, 163, 212, 229
Eritrea, 13, 104
Ethiopia, 129
European Union (EU), xv, xviii, 173, 195, 198, 203, 209, 215, 216, 231, 232, 238
  EUCAP Sahel Mali (2015–), xix, 216
  EUTF for Africa, 104
  EUTM Mali (2013–24), 3, 156, 216
  G5 Sahel project, 34–6, 94, 216
  Horizon 2020 programme, 20, 21

Niger, relations with, 80, 97, 100–103, 107, 109
Takouba Task Force (2020–22), 202
Executive Outcomes, 205, 207

FAMA, 52, 109, 199, 208, 216, 220
family law code, 177, 185, 186–7
farmer–herder conflicts, *see* land rights
FC-G5S, 35
FEDAP-BC, 67, 68
Flame of Peace Monument, Timbuktu, 28, 33
Fomba, Bakery, 227
food security, 88–9
Forces Nouvelles, 70–71, 72
fragile states, *see* weak states
France, xv, xvii, xviii, xx–xxi, 34, 195–6, 202–4, 215, 232
  Burkina Faso, relations with, xx–xxi, 3, 34, 59, 61, 195, 200, 203, 231
  colonialism, *see* colonialism
  G5 Sahel project, 34–6, 94, 216
  Mali, relations with, *see* Franco–Mali relations
  Niger, relations with, xx–xxi, 3, 34, 80, 195, 196, 202, 203, 231
  Operation Barkhane (2014–22), *see* Operation Barkhane
  Operation Serval (2013–14), xix, 3, 29–30, 33, 41, 46, 90, 116, 180, 216
  Takouba Task Force (2020–22), 202
  withdrawal (2022–3), 4, 10, 195, 199, 200, 202, 203, 217–19, 225–6, 231

269

INDEX

Franco–African Summit (1996), 71
Franco–Mali relations, xv, xx, 3–5, 32–4, 36, 44, 52, 157–8, 173, 195–6, 202–4, 209, 238
  neopatriotism and, 197, 198, 199, 231, 236
  withdrawal (2022), 4, 10, 195, 199, 203, 217, 218–19, 225–6, 231
Freedom House, 225
FRONTEX, 100–101
Fulani people, xx
  in Burkina Faso, 56, 75–6, 77
  in Mali, 27, 42–3, 46, 47, 51, 115, 116, 118, 141, 146, 148, 168–72
  in Niger, 84, 86, 90, 91, 93, 95

G5 Sahel project, 34–6, 94, 216
Gaddafi, Muammar, 29, 36, 39–40, 86, 107, 147, 155, 215
Gao, Mali, 27, 30, 33, 45, 46, 90–91, 136, 143, 145, 164, 179, 211
Gatrone, Libya, 102
Gbagbo, Laurent, 158
Germany, 34, 132, 133
Ghana, xix, xx, 5, 44, 57, 134, 231
Ghana Empire (c. 100–1200s), 143, 161–2, 163, 229
Ghanda Koy, 149–50, 157
globalisation, 12
Goïta, Assimi, 59, 159, 197–9, 201, 202, 204, 209–27, 231
  approval ratings, 21, 209, 227, 231, 235, 237
  constitutional referendum (2023), 192
  coup d'état (2020), 55, 177, 189–90, 195, 198, 209, 217, 224
  coup d'état (2021), xv, 34, 217, 218
  dissent, suppression of, 225–6
  inter-Malian dialogue, 226–7
  international relations, 4, 215–24, 225, 226
  mythmaking, 210–15, 224–5, 237
gold, xvi, 56, 88, 128, 130, 136–9, 140, 162, 163–4, 167
Gorouol River, 88
Gourma people, 84
Gourma, Mali, 50, 52
Gouroubi River, 88
Gramsci, Antonio, 11
Granada, Spain, 164
Group for Preaching and Combat (GSPC), 38, 40, 132
Groupe Autodéfense Touareg Imghad (GATIA), 47, 91, 138
Guevara, Ernesto 'Che', 59
Guinea, 58
Guinea-Bissau, 134

hadith literature, 48
Haftar, Khalifa, 206
Haidara, Cherif Ousmane Maidani, 121, 182, 184, 225, 237
Hamallah, Cheik, 183
Hamawiyya Brotherhood, 183
Hassani Arabs, 150
Hausa people, 84, 97, 98
Haut Conseil Islamique Malien (HCIM), 177, 182, 184, 186, 187
herder–farmer conflicts, *see* land rights
heterarchy, 19

INDEX

High Authority for Consolidation of Peace (HACP), 92–3, 97
historic blocs, 11
Hobsbawm, Eric, 129, 133
Hollande, François, 29, 196
homosexuality, 177, 185, 187–8
Horizon 2020 programme, 20, 21
hostage taking, 40, 69, 72, 130, 132, 133
Human Development Report (2022), 56, 79, 211
human trafficking, 24, 63, 96, 102–3, 155
Hüsken, Thomas, 19
hybridity, 125–40

Ibn al-Jawziyya, 49
Ibn Taymiyyah, 49
identity, xvi, 14, 209–13, 221
Ifoghas Tuaregs, 39, 41, 153
infant mortality, 60
informal governance, 14
Inner Delta region, 27–8, 42, 51, 115, 167, 168, 170
insecure spaces, 12
insurgencies, 12–20
    governance and, 14–20, 83–4, 114
    resource mobilisation, 128–30
inter-communal conflicts
    in Burkina Faso, 75–8
    in Mali, 41, 42, 46, 52, 89, 90, 116–19, 168, 189
    in Niger, 45, 86, 89
International Committee of the Red Cross (ICRC), 86
international community, 7–8, 11, 17, 18–19, 210, 215–17
    donors, 10, 24–5, 35, 67, 80, 209
International Monetary Fund (IMF), 61

International Organization for Migration (IOM), 102, 103, 105
Iran, 196
Iraq, 17
Irayaken clan, 39
iron, 88
Islam, 143, 162, 166–72
    quietism, 185
    Salafism, *see* Salafism
    Sharia law, 41, 48, 95, 169, 170, 175, 183, 185
    Shi'ism, 48, 49
    Sufism, 49, 97, 121, 166, 169, 175, 183, 186, 193, 225, 237
    Sunnism, 48, 56, 121, 175, 182
    Wahhabism, 49, 97, 121, 166, 175, 177, 185, 186
Islamic Front of Azawad (FIAA), 150
Islamic Institute of Missira, 187
Islamic Legion, 39–40, 149
Islamic Movement for Azawad (IMA), 154, 157
Islamic Salvation Front (FIS), 132
Islamic State (IS), 10–11, 25, 45–53, 58, 114, 232
    in Mali, 10–11, 25, 45–53, 109–10, 138, 232
    in Niger, 81, 84, 87, 89, 90–94, 95, 109–10
    al-Qaeda, relations with, 47–53, 58
Issoufou, Mahamadou, 79, 93, 108, 201
Italy, 98
Izala, 98

Jackson, Robert, 63, 126
Jama'at al-Tabligh, 40, 42
Jama'at Nusrat al-Islam wal Muslimeen (JNIM), 37, 39,

INDEX

47–53, 109–10, 138, 171, 176, 232
Bamako attack (2024), 196–7
Battle of Tinzaouaten (2024), 30, 196
Islamic State, relations with, 47–53, 232
Katiba Macina, relations with, 42, 43–4
Jeddah, Saudi Arabia, 40
jihadist movements, xvi, xix, xx, xxi, 3, 5, 18, 32, 111–23, 165, 166–72, 232–4
  in Burkina Faso, 57, 76–9, 216, 233
  enabling environments and, 87, 111–23
  governance services, 18, 84, 89–90, 93
  land conflicts and, 27–8, 42–3, 46, 51, 82, 84–7, 89–90, 92, 95, 118–19, 168, 200
  in Mali, *see under* Mali War
  in Niger, xvi, xviii, xix, 56, 80–98, 216, 233
  resource mobilisation, 128, 132–40
Jowros, 43, 51, 168
June 5 Movement, 189

Kaarta Kingdom (c.1650–1890), 143
Kaboré, Roch March, 67, 75, 76
Kafando, Michel, 74
kafir, 48
Kanazaoé, Oumarou, 68
Kankan Musa, Emperor of Mali, 163
Kanouri people, 97
Kati, Mali, 190
Katiba Macina, xix, 27–8, 39, 41–3, 44, 47, 50, 51–2, 116, 119, 176, 216
  Macina Empire and, xix, 141, 167–72
Kawar, Niger, 101
Kayes, Mali, 7, 167, 189
Keita, Ibrahim Boubacar, xvi, 26, 30–32, 156, 177, 181–5, 188–91, 209, 216, 217, 231
Keita, Karim, 189
Keita, Modibo, 144, 148, 237
Kenedougou Kingdom (c. 1650–1898), 143
Kenya, 13
Kharijites, 48–9, 52
Khassonke people, 143
Kidal, Mali, 15, 30, 33, 40, 134, 145, 146, 148, 150, 151, 152–5
  FAMA capture (2023), 199, 208, 225, 226
kidnappings, *see* hostage taking
Klute, Georg, 19
Koglwéogo people, 77, 78
Konaré, Alpha Oumar, 145, 151
Konaté, Doussouba, 227
Konna, Mali, 27, 29
Kouffa, Hamadoun, xix, 39, 41–3, 47, 51, 52, 141, 168, 170, 176
Koulikoro, Mali, 7
Kouroukan Fouga, 212, 213, 221
kufr, 48

Laayoune, Western Sahara, 45
Lake Chad Basin, 57–8, 164
land rights, xviii, xx, 6–7, 26–8, 42–3, 51, 82, 84–7, 89, 115–23
  jihadism and, 27–8, 42–3, 46, 51, 82, 84–7, 89–90, 92, 95, 118–19, 168, 200
Lassana, Soufi, 121
Lavrov, Sergey, 208
lead, 56

INDEX

Lebanon, 149
Lenin, Vladimir, 59
liberation insurgencies, 13, 17
Liberia, 13, 58, 70, 73, 155
Libya, 15, 23, 38
   Civil War (2011), 29, 36, 40, 86, 107, 147, 155, 215
   Islamic Legion, 39–40, 149
   migration through, 98, 99, 100, 102, 103, 104
   Tuaregs in, 29, 36, 39–40, 147, 149, 150, 155
   Wagner Group in, 206
limestone, 56
Liptako-Gourma region, 46, 81, 137–8
literacy, 60
Lonely Planet, 166
Lovejoy, Paul, 162, 164, 166, 169, 172, 230

M5 alliance, 189
Macina Empire (1818–64), xix, 42, 141, 143, 165, 167–72, 229
Macron, Emmanuel, 4, 236
Madagascar, 59
Maïga, Abdoulaye, 224, 226
Maïga, Choguel Kokalla, 189, 198, 210, 218, 219, 220, 224, 234
Maïga, Soumeylou Boubéye, 188
Mali, xv, 23–53
   Agacher Strip dispute, 55
   Algiers Agreement (2015), 4, 91, 225
   AoSS formation (2023), 55, 174
   Burkina Faso, relations with, 70, 71, 72, 197
   cigarette smuggling in, 134–6, 165
   Civil War (2012–), *see* Mali War

   constitution, 145, 175, 180, 190, 192, 199
   coup d'état (2012), 36, 144, 147, 156–9, 176
   coup d'état (2020), 55, 177, 189–90, 195, 198, 209, 217, 224, 234
   coup d'état (2021), xv, 34, 217, 218
   decentralisation programme (1992–), xix, 32, 131, 141, 151–3
   democratisation, 32–3, 143, 158, 179–80, 217
   drug trade in, 134, 136, 146, 153, 154
   ECOWAS withdrawal (2024), 55–6, 174
   European Union, relations with, xix, 3, 156, 209, 215, 216
   family law code, 177, 185, 186–7
   France, relations with, *see* Franco–Mali relations
   G5 Sahel project, 34–6, 216
   Goïta presidency (2021–), 4, 55, 59, 159, 198–9, 202, 209–27, 235, 237
   gold mining in, 137–9, 163, 206
   inter-communal conflicts, 41, 42, 46, 52, 89, 90, 116–19, 168
   Keita presidency (1960–68), 144, 148, 237
   Keita presidency (2013–20), xvi, 26, 30–32, 158, 177, 181–93, 209, 216, 217
   Konaré presidency (1992–2002), 145, 151
   land rights in, 26–8, 42–3, 46, 51

INDEX

March Revolution (1991), 144–5
National Pact (1992), xvi, xix, 32, 141, 147, 151–3, 154, 159
Niger, relations with, 197, 201
organised crime in, 8–9, 12, 32, 134–6, 146, 153, 154
peace agreement (1996), 33, 40, 131, 150, 153
population growth, xviii, 26, 230
poverty in, 24, 26, 118, 211, 229
presidential elections (2013), 30, 177, 180–81, 191
presidential elections (2018), 30–32, 177, 180, 181–5, 188, 189
religious leaders in, 176–7
Russia, relations with, xv, xvi, xx–xxi, 3, 4, 10, 30, 173–4, 195–208, 217, 226, 231
secular state, 156, 175
state weakness, 8–12, 24–5, 28
Touré presidency, first (1991–2), 145, 151
Touré presidency, second (2002–12), 29, 156, 158, 177, 215
Traoré presidency (1968–91), 144–5, 186, 237
Tuareg rebellion (1962–4), 36, 147, 148–9
Tuareg rebellion (1990–5), xix, 15, 36, 131, 147, 149–50, 154, 155
Tuareg rebellion (2006), 147, 151
Tuareg rebellion (2012–15), 28–9, 30, 36–7, 39–41, 45, 91, 131

Wagner Group in, xv, xvi, 3, 4, 30, 196, 198, 203–8, 217, 220
Mali Empire (c. 1235–1610), 163, 212, 224, 229
Mali Koura Hope, 189
Mali War (2013–), xvi, xix, 3–5, 28–53, 215–16
  AFISMA (2013–), 3, 33
  Ansar ed-Dine insurgency, 36–7, 39–41, 50, 76, 136, 147, 154, 155
  Battle of Tinzaouaten (2024), 30, 196
  ECOWAS withdrawal (2024), 55–6, 174
  internationalisation of, 32, 33
  Islamic State insurgency, 10–11, 25, 45–53, 109–10, 138
  JNIM insurgency, 37, 39, 43–4, 47–53, 109–10, 138, 171, 176, 196
  Katiba Macina insurgency (2015–), *see* Katiba Macina
  MINUSMA (2013–23), *see* MINUSMA
  MNLA rebellion, 28–9, 30, 36–7, 45
  MOJWA insurgency, 27, 29, 37, 45–6, 50, 90, 136, 147, 155
  Operation Barkhane (2014–22), *see* Operation Barkhane
  Operation Serval (2013–14), xix, 3, 29–30, 33, 41, 46, 90, 116, 180, 216
  Qaeda insurgency, 10–11, 18, 25, 29, 37–9, 43, 72, 83, 147, 155
  self-defence groups, 41, 47, 116–19
  spillover effects, 23, 25, 57–8,

INDEX

59, 79, 82, 86–7, 89–90, 94, 95
Tuareg rebellion (2012–15), 28–9, 30, 36–7, 39–41, 45, 91, 131, 149, 176, 215
Wagner Group intervention, xv, xvi, xxi, 3, 4, 30, 196, 198, 203–8
Yattabaré murder (2019), 187–8
Mali-Mètre, 21, 205, 227, 231
Maliki school, 182
Malinke people, 115, 146, 210, 212
Mande language, 146
manganese, 56
Manimory, 213
Mano River Basin, 34, 57, 58, 70
March Revolution (1991), 144–5
Mariko, Oumar, 157, 189
Marxism, 59, 199, 236
Mau Mau rebellion (1952–60), 13
Mauritania, 23, 33, 34, 36, 38, 72, 134, 150, 161, 162
measles, 60
Mecca, 163, 164
mediation industry, 71–3
Mékrou River, 88
Melanesia, 126–7
Ménaka, Mali, 45, 91, 232
meningitis, 60
Mentouri University of Constantine, 45
migration, xvii, xx, 3, 24
  in Mali, 7, 35, 155
  in Niger, 80, 98–110
Milestones (Qutb), 49
Military Personnel Resources Incorporated, 205
minerals, 56, 57, 88, 89, 96, 206
MINUSMA (2013–23), xix, 3, 10, 32, 33, 41, 53, 157, 174, 176, 210, 216, 235
  withdrawal (2023), xv, xvii–xviii, 173, 195, 199, 218, 219–21, 225, 226, 231
monopoly on violence, 8, 10, 76
Mooré, 60
Moorish people, 146, 150
Mopti, Mali, 6–7, 20, 29, 42, 50, 51, 112, 116, 119, 167, 169, 199, 216, 232
Morho Naba, 61
Morocco, 34, 59, 162, 166
Mossi people, 56, 61, 75–6, 94
al-Mourabitoun, 41, 43, 46–7, 50
Movement for Development in Mali, 181
Movement for National Liberation (MNLA), 28, 29, 30, 36, 40, 91, 147, 149, 155, 157
Movement for Oneness and Jihad (MOJWA), 27, 29, 37, 45–6, 50, 90, 136, 147, 155
Movement for the Salvation of Azawad (MSA), 90
Muhammad, Prophet of Islam, 183
Muhammadu, Chérif Bouyé of Nioro, 183–5, 186, 187, 188
al-Mulathameen, 46
Museveni, Yoweri, 13

al-Naba, 52
narco-terrorism, 8, 12, 128
National Alliance of the Tuareg (NATM), 29
National Committee for Recovering Democracy (CNRDRE), 29
National Movement of Azawad (MNA), 29
National Pact (Mali, 1992), xvi,

xix, 32, 141, 147, 151–3, 154, 159
neoliberalism, 12, 127, 143
neopatrimonialism, *see* patrimonial politics
neopatriotism, 158, 197–201, 202, 231, 236
Niafunké, Mali, 42
Niamey, Niger, 56, 80
nickel, 56
Niger, xv, xvi, xvii, xviii, 5, 20, 23, 79–110
   Agadez region, 24, 80, 81, 96–110
   AoSS formation (2023), 55, 174
   banditry in, 94, 102
   Bazoum presidency (2021–3), xviii, 55, 79–80, 101, 107, 109, 197–8, 201–2
   Boko Haram in, 58, 98
   Burkina Faso, relations with, 71, 72, 201, 231
   coup d'état (2023), xv, xviii, 5, 25, 55, 80, 107–10, 195, 197–8, 201–2, 224, 234
   drug trade in, 134
   ECOWAS withdrawal (2024), 55–6, 174
   France, relations with, xx–xxi, 3, 34, 80, 195, 203
   G5 Sahel project, 34–6, 94
   inter-communal conflicts, 45, 86, 89
   Islamic State in, 81, 84, 87, 89, 90–94, 95, 109–10
   Issoufou presidency (2011–21), 79, 93, 100–103, 106, 108, 201
   jihadist insurgency (2015–), xvi, xviii, xix, 56, 80–98, 216, 233
   land rights in, 82, 84–7, 88, 89–90, 92, 95
   Loi 2015–036 (2015), 100–103, 109
   Loi 2016–036 (2016), 106
   Loi 58–31 (2002), 81
   Mali War (2012–) and, xvi, 4, 25, 46, 52, 53, 82, 86–7, 89–90, 94, 95
   Mali, relations with, 197, 201
   migration in, 80, 98–110
   mineral production, 88, 89, 96, 206
   Movement for Justice (MNJ), 96
   Operation Barkhane (2014–22), xix, 3, 4, 33, 90, 94, 202
   population growth, xviii, 230
   al-Qaeda in, 38, 96
   Russia, relations with, xx–xxi, 3, 173–4, 195
   Security and Defence Forces (SDF), 85–6, 92, 94
   state weakness, 24, 80, 87
   Tillabéri region, xvi, 20, 45, 46, 47, 56, 80–95, 216
   Tuareg people in, 25, 72, 80, 84, 92, 96, 97, 107
   Wagner Group in, 206
Niger River, 6–7, 29, 88
   Inner Delta region, 27–8, 42, 51, 115, 167, 168, 170
Nigeria, 34, 58, 155
Nigerien Party for Democracy and Socialism, 79
Nioro, Mali, 183
Nkrumah, Kwame, 211
Norwegian Research Council, 20
Nugent, Paul, 62

Observatoire des Réligions, 97
Olson, Mancur, 18

INDEX

Operation Barkhane (2014–22), xix, 3, 4, 33, 39, 41, 53, 90, 94, 116, 133, 216, 233
  withdrawal of (2022), 199, 202–3
Operation Serval (2013–14), xix, 3, 29–30, 33, 41, 46, 90, 116, 180, 216
Organisation of African Unity (OAU), 71
organised crime, *see* crime
Ouagadougou Political Agreement (2007), 70, 72
Ouagadougou, Burkina Faso, 58, 65, 74, 76
Ouattara, Alassane, 74, 222
Ouédraogo, Ablassé, 72
Ouédraogo, Alizéta, 68
Ouédraogo, Kadré Désiré, 72
Ould Ali, Hanoune, 16
Ould Daya, Dina, 16
Ould Limam Chafi, Moustapha, 72
Ould Mataly, Mohamed, 16
Ould Tahar, Chérif, 136

pastoralism, xviii, xx, 6–7
  in Mali, 26–8, 42–3, 46, 51, 115–23, 168, 171
  in Niger, 82, 84–7, 88, 89, 90, 92, 95
patrimonial politics, 10, 15–16, 17, 19, 32, 126–30
  in Burkina Faso, 58, 62–9, 70, 71, 72, 73, 75, 76, 78–9, 200
  in Mali, 127, 130, 131, 150–51, 159, 178, 179–80, 192–3
  in Niger, 83, 108
Patriotic Movement for Safeguard and Restoration, 200
phosphate, 88

Platform Against Corruption, 189
PNDS-Tarrayya, 108
polio, 60
Polisario Front, 45
Polynesia, 126–7
Popular Front for Liberation of Azawad (FPLA), 150
Popular Movement of Azawad (MPA), 40, 150
Popular Revolutionary Tribunals, 60
population growth, xviii, xx, 18, 26, 56, 57, 167, 173, 230
poverty, xvii, 3, 24, 26, 113, 118, 211, 229
preventing and countering violent extremism (PCVE), 97
PREVEX, 20
Prigozhin, Yevgeny, 207
privatisation, 12
Protocol on Transhumance (1998), 84
Putin, Vladimir, 195, 196, 203, 204, 236

Qadiriyya, 97, 175
al-Qaeda, 10–11, 18, 25, 29, 37–9, 43, 58, 72, 83, 114, 147, 155, 232
  Islamic State, relations with, 47–53, 58
  resource mobilisation, 132–6, 138, 154–5
Quran, 48, 50, 97, 148, 169
Qutb, Sayyid, 49

Radisson Blu attack (2015), 198
Rally for Mali, 181
Ranger, Terence, 129
Red Army Faction (RAF), 129
reform insurgencies, 13

INDEX

refugees, xvii, 3, 71, 98, 100, 103, 104
Régiment de sécurité présidentielle (RSP), 64, 66–7, 73–5, 76
regional arrangements, 34–6
religious leaders, 176–88
Revolutionary Army for Liberation of Azawad (ARLA), 150
right of way, 14–15
Rimbé class, 43, 51
Rosberg, Carl, 63, 126
Rougha, 77
Rouji, Mohamed, 16
Russian Federation, xv, xvi, xx–xxi, 4, 10, 30, 172, 173–4, 192, 195–208, 217, 226, 231–2
   Africa Initiative, 192, 204
   coup-proofing and, 174, 197, 200, 206, 235
   'moment' in Sahel, 196, 232, 237–9
   Ukraine War (2022–), xvii, 196, 238
   Wagner Group, *see* Wagner Group
Rwanda, 147

Sahel region, 23–4
Sahlins, Marshall, 15, 63, 126–7, 178, 180
al-Sahraoui, Adnan Abou Walid, 87, 90
Sahrawi people, 45, 150
al-Sahrawi, Abu Walid, 45–7, 90, 91–3
Salafism, 38, 50, 97–8, 140, 159, 162, 166, 172–5, 197, 233
   Ansar ed-Dine, 41, 50, 133, 136
   Dicko, 178–9, 183
   Islamic State, 50, 110
   JNIM, 42, 110

Katiba Macina, 50, 51, 168
MOJWA, 50
al-Mourabitoun, 50
al-Qaeda, 45, 50
Sufism and, 121, 166, 179, 193
Sankara, Thomas, 57, 59–61, 65, 197, 213, 224, 225, 226
Sankoh, Foday, 13
Sanogo, Amadou Haya, 29, 156, 157
Saudi Arabia, 40
Séba, Kémi, 204
secularism, 9, 16, 40, 48, 129, 139, 148, 156, 175
Security and Defence Forces, Niger (SDF), 85–6, 92, 94
Ségou Empire (1712–1861), 165
Ségou, Mali, 7, 112, 120–22, 165, 189, 199
Sekou Amadou, Macina Caliph, 169
self-defence groups, 41, 47, 77–8, 116–17
Senegal, 134, 161, 165, 167
separatist insurgencies, 13, 17
Sharia law, 41, 48, 95, 169, 170, 175, 183, 185
Shia Islam, 48, 49
Sierra Leone, 13, 58, 70, 73
Sikasso, Mali, 7, 189
Sirba River, 88
Sissoko, Cheick Oumar, 189
slavery, 148, 163
social banditry, 129, 133
social contract, 209, 210, 211, 214–15, 224
social media, 192, 199, 204, 207, 225
social mobility, 12, 114, 115, 122
Somalia, 104, 210, 229, 235
Songhay Empire (c. 1430s–1591), 164–5, 166, 230

278

INDEX

Songhay people, 84, 94, 115, 116–17, 118, 146, 148, 149, 157, 211
Soninke people, 146
South Africa, 205, 207
spillover effects, 23, 25, 57–8, 59, 79, 82, 86–7, 89–90, 94, 95
sporadic governance, 18, 84
state capture, 12
Strategic Framework (CSP-DPA), 196
Sudan, 104, 107
Sufism, 49, 97, 121, 166, 169, 175, 183, 186, 193, 225, 237
Sundiata Keita, Emperor of Mali, 163, 212, 229
Sunjata, 210, 212–13, 221, 224, 225
Sunni Islam, 48, 56, 121, 175, 182
Sylla, Boubacar Sidiki, 219
Syria, 17, 30, 197

Tablighi Jamaat, 40, 42
takfir doctrine, 48–50
Takouba Task Force (2020–22), 202
Taliban, 233
Tall, al-Haji Umar, 121, 169
Tall, Mountaga, 189
Tamacheq language, 150
Tamanrasset, Algeria, 104–5, 134
Tanout, Niger, 101
Tapoa River, 88
taxation, 7, 8, 26, 117, 148, 170, 214
Taylor, Charles, 13, 70
Tchiani, Abdourahamane, 55, 80, 201–2
Tijaniyya Brotherhood, 121, 169, 175, 183
Tillabéri, Niger, xvi, 20, 45, 46, 47, 56, 80–95, 109
Timbuktu, Mali, 28, 30, 33, 143, 145, 163–4, 168, 171, 179, 189, 211
Tindouf, Algeria, 45
Tinzaouaten, Mali, 30, 196
Togo, 5, 44, 57, 72, 231
Tonga Tonga, Mali, 47
Toucouleur Empire (1848–93), 121
Touré, Amadou Toumani, 29, 145, 151, 156, 177, 215
trans-Saharan trade, 134, 154–5, 161–2, 163, 164–5, 166
transfers of power, 8
transhumance, 82, 84–6
Traoré, Dioncounda, 157
Traoré, Ibrahim, 55, 59, 197, 199–201, 202, 203, 204, 206, 224, 225
Traoré, Moussa, 144–5, 186, 237
Tuareg people, xvi, xix, 25, 27, 80, 84, 86, 145, 146–55, 156
  Battle of Tinzaouaten (2024), 30, 196
  Islamic State conflict (2014–), 47, 50, 90–91
  Macina rebellion (1840–46), 171
  Mali rebellion (1962–64), 36, 147, 148–9
  Mali rebellion (1990–95), xix, 15, 36, 131, 147, 149–50, 154, 155
  Mali rebellion (2006), 147, 151
  Mali rebellion (2012–15), 28–9, 30, 36–7, 39–41, 45, 91, 131, 149, 176, 215
  Niger rebellion (1990–95), 92, 107
  Niger rebellion (2007–09), 72, 96, 97
  pyramid hierarchy, 148
Tukulor Empire (1852–93), 167
Turkey, 196, 200

279

INDEX

Uganda, 13
Ukraine, xvii, 70, 196, 238
umma, 51
unemployment, 57, 87, 89, 96, 111, 115, 119, 122, 173, 230
ungoverned space, 8–9, 95
Union for the Republic and Democracy, 181
United Arab Emirates (UAE), 137
United Front to Safeguard Democracy (FDR), 156–7
United Kingdom, 203
United Movements and Fronts of Azawad (MFUA), 150, 151
United Nations (UN), xv, xx–xxi, 17, 18–19, 198, 209, 211, 218–21, 231, 235, 238
    Development Programme (UNDP), 26, 56, 58, 79, 113, 211
    High Commissioner for Refugees (UNHCR), 103, 104, 106
    Human Development Report (2022), 56, 79, 211
    International Organization for Migration (IOM), 102, 103
    MINUSMA (2013–23), *see* MINUSMA
United States, 109, 135, 202, 203, 205
Upper Volta (1958–84), 59–60, 65
uranium, 96, 165
Urgences Panafricanistes, 218, 219
Uthman dan Fodio, 169

violent entrepreneurs, 11, 27, 76–9, 82, 87, 114, 126, 128–30
Voltaic peoples, 146
Volunteers for Defence of the Homeland (VDF), 200

Wagadou (c. 100–1200s), *see* Ghana Empire
Wagner Group, xv, xvi, xxi, 3, 4, 175, 198, 200, 203–8, 217, 220, 238
    Africa Corps, xxi, 207, 217
    Battle of Tinzaouaten (2024), 30, 196
    coup-proofing, 174, 197, 200, 206, 235
    Moura massacre (2022), 220
al-Wahhab, Muhammad, 49
Wahhabism, 97, 121, 166, 175, 177, 185, 186
warlords, 13, 17, 83
Water and Forest Agency, 42, 168
water sources, 6, 7, 27, 42, 76, 88–9, 98, 111, 112, 115–16, 118, 168
weak states, xvii, 3, 7–8, 24–5, 57–8, 62, 63, 65, 69, 227
    Burkina Faso, 24, 56–8
    enabling environments and, 114, 115, 117
    Mali, 8–12, 24–5, 28
    Niger, 24, 80, 87
Weberian state, 9–10, 139, 213, 228
Well of Hope, Niger, 101
West African Economic Union (WAEMU), 223
Western Sahara, 45, 150
women, 95, 177, 186
World Bank, 26, 61, 209, 231
World Trade Organization (WTO), 72

Yattabaré, Abdoul Aziz, 187–8
Yèrèwolo Debout sur les Remparts, 218
Yusuf, Mohamed, 98

Zarma people, 84

INDEX

Zerbo, Saye, 60
Zerouate, Mauritania, 134
Zida, Yacouba, 74–5
Zimbabwe, 129
zinc, 56
Zinder, Niger, 101